D0436367

DEVOTION

Also by Adam Makos

Spearhead

A Higher Call

Makos, Adam,
Devotion : an epic story of
heroism and friendship ; adapt
2022]
3305254709235
a   05/31/23

...AKOS

DEVOTION

An Epic Story of Heroism and Friendship

ADAPTED FOR YOUNG ADULTS

Delacorte Press

Text copyright © 2022 by Adam Makos

All rights reserved. Published in the United States by Delacorte Press, an imprint of Random House Children's Books, a division of Penguin Random House LLC, New York.

This work is based on *Devotion: An Epic Story of Heroism, Friendship, and Sacrifice,* copyright © 2015 by Adam Makos. Published in hardcover in the United States by Ballantine Books, an imprint of Random House, a division of Penguin Random House LLC, New York, in 2015.

Delacorte Press is a registered trademark and the colophon is a trademark of Penguin Random House LLC.

Jacket and interior photo credits can be found on pages 345–347.

Visit us on the Web! GetUnderlined.com

Educators and librarians, for a variety of teaching tools, visit us at RHTeachersLibrarians.com

Library of Congress Cataloging-in-Publication Data is available upon request.
ISBN 978-0-593-48145-5 (hardcover) — ISBN 978-0-593-48146-2 (lib. bdg.) — ISBN 978-0-593-48147-9 (ebook)

The text of this book is set in 11-point Apollo MT Pro.
Interior design by Cathy Bobak
Interior map by Bryan Makos of Valor Studios, Inc.

Printed in the United States of America
10 9 8 7 6 5 4 3 2
First Edition

Random House Children's Books supports the First Amendment and celebrates the right to read.

Penguin Random House LLC supports copyright. Copyright fuels creativity, encourages diverse voices, promotes free speech, and creates a vibrant culture. Thank you for buying an authorized edition of this book and for complying with copyright laws by not reproducing, scanning, or distributing any part in any form without permission. You are supporting writers and allowing Penguin Random House to publish books for every reader.

To the veterans of the forgotten victory in Korea, 1950–1953

≡ Contents ≡

▰ PART II ▰

≡ Introduction ≡

From across the hotel lobby, I saw him sitting alone, newspaper in hand.

He was a distinguished-looking older gentleman. His gray hair was swept back, his face sharp and handsome. He wore a navy blazer and tan slacks, and his luggage sat by his side.

The lobby was buzzing, but no one paid him any special attention. It was fall 2007, another busy morning in Washington, D.C. I was twenty-six at the time and trying to make it as a writer for a history magazine.

The day before, I had heard the distinguished gentleman speak at a veterans' history conference. I had caught part of his story. He was a former navy fighter pilot who had done something incredible in a war long ago. It was a feat so superhuman that the captain of his aircraft carrier stated: "There has been no finer act of unselfish heroism in military history."

President Harry Truman had agreed and invited this pilot to the White House. His deeds appeared in magazines and even a Hollywood movie. And now here he was—sitting across the lobby from me.

I wanted to ask him for an interview but hesitated. A journalist should know their subject matter, and I was unprepared.

He had flown a fighter plane known as a Corsair, that I knew. Apparently, he had fought alongside World War II veterans. He was a member of the Greatest Generation, too—the popular name for those born between 1901 and 1927.

But he hadn't fought in World War II.

He had fought in the Korean War.

To me, the Korean War was a mystery. It is to most Americans; our history books label it the "Forgotten War."

Only later would I discover that the Korean War was practically an extension of World War II, fought just five years later between nations that had once called themselves allies. Only later did I discover a surprising reality: *The Greatest Generation actually fought two wars.*

The gentleman was folding his newspaper to leave. It was now or never.

I mustered the nerve to introduce myself. We shook hands. We made small talk about the conference, and finally I asked the gentleman if I could interview him sometime for a magazine story. I held my breath. Maybe he was tired of interviews? Maybe I was too young to be taken seriously?

"Why, sure," he said robustly. He fished a business card from his pocket and handed it to me. Only later would I realize what an opportunity he'd given me. His name was Captain Tom Hudner. And that's how *Devotion* began.

★ ★ ★

True to his word, Tom Hudner granted me that interview. Then another, and another, until what began as a magazine story blossomed into this book. I discovered that Tom and his squadron weren't your typical navy fighter pilots. They were specialists in ground attack, meaning they were trained to carry out airstrikes against the enemy—and to give backup to Marines who fought battles on the ground. So what began as the story of fighter pilots became a bigger story: an interwoven tale of flyboys in the air, Marines on the ground, and the heroes behind the scenes—the wives and families on the home front.

Over the next seven years, from 2007 to 2014, my staff and I interviewed Tom and the other real-life "characters" of his story more times than we could count. All told, we interviewed more than sixty former navy carrier pilots, Marines, their wives, their siblings.

Over those seven years we worked as a team—the book's subjects, a team of historians, my staff, and I—to piece together this story. Our goal was for you not just to read *Devotion* but to experience it. To construct a narrative of rich detail, we needed to zoom in close. Our questions for the subjects were countless. When a man encountered something good or bad, what did he think? What facial gestures corresponded with his feelings—did his eyes lift with hope? Did his face sink with sorrow? What actions did he take next?

More than anything, we asked: "What did you say?" I love dialogue. There's no more powerful means to tell a story, but an author of a nonfiction book can't just make up what he wants a character to say. This is a true story, after all, so I relied on the dialogue recorded in the past and the memories of our subjects, who were there.

I owe a debt of gratitude to these real-life "characters" of *Devotion,* people you'll soon meet and never forget—Tom, Fletcher, Lura, Daisy, Marty, Koenig, Red, Wilkie, and so many others. *Devotion* was crafted by their memories as much as it was written by me.

This book also required another level of research. I needed to see the book's settings for myself—all of them. So I hit the road and followed the characters' footsteps to the places where they grew up, flew, and fought—from Massachusetts to Mississippi, to the French Riviera and Monaco, and back to the battlefields of the Korean War. I had been to South Korea before, but never to that mysterious land above it—North Korea.

But before the book was done, my staff and I went there, too. We traveled to China and then into that misty place known as the "hermit kingdom," the land where some Americans enter and later fail to reemerge.

As the book neared completion, I struggled for a way to describe this interwoven story to you, the reader. *Devotion* is a war story, sure. But it's also a *love story.* It's the tale of a mother raising her son to escape a life of poverty and of a newlywed couple being torn apart by war.

It's also an *inspirational story* of an unlikely friendship. It's the tale of a white pilot from the country clubs of New England

and a Black pilot from the Jim Crow South who formed a deep friendship during a deeply racist era.

As I was editing the last pages of this manuscript, the answer hit me.

It's all those things.

This is an American story.

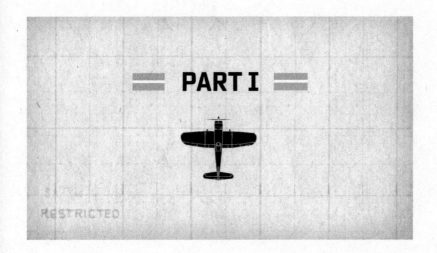

PART I

RESTRICTED

CHAPTER 1

GHOSTS AND SHADOWS

December 4, 1950
North Korea, during the first year of the Korean War

In a flash, a Corsair fighter plane burst around the edge of a snow-covered valley, turning sharply. The plane's engine snarled. A bomb hung from its belly, and rockets dangled from its wings.

Another roar shook the valley. A second Corsair blasted around the edge. Then came a third, a fourth, a fifth, and more until ten planes had fallen in line.

The Corsairs dropped low over a snow-packed road. They glided between ice-capped hills and dead trees. It was official: they were now flying far behind enemy lines.

From the cockpit of the fourth Corsair, Lieutenant (Junior Grade) Tom Hudner reached to the switches above the plane's instrument panel. With a flick, he armed his eight rockets.

Tom was twenty-six and a navy carrier pilot. His white helmet and raised goggles framed the face of a movie star—ice-blue eyes, a chiseled nose, and a cleft chin. He dressed the part, too, in a dark brown leather jacket with a reddish fur collar. But Tom could never cut it as a star of the silver screen—his eyes were too humble.

At 250 miles per hour, Tom chased the plane ahead of him. It was nearly 3 p.m. Dark clouds draped the sky. Tom glanced from side to side and checked his wing tips as the treetops whipped by. Beyond the hills lay a frozen lake called the Chosin Reservoir. The flight was following the road up the reservoir's western side.

The radio crackled in Tom's earphones. The flight leader was calling the base. His report? "All quiet, so far."

"Copy that," replied a tired voice. Seven miles away, at the foot of the reservoir, a Marine air controller was shivering in his tent at the American base. His maps revealed a dire situation. The enemy had the Marines surrounded. To top it off, it was one of the coldest winters on record.

The engine droned. Tom edged forward in his seat, his eyes settling on the Corsair in front of him.

In the plane ahead, a pilot peered through the rings of his gunsight. The man's face was slender beneath his helmet, his eyebrows angled over honest dark eyes. Just twenty-four, Ensign Jesse Brown was the first African American carrier pilot in the U.S. Navy. The military had only recently desegregated, and the treatment of military men of color was still often exclusionary, sometimes even downright hostile. Somehow, Jesse had been able to overcome that.

Jesse had more flight time than Tom, so in this squadron, that meant he took the lead. Jesse dipped his right wing for a better view of the neighboring trees. Tom's gut tensed.

"See something, Jesse?" Tom radioed.

Jesse snapped his plane level again. "Not a thing."

The enemy was undoubtedly there, tucked behind trees, grasping rifles, holding their fire so the planes would pass. The enemy weren't just anyone; they were the White Jackets, troops from the People's Volunteer Army—Chinese Communist soldiers. By now their methods were well known. They hid by day and attacked by night. The week before, they had first attacked the American base. Nearly a hundred thousand White Jackets were now laying siege to it, with more arriving.

The base's ten thousand men had fought back—some U.S. Army soldiers, some British Royal Marine Commandos, but mostly U.S. Marines. Their survival in the war now hinged on airpower—the Corsair pilots knew it. Every White Jacket they could attack from the sky now would be one fewer trying to shoot an American Marine that night.

But the pilots couldn't just bomb a grove of trees on a hunch. They needed to spot the enemy first. "Heads up, disturbances ahead!" the flight leader radioed.

Finally, something, Tom thought.

Small boulders dotted the snow beside the road.

"Watch the rocks!" Jesse said as he zipped over them.

"Roger," Tom replied. He wrapped his index finger over the trigger of the control stick. Then he squinted down at the boulders to see if anyone was there. It was well known that the White Jackets would sometimes drop to the ground when American planes flew overhead. That way, they would blend into their surroundings; their stained uniforms looked like gray stone, and the side flaps of their caps hid their faces.

The rock pile passed behind Tom's wings. He glanced into his rearview mirror. Behind his tail flew a string of six more Corsairs. Now, if any of the White Jackets took a shot at them, Tom's buddies would deal with it.

Tom trusted the men behind him, just as Jesse entrusted his life to Tom.

After two months of flying combat together, the two of them were as close as brothers, although they hailed from different worlds. A sharecropper's son, Jesse had grown up dirt-poor, toiling in the fields of Mississippi, whereas Tom had spent his summers boating at a country club in Massachusetts as an heir to a chain of grocery stores. In 1950 their friendship was genuine, but ahead of the times.

Tom caught the green blur of a vehicle beneath his left wing. Then another on the right.

He leaned from side to side for a better view.

Abandoned American trucks and jeeps lined the road. Cannons jutted here and there, their barrels frosty with ice. Splashes of pink colored the snow below. It was a terrible sight. The day before, the Marines had been attacked right here. In subzero conditions, their spilled blood turned pink.

"Bodies, nine o'clock!" the flight leader announced as he flew past a hill on the left. "God, they're everywhere!"

Sun warmed the hillside, revealing bodies stacked like sandbags across the slope. Mounds of dead men poked from the snow, their frozen blue arms reaching defiantly. Tom's eyes tracked the carnage as he flew past.

Are they ours or theirs? he wondered.

Just the day before, he had flown over and seen young Marines down there, waving up at him. He had heard rumors of the horrors they faced after nightfall. Nighttime was when the enemy charged in seemingly endless human waves. It was also when the temperature dropped to twenty below—meaning the boys' weapons froze and they were reduced to fighting with bayonets and fists. It was something the pilots, who slept safely each night on a carrier, didn't have to deal with at all.

Aboard their aircraft carrier, Tom and the other pilots had become accustomed to starting each morning with the same question: "Did our boys survive the night?"

As the flight raced ahead, the pilots scanned for signs of life. Four Corsairs had changed direction to search for the enemy elsewhere.

The remaining planes followed the same road farther into hostile territory. The clouds ahead were growing stormier. Trees swayed ominously in the wind.

"Possible footprints!" Jesse announced. Tom glanced eagerly forward.

"Nope, just shadows," Jesse muttered as he flew overhead.

Tom could tell that Jesse was frustrated, too. They both should have been far from this winter wasteland. Tom should have been sipping a scotch in a warm country club back home and Jesse should have been holding his baby daughter on his lap under a Mississippi sun. Instead, they'd both come here as volunteers.

It wasn't the risk that bothered them—they were frustrated because they wanted to do something, anything, to defend the Marines at the base. The night before, Jesse had written a letter to his wife, Daisy, saying: "Knowing that he's helping those poor guys on the ground, I think every pilot on here would fly until he dropped in his tracks."

From a field below, a voice barked a command. Just then, a dozen rifles and submachine guns rose up. Arms aimed skyward—arms wrapped in white quilted uniforms.

The White Jackets. They had heard the planes coming and taken cover.

The shadow of the first Corsair passed overhead. The second shadow zipped safely past, too. Jesse's Corsair was next.

But just then, the White Jackets' rifles and submachine guns fired a volley, sending bullets rocketing upward.

Tom's plane flew over the enemy next, then two more Corsairs in quick succession at 250 miles per hour.

Over the roar of their 2,250-horsepower engines, none of the pilots heard the gunshots.

The flight leader ordered the men to re-form over the surrounding mountains.

Tom and Jesse tucked in behind the leader and his wingman. The trailing two Corsairs wedged in behind them. From the rear of the formation, a pilot named Koenig radioed with alarm. "Jesse, something's wrong—looks like you're bleeding fuel!"

Jesse spun in his seat, trying to see behind his tail. He looked toward Tom across the space between their planes.

Tom saw a white vapor trail slipping from Jesse's belly. "You've got a streamer, all right," Tom said.

Jesse nodded. He glanced at his plane's fuel selector switch. The handle was locked properly, so that wasn't the problem. Next, he studied the instrument panel. The needle in the oil pressure gauge was dropping.

Jesse glanced at Tom with a furrowed brow. "I've got an oil leak," he announced.

Tom's face sank. The hole in Jesse's oil tank was a mortal wound. With every passing second, the oil was draining.

"Losing power," Jesse said flatly.

"Can you make it south?" Tom asked.

"Nope, my engine's seizing up," Jesse said. "I'm going down."

Jesse's propeller sputtered and his plane pitched forward into a rapid descent. Instinctively, Tom held formation and followed him down, frantically scanning the terrain for a suitable crash site. All he saw were snowy mountains and valleys studded with dead trees. *This can't be happening,* Tom thought. Jesse would never survive a crash in this terrain and if he did, the cold would kill him.

Tom's face twisted. Jesse was going down seventeen miles behind enemy lines. If he survived the crash, the enemy would surely double-time it to capture him—and if they didn't shoot him on sight, they'd surely torture the captured pilot.

Tom needed to do something to help his friend, and fast.

CHAPTER 2

THE LESSON OF A LIFETIME

Twelve years earlier, spring 1938
Fall River, Massachusetts

The cafeteria of Morton Junior High buzzed with chattering voices. Some students stood in lunch lines, while others sat and ate from tin lunch pails.

Thirteen-year-old Tom Hudner set his tray on a table and sat next to his friends. They were all eighth-grade boys, just like him. He wore a white polo shirt and khakis. His chin was strong, and his eyes were blue and honest. Tom and the other boys still sat away from the girls. Morton Junior High was a place of rules and playground codes, and to sit with girls would invite ridicule. Tom was a rule follower by nature.

Tom bought lunch every day for thirty-five cents, a perk of having wealthy parents. He chewed silently and listened far more than he spoke. During a lull in the conversation, his gaze shifted. Outside the cafeteria's windows, the school's bullies were gathering in a corner of the courtyard where kids played after lunch.

They were sons of Portuguese fishermen, immigrants who had settled in Fall River. Tom stood up to get a better view. The boys were tossing around a pair of eyeglasses, each one trying them on and laughing. At the center of the circle, Tom could see another kid haplessly lunging to snatch his glasses back. The kid was overweight and wore his hair slicked to one side. Tom recognized him as Jack. Other students often ridiculed Jack for being quick to cry, but Tom was friends with him, and most everyone else for that matter.

Tom alerted the boys around him: "Someone should tell the teacher." He looked around, but the teacher was nowhere to be seen. Outside, Jack was turning red and about to cry. The boys around Tom scowled, not because of their affection for Jack.

"Portugee rats!" one said.

"Dirty boat hoppers," whispered another with a cruel hiss. "They should go back to where they came from." The school-children even had a name for the industrial borough near the waterfront that the immigrants called home: "Portugee-ville."

The Portuguese kids were working-class and darker-skinned. For those reasons alone, Fall River's mostly white, privileged families looked at them with distrust. To Tom, the judgments seemed prejudiced. Still, in this moment he felt he should stand up against the Portuguese kids for bullying Jack. "We should do something," he blurted.

Nobody moved.

One of Tom's friends shrugged and looked away. "I'm not getting mixed up in this," he muttered.

"Yeah, I barely know Jack, anyhow," said another.

One by one, Tom's friends sat down. Only Tom remained standing. Outside, he saw that Jack was now blubbering like a baby.

"Come on, guys," Tom pleaded.

"He's your friend, not ours," a boy said.

"If you feel so bad for him, you should do something about it!" another added.

"Okay, fine," Tom said. He sighed and walked toward the door.

Tom stepped out into the pale afternoon sunlight and approached the bullies. "Hey, fellas," he said. The Portuguese kids stopped laughing at Jack and turned, some grinning, some glaring. Tom's stride slowed. His mind raced.

"You say something?" called one of them.

Tom stopped and tried to smile. "I don't think Jack's enjoying this very much," he said. It was the only thing that came to mind.

One of the bullies emerged from the group and sauntered closer. The teen was short and stocky, with a rough-and-tumble way about him. Tom recognized him as Manny Cabral, the group's leader. Unlike Tom's polished, expensive clothes, Manny's brown slacks were patched from wear, and his dark T-shirt had a stretched-out neck. He walked over and stood with his nose nearly touching Tom's.

"I think you should stay out of our business," Manny said.

"C'mon, he's crying," Tom said quietly. Out of the corner of his eye, he saw Jack running away, fumbling with his glasses.

"We were only having fun," Manny said, gesturing to his

buddies. When he looked back at Tom, his voice lowered. "So what are you going to do about it?"

Tom's heart pounded. He had never been in a fight but felt Manny was suggesting it. He wanted to tell Manny to let it go, but Manny spoke first.

"We'll settle the matter later," he said casually. His eyebrow lifted, seemingly with a change of heart. "After school, outside."

Tom gulped.

"You gonna show?" Manny asked.

Tom's eyes darted from Manny to his gang to the circle of students that had gathered to watch the spectacle.

Just say no, Tom thought. But he knew that wasn't an option. If he said no, the boys would never leave him alone.

"Okay, I'll be there," he said.

Manny smiled and walked away. His buddies followed, all laughing and talking loudly. Tom plodded back toward the cafeteria. The boys at his table congratulated him for acting tough. Tom looked down at his cold food and shook his head. "I've got to fight Manny after school." Just saying the words made him light-headed. Tom's friends assured him he didn't need to worry; they would back him up.

Tom thought of his father, Thomas Hudner Sr., and how he would react. His father ran a chain of eight grocery stores called Hudner's Markets and always said that the Portuguese immigrants were dedicated workers, people committed to building a new future for themselves. Senior wouldn't be happy about his son getting in a fight—that much was for sure. But Tom remembered something else his father had told him: *Always assume the*

best of people. But if a guy proves he's no good, then don't hesitate
to give him what he deserves.

When the bell rang at the day's end, Tom's buddies surrounded him in the hallway. They slapped his back as if he were a football player about to take the field. Tom closed his locker and trudged out through the double doors.

Fifty yards away stood the white flagpole and a large cluster of students. At the center of the crowd stood Manny Cabral and his friends. Tom's heart began to race. He glanced over his shoulder toward where his own friends were. But to his surprise, they were gone. They had fled across the street and seemed to be watching and whispering from afar.

All eyes were on him.

Tom was alone.

He stopped, set down his books, and took off his jacket to keep it clean. As he stepped toward Manny Cabral, the crowd hushed. Tom raised his fists and turned his palms inward, thinking of pictures he'd seen of boxers. His fists trembled.

"Whip him, Manny!" yelled a Portuguese kid.

"Yeah, beat him good!" urged another.

Tom noticed the strangest thing—despite the presence of his own supporters, no one was cheering for him. They were too afraid.

Manny stepped forward and raised his fists like a professional fighter. He dropped his chin and scrunched his face, eyebrows low.

"Slug him, Manny!" someone yelled. Manny bobbed lightly, as if he was waiting for the perfect moment. Tom was too terrified to throw the first punch. His fists shook.

Manny raised an eyebrow. His expression loosened, he raised his chin and dropped his fists. His fingers uncurled.

Tom kept up his guard.

Manny stepped toward Tom and thrust forward his right hand. His palm was open.

Tom lowered his fists and looked down at Manny's outstretched hand, confused.

"Go ahead, shake," Manny said.

The crowd grew silent. Tom unclenched his fists. He reached out his trembling hand and took Manny's hand in his. They shook up, then down just once.

Manny turned to his friends. "He's okay," he said. "It's all right between us." Then he turned and walked away. The others lingered, speechless, then followed him down the street.

Tom watched the students disperse. Across the street, his friends had disappeared. Tom gathered his books and jacket and began to walk home. His adrenaline was surging. Before he knew it, he found himself running. He ran right up Highland Avenue toward his home on the hill. At the top of the hill, he hung a right and saw his house, a three-story Victorian with gray wooden shingles and tall windows. The Hudner family had prospered even during the Great Depression because everybody always needed groceries. Tom's face tightened as he ran up to the porch and entered his home.

Inside, he untied his oxford shoes and placed them on a

doormat. His mother was away, probably playing bridge, and his father was still at work.

Tom snuck up the staircase, past his father's pennants from Andover prep school and Harvard University. On the second floor, where his parents and younger brothers and sister had their bedrooms, Tom turned the corner and kept going. He followed another staircase to the third floor, to his own room. The ceiling was sharply angled and a rectangular window overlooked the street below. A crucifix hung next to the doorway and a Boy Scout poster hung on the wall. A baseball glove sat perched on his bedpost.

Tom tossed his books on his desk and flopped onto the bed. A model of an old schooner sat on his dresser along with a copy of his favorite book, *Beat to Quarters,* the tale of a British sea captain named Horatio Hornblower. Comic books littered Tom's nightstand, their covers filled with colorful scenes of pirates and sea monsters. Tom loved ships and sailing.

As he lay back, he could still see Manny's upraised fists and feel Manny's palm when they shook. The boy had handed him a challenge, to rise above a human's judgmental nature.

Then the thought hit Tom.

What if Manny hadn't been such a good guy after all?

Tom stared at the ceiling. Taking a chance—even to do the right thing—had almost cost him his front teeth. *Never again,* he decided.

From now on, Tom Hudner would be playing it safe.

CHAPTER 3

SWIMMING WITH SNAKES

A year later, April 1939
Lux, Mississippi

The late-afternoon sun cast long shadows as a father and his three boys trudged along a dirt road. On one side of the road stood tall pines and leafy trees with thin white trunks. On the other lay parched brown fields. The air was hot and muggy.

Twelve-year-old Jesse Brown and his father, John Brown, were pulling mules by the reins. Jesse was handsome and slender, with sharp eyebrows and steady eyes. Behind Jesse came his younger brothers—Lura, who was nine, and Fletcher, who was seven. The younger boys staggered barefoot in the heat, carrying hoes. Each had spindly legs that stuck out from overalls that their mother had cut into shorts. Lura's face was square and lean, whereas Fletcher's was rounder.

Only Jesse's father wore shoes, but they were falling apart. John Brown was built solidly, with a thick chest and muscular arms. Sweat poured down his face. He kept his eyes focused contentedly forward. That night there would be food on his family's table. It was the Great Depression, and Mississippi was the poorest state in the nation. Not everybody was so fortunate.

Jesse's eyes drooped from sleepiness while his brothers struggled to walk in a straight line. Planting season had come in the Deep South and they'd all been at work since 4:30 a.m. The fields lay in Lux, Mississippi. While local white children remained in school, Jesse and his brothers were given a "spring break" from their one-room schoolhouse that was the exact opposite of a vacation. This was the time when they and other Black students were forced to toil in the fields. The days were unspeakably grueling, for adults as much as for children. For eleven hours that day, Jesse and his brothers chopped plants until their backs ached and their hands were covered in blisters.

Now they were headed home to do their chores; there was firewood to chop and chickens to feed and a garden to maintain. The home garden was everything to the Brown family, because it was actually theirs.

As a sharecropper, John Brown wasn't legally entitled to own the thirty acres that his family farmed and labored on. This was common in the segregated Jim Crow–era South. A white landowner rented the land to the Browns, and took a heavy cut of the crops they harvested. Furthermore, the white landowner also owned the town's general store where the Browns rented their tools and bought seeds. Throughout the year, the store ran a tally of the family's purchases. At year's end when the bill was presented, the landowner always adjusted it to erase the Brown family's yearly profit. For John Brown, it was a no-win life, one he hoped his boys would escape.

The father and sons approached a roadside footpath that led into the woods. Lura and Fletcher perked up and grinned. With a fresh bounce in their steps, the boys tapped Jesse's arm and motioned toward the woods. Every day they came to him at this same spot, with the same pleading eyes.

"Ask him!" Fletcher whispered.

Jesse knew what his brothers were hinting at. He shook his head. They still had to bring in the mules and do their chores.

The faces of the younger boys sank.

"C'mon, ask him—please!" Lura whispered.

Jesse looked down at his younger brothers. He felt exhausted. He steered his mule closer to his father.

"Pa," Jesse said. "Do we have time for a quick break?"

Fletcher and Lura hurried forward and beamed at their father.

John Brown stopped to wipe his brow. He stroked the face of his panting mule, its eye half-closed.

John Brown looked at his boys and saw their raised eyebrows. His lips broke into a smile. "I'll handle the mules," he said. "Just do your chores when y'all get home."

The boys glanced at one another with fresh life in their eyes. Jesse handed his father the reins of his mule and the boys handed him their tools.

Lura and Fletcher took off skipping toward the forest path with Jesse following.

"Hold your horses!" Jesse called. At the trailhead he grabbed a stick from the ground, swung it through the air, and saw that it was good and steady. Jesse warned Fletcher and Lura to stay behind him.

Then he led the boys into the woods.

Jesse walked slowly and swept the path ahead with the stick. The trail wasn't used much, and weeds crisscrossed the dirt. Jesse strained to hear the hiss of a cottonmouth over the buzzing from insects and croaking from bullfrogs. Cottonmouths were the thick brown-black vipers that infested the backwoods. They were poisonous, even more than rattlesnakes. Fletcher tried to race ahead, but Jesse stopped him. "Get back here, Mule!" Jesse shouted. He had nicknamed Fletcher "Mule" because the boy had a mind of his own. Fletcher stopped and grinned.

With his brothers behind him, Jesse resumed the march. He watched the trail, unblinking. In the center of the woods, he led the boys to a pond of water. It was brown and a thin layer of green scum floated around the edges. The boys stood a few moments and watched a snake cross the pond. Only its triangular head swam above the surface.

The boys knew how to get the snakes out of their swimming hole. Jesse unhooked his overalls. He hadn't even stepped out of them before Fletcher took off, naked as the day he was born, running down the dirt hill. Legs flailing, Fletcher jumped straight into the center of the pond. Lura followed and Jesse plunged in last.

The muddy pond felt as warm as bathwater and the brothers

splashed and paddled around, hooting and hollering to make as much ruckus as possible. The cottonmouth didn't like the disturbance. It slithered in retreat up the bank. Keeping the noise up was the best way to keep the snakes on the banks.

Dripping wet, the boys walked down the same dirt road as before, talking happily and feeling clean.

Jesse smiled with amusement as he listened. Fletcher often jabbered about his girlfriends, whereas Lura knew all the current events from the newspapers left over after his paper route. For this reason, the family had nicknamed Lura "Junior" because he was like a junior Jesse, always reading.

The brothers got quiet. Behind them, around the bend, came the sound of a bus. The road was narrow, so Jesse led his brothers to the side and glanced back.

A school bus burst around the corner. It shifted gears and picked up speed. Jesse edged his brothers farther into the weeds.

From the windows toward the back of the bus, a half dozen white faces poked out, sporting mops of brown, blond, and red hair. The kids in the bus shouted a chorus of hateful slurs.

"Heya, niggers!"

"Dirty niggers!

"Looky here, niggers!"

As the bus roared past, the kids spat at Jesse and his brothers. Spit splattered on Jesse and his brothers and stuck to their bare chests and arms as they tried to cover their faces. Dust and hot diesel exhaust enveloped the boys as the bus roared away.

The kids in the bus stared back and pointed, laughing and whooping.

Jesse and his brothers frantically tried to wipe away the spit. Fletcher began to cry. He and Lura looked to Jesse for an answer. Jesse glared at the cloud of dust where the bus had been. He clenched his jaw and tightened his fists. He seldom lashed out and never cursed; instead he became tense to the point of shaking. He was "PO'd," as he called it.

The brothers resumed their walk home in silence. It wasn't the first time they'd encountered racism, but usually it was a curse or an angry eye when they walked into a store. Never had anyone spat on them. Never had they been this violated.

Lura's eyebrows sank over his eyes with disgust. "I know what I want to be when I grow up," he said, breaking the silence. "A Greyhound bus driver—so I can get the hell out of Mississippi."

Jesse nodded. He was thinking the same thing.

CHAPTER 4

THE WORDS

Several days later
Lux, Mississippi

Chop. Jesse Brown took a step, then his hoe struck earth again. *Chop.* With his back hunched, Jesse hoed the weeds between the high cotton plants. Sweat dripped down his back, turning his overalls deep blue. He squinted at the acres of leaves ahead. The rows of green seemed endless, and the pine trees closing around the field made it feel like a prison.

In a nearby row, Fletcher swatted his face. Gnats buzzed his ears and darted for his eyes. Only seven years old, he often lagged behind. Lura, at nine, could keep time with his older brother, but he was away that day with their father.

Alongside Jesse and Fletcher, six other farmhands hoed the weeds. For fifty cents a day, each helped the Browns during planting season. Women wore breezy cotton dresses and worked alongside men dressed in overalls and T-shirts. The adults all wore wide-brimmed straw hats.

The sun was white-hot overhead. Steamy air settled in the fields and breathing became difficult. Time seemed to stand still.

Lost in a daydream, Jesse often hummed to himself. Fletcher and others would glance over to try to discern the tune. Sometimes Jesse hummed a slow folk song and other times a radio jingle.

Over the sound of his humming, Jesse didn't hear it coming. No one else heard it, either.

Then, from across the field came a shout. A farmhand was pointing frantically toward the edge of the field. The man dropped to the dirt. Others did, too.

Jesse turned just in time to see a sleek blue airplane traveling toward him at treetop height. Its wings were low and yellow and its engine was round—but the plane's propeller wasn't whirling. It was fixed straight across.

It was *aiming* for him.

Fletcher was already down. Jesse dropped to the earth, too. He buried his nose in the dirt. Just when he thought the plane would smack into the field, its engine whined, coughed, and bucked to life. Jesse felt the gust of hot exhaust as the plane roared over him. He stood and studied the machine.

The plane ascended, whistling toward the clouds. The pilot jerked the wings and wagged the red-and-white-striped rudder. It was a stunt. The plane had never been in danger of crashing.

"It's that fool Miley boy again!" one of the farmhands yelled. Miley was a neighboring landowner whose son was training to be a pilot.

Jesse envisioned the pilot and a redneck buddy having a

good laugh at the Black folks they had scared senseless. At the far end of the field, the plane turned above the pines. It was circling back for another pass.

"Head for the trees!" someone shouted.

The farmhands sprinted for safety. Jesse didn't move.

He shaded his eyes with his hand and watched the distant airplane coming around. Fletcher stayed, too. If Jesse wasn't going to run, then neither was he, even though he was shaking.

A male farmhand darted out and hollered, "Fletcher! Jesse! Git your asses over here! That boy's gonna kill you!"

Fletcher's knees began to bend in terror, but Jesse didn't flinch. The plane zoomed over the field, aimed at them. Its engine was alive. Its silver propeller blades whirled at shoulder height, and its wheels threatened to skim the ground.

Jesse stood tall and stared right at the oncoming plane. Its wings stretched. Fletcher hit the dirt and covered his head with his hands.

Just before the plane could cut Jesse in two, its nose pitched up. The pilot gunned the engine and the machine's wheels soared over him. Jesse's hands reached toward the wheels as the plane passed above his fingertips. Its engine's blast blew soil around the boys. Jesse shielded his eyes and then waved vigorously at the plane as it shrank in the distance. The farmhands ran to his side.

"Did you see that?" Jesse said. "A BT-9! I've only ever read about them."

"You're crazy!" one of the farmhands shouted. "That boy was trying to kill you!"

Jesse laughed and explained that the pilot would never have hit him—at that altitude the pilot would have crashed if he'd tried.

The other farmhands insisted that the pilot was out to get them. "He was up there laughing, yelling, 'Run, niggers, run!'" one man said.

Jesse brushed the comment off with a grin. "When I get my plane I'll probably do the same thing to you!"

The farmhands broke into laughter. In front of them stood a barefoot twelve-year-old boy dressed in stained overalls.

"Child, throw that idea straight out of your mind!" said a female field hand. "If Negroes can't ride in aeroplanes, they sure ain't gonna be flying one."

Jesse's smile faded. He returned to chopping, but this time he didn't hum. His shoulders tightened and his chin tucked. He was PO'd that the white pilot thought he had the right to rattle the Black workers. And he was PO'd because the farmhands just might be right.

Several days later, after the farming was done, Jesse, Fletcher, and Lura walked on the dirt road, heading home to their chores. A summer storm was brewing.

Behind them came the distinctive sounds of a gear shifting and an engine rattling.

Jesse pulled Fletcher off the road and Lura followed. Jesse looked his brothers in the eyes. "If I say to run, then you run— get it?"

The younger boys nodded.

Jesse scoured the ground until he picked up a dried corn-stalk about four feet long. He shook off the dirt and ran back to the roadside, the stalk in hand.

As the school bus neared, the windows slid back and the same faces emerged. Jesse stood to the side of the bus's path and gripped the cornstalk like a bat. As the bus passed, he swung the cornstalk and smacked the first face that jutted from the windows.

The face shrieked and reeled back inside. The boy's friends yelled at the bus driver to stop. The bus made a grinding sound and stopped. Jesse lowered the cornstalk. The boys in the back of the bus swore until a male voice barked, "Shut up!" The bus door banged open.

A white man in suspenders stepped out, spat tobacco juice, and strode toward Jesse. The bus driver was older, with broad shoulders and big fists. Lura shielded Fletcher and glanced nervously up at Jesse, waiting for the order to run. Jesse remained still, his eyes fixed on the approaching driver.

"What in the hell just happened here?" the driver asked, his eyebrows narrowing.

"Sir," Jesse said. "Every day when you pass us, those boys stick their heads out and spit on us."

The driver's eyebrows lifted. He turned and stared at his bus. The boys were leaning halfway out the window, like dogs with dangling tongues.

"C'mon, let him have it!" yelled the crying boy whose face Jesse had smacked.

The driver turned and studied Jesse from head to toe, taking in the sight of the boy's bare feet and patched overalls. The driver then glanced at Fletcher and Lura, who were looking up with frightened eyes.

"Well, that won't happen anymore," the driver said.

The man turned and strode back to his bus. The door slammed harder than before. The boys' heads disappeared from the windows. Through the open windows of the bus Jesse and his brothers heard the driver chewing the kids out. Soon enough, the bus started and drove off with a grind and a roar.

When the bus was out of sight, Jesse and his brothers resumed walking home. The storm clouds still brewed in the distance, but things felt different.

After a few silent paces, Fletcher looked over at Jesse. His eyebrows were arched in astonishment. Jesse smiled, shrugged, and raised his hands, palms out.

His younger brothers broke out in laughter.

The rain was falling hard by the time Jesse and his brothers reached home, a cabin nestled in a thin grove of trees. The cabin was made of pine boards and a rusted tin roof. Kerosene lamplight flickered in the windows. Behind the home were a garden fence and some railroad tracks. When trains raced by at night, the cabin shook.

Jesse and his brothers entered through the rickety front door.

John Brown was lumbering around the main room, placing

glass jars under leaks from the roof. The cabin's main room was for living, cooking, and sleeping. At night, Jesse's parents slept there on a pull-out bed, while the children slept in a smaller room in back. An outhouse served as the bathroom.

Jesse and his brothers wiped their bare feet with a rag that was kept near the door. Their brown shoes sat nearby and were being saved for Sundays, when the family attended church services. Jesse's shoes had holes and so did his brothers' shoes, but the holes had been filled with patches of cardboard and painted over with shoe polish.

Julia Brown, the boys' mother, was cooking on a wood-burning stove on the other side of the room. She was petite and trim and wore her short black hair curled behind her ears. Her face was strong and certain, with high cheekbones and intelligent eyes.

The boys greeted their mother.

"Hi, loves," she said back, her smile wide.

Jesse and his brothers ran to the smaller room in the back of the cabin. Between two beds sat a lantern on top of an apple box. The boys' books and magazines lay in piles next to their beds. Jesse gathered up his dog-eared copies of *Popular Aviation* and stacks of how-to books—how to do magic, jujitsu, woodworking, and athletics—while Fletcher scooped up his mystery novels and Lura rescued his newspapers to protect them from the rain.

Jesse and his brothers helped their father put jars under the leaks. On a clear night, they could see stars through the cracks, but now all they saw were flashes of lightning. With the leaking roof under control, the boys congregated near their mother. The warmth from the cast-iron stove dried their skin. Julia was almost finished with supper. Jesse's favorite dish was his mother's chicken pot pie.

"How was your day, boys?" Julia Brown asked.

Jesse shot his brothers a quick glance and answered for them. He told his mother that they had made good progress on the field. On their walk home, Jesse and his brothers had agreed not to mention the cornstalk incident.

Jesse knew that his actions had been dangerous. In the Depression-era Deep South, having the bravery to stand up to a white kid could mean trouble. White folks had money, power, and the police on their side. The white kid might go home and come back with his father and his father's friends, or worse. There'd been a lynching six months earlier, just thirty miles down the road.

After dinner, Jesse, Fletcher, and Lura sat around the table with their mother and enjoyed dessert. The family grew their own sugarcane and made syrup, so sweets were never in short supply. Sweet potato pie was a family favorite.

John Brown rocked in a chair while reading a newspaper. While he read, he sipped sweet tea from a mason jar. Beside him, a record player played music softly. As a young man, John had served in an all-Black army cavalry unit during World War I, a unit that had been set to deploy overseas, but the war ended before they could ship out. Now, he served as deacon for the family's small Baptist church.

After dessert, the boys and their mother always played what she called the "word game," Julia's attempt to make up for the schooling her boys missed during planting season. Before she married John Brown she had taught public school, and when Jesse and her boys were old enough, she resumed teaching Sunday school at the church.

Jesse, Lura, and Fletcher passed around a dictionary. Each chose a word and read its definition. Julia then attempted to spell it. The harder the word, the greater the challenge, and the boys groaned time and again as she spelled every word correctly. The boys' older brother Marvin was away on scholarship at the all-Black Alcorn College, intent on becoming a science teacher. But when he came home, even he couldn't stump his mother. Embedded in the game was Julia's hope that through education her boys could escape the fields forever.

Fletcher took the dictionary. He usually chose a word pertaining to medicine, as his dream was to be a doctor. His mother had always told him he could do anything he set his mind to—provided he got an education. When Lura took his turn, he often chose a word relating to geography. Jesse was usually the most excitable player. He'd look up aviation terms like *dihedral* and *dirigible*. But that night, he was mellow. His mind was in another place as the day's events chewed at him.

"People judge you by the words you use," Julia reminded Jesse and his brothers. "So choose the right words and say them correctly, the way they're spelled. No *ain't*. No *whatcha doin'*."

Frustrated, Jesse pushed aside the dictionary. "Mama, sometimes people don't judge you by the words you use. They just judge you." He folded his arms.

"Of course they do," Julia agreed. She could see that Jesse was holding something back.

She looked him in the eyes.

"Well, I've been called a 'dumb nigger' by a dozen different people," Jesse said, "and that's just this week."

John Brown looked up from his paper. Fletcher and Lura glanced at the floor.

Jesse's mother leaned across the table. "When someone calls you a 'nigger,' then you feel sorry for him," she said. "You have to pity him because his mind has such a sorry way of expressing itself."

Jesse frowned and looked away. He knew his mother had endured far worse than he had, that she had encountered every sort of verbal abuse.

Julia smiled and put a hand on Jesse's shoulder. "Even when folks call you the most hateful things, they're still only words," she said. "Words can have all the power in the world or—none at all. That's up to you."

Later on, sometimes Jesse would face the mirror on the wall near the kitchen and practice shrugging away insults without flinching. He knew more of them were sure to come. For what he dreamed of doing, the insults would be coming in planeloads.

CHAPTER 5

THE RENAISSANCE MAN

Five years later, spring 1944
Near Lux, Mississippi

Under his breath Jesse sang as he weeded the young watermelon plants. Lura, Fletcher, and John Brown worked nearby as the sun was setting. It was a weekend evening and only the Brown family was still toiling in the fields.

Lura, Fletcher, and John Brown stopped and looked at Jesse. Each was trying to discern the tune he was singing. It was a strange song, almost operatic, probably something he'd learned in school.

A year earlier, Jesse had moved into the nearby city of Hattiesburg to attend a better high school for Black kids, and his parents had arranged for him to stay with his aunt and uncle. By now, he was eighteen and in his senior year. Still, every Saturday morning he walked home to help his family and every Sunday night he walked back to the city to begin the school week.

The words from Jesse's mouth sounded foreign.

"What in the heck are you singing?" Fletcher blurted from his row. "Ain't nobody happy in these damn fields!"

Jesse looked up and beamed a guilty smile. "I'm practicing a song for choir," he said. "Leander and I are going to sing in an assembly." Leander was his school friend.

"In front of the whole school?" Lura said, and raised an eyebrow.

Jesse nodded sheepishly.

Fletcher was intrigued. "If you're gonna sing in front of all them, at least let us hear it first!"

"Come on, son," Jesse's father said encouragingly. "Practice on us."

Jesse looked at the leafy plants near his foot. "Nah, I'm too tired," he said.

They were all tired, but Jesse especially. His weeks were grueling.

In school, he maintained a top-three ranking in his class, ran track in the spring, played football in the fall, and still every evening reported to the Holmes Club, a bar and honky-tonk south of Hattiesburg. There, he worked until midnight, carrying beers to tables of rowdy soldiers. World War II was raging. Every so often Jesse needed to dodge a fistfight or deal with a drunken soldier's racist slurs.

Jesse planned on fighting in World War II himself, if the war continued. He wanted to enlist as an officer, which required higher education. Otherwise, he could end up slinging corned beef hash in a mess tent or driving shells to the front lines, the jobs Black soldiers usually received. So Jesse had applied to The

Ohio State University in hopes of attending the same university as his idol—Olympic track star Jesse Owens—*if* the university would grant him admission.

Lura and Fletcher stopped picking weeds. They folded their arms and insisted that Jesse sing before they would return to work.

Jesse knew he couldn't talk his way out of giving them a performance. Besides, they heard him sing every Sunday in the church choir.

He cleared his throat and stood straight. The rows of plants separated him from his father and brothers like seats in a theater.

He began to sing.

"Ave Maria . . . gratia plena . . ."

His baritone voice was deep and smooth, and each Latin word rolled perfectly off his tongue and danced across the field.

"Maria . . . gratia plena . . ."

The song was "Ave Maria," by Schubert, a musical prayer to the Virgin Mary.

Jesse's last lyric trailed softly to silence. He wiped his brow and an embarrassed grin spanned his face. After a stunned pause, Fletcher, Lura, and John Brown clapped and cheered. Jesse jokingly bowed across the rows of plants.

CHAPTER 6

THIS IS FLYING

Nearly three years later, January 1947
U.S. Territory of Hawaii

The silver SNJ trainer plane flew low and fast over the waters of Pearl Harbor off the island of Oahu, Hawaii. The plane was stubby, with square wings and a round nose. NAVY was painted on each flank.

In the backseat, Tom Hudner eagerly leaned over the cockpit railing to see the harbor. He was now twenty-two. His chin and jaw had thickened, his face had grown more rugged. His blue eyes drank in the lush fields and the harbor below.

Tom wore a black tie over his tan shirt. Clipped to his shirt was a gold collar bar—the badge of an ensign, the entry-level officer grade in the U.S. Navy. Tom was a sailor now, and this was his first real plane ride.

The growl of the engine filled his ears. Ahead, navy warships were anchored in the harbor's center. The pilot approached a cruiser ship. It was the USS *Helena*—and she looked peaceful way down there, with sailors milling about her deck. As a junior officer, he had called her home for the past six months.

The sailors waved upward as the SNJ soared overhead. The pilot steered the plane into the island's heart for some sightseeing. Tom marveled at the rich green mountains and knew he had made the right choice when he chose the navy.

Four years earlier, in 1943, he had preregistered to attend Harvard University. His father was a Harvard man, and everyone expected Tom to follow in his footsteps. But to his family's surprise, Tom contacted his congressman and secured a nomination to the Naval Academy. He was accepted and had graduated in May 1946, just nine months after World War II ended. All graduates were required to take their first posting aboard a ship, and Tom wound up on the *Helena*.

The plane began bucking in the rough mountain air. Tom floated from his seat and got a plunging feeling in his gut. His smile retreated and his head felt heavy. The pilot pointed out a waterfall. Tom looked where he was told. His vision was becoming blurry. Tom lowered his chin and braced his arms against the cockpit walls. Sweat slipped from his helmet. "Sir, I'm not feeling so good," he said over the intercom.

The pilot leveled the plane. "Sorry, Tom, these mountains have some chop because of the coming storm—I'll turn us around."

Tom tried to focus his gaze ahead, but his vision seemed to float. He opened his shirt and sucked in deep breaths, thirsty for fresh air.

The plane leapt and dipped again. Tom closed his eyes, but his head was spinning. He gagged and then shot a hand to his mouth. He scanned the cockpit frantically for an airsickness bag but found none. He knew enough about flying to know that ground crewmen hated nothing more than to have to clean up a pilot's puke. *I can't do this to them,* Tom thought.

With a hand across his mouth, Tom leaned over the right ledge of the canopy and vomited down the side of the plane.

Finally, he flopped back inside the cockpit.

Tom vowed there wouldn't be a "next time." As far as flying went, he had made up his mind—he just wasn't built for it.

Three months later

Tom passed through the officers' club wearing a crisp blue blazer over a white shirt and black tie. The club looked like an upscale steakhouse, but it was decorated with palm leaves and tiki statues.

Tom approached a round table and took a seat with his buddies—Carl, Bill, and Doug. Tom's friends were well-mannered and neatly groomed, with their hair slicked back. They were ensigns, too. Each night, they enjoyed drinks in the club after a day's work.

On this night, all the men turned to him. Carl spoke up as if he had an announcement to make. "Tom," he said. "We're done with paper pushing. We're doing it, we're putting in our chits for aviation."

A "chit" was an official letter, in this case requesting admission to flight training. It was common knowledge that the navy needed pilots, because so many veterans had left the service after World War II.

"That's wonderful, guys," Tom said. "I hope you get in."

Carl leaned across the table. "You don't get it—we want you to apply with us!"

The others studied Tom's face, eager for his answer.

Tom's smile dropped and he told his buddies about his airsickness.

They reassured him that the airsickness was a onetime thing.

"Think about it, Tom," Carl said. "What's the first thing you see when a fella approaches you?"

Tom shrugged.

"Gold wings!" Carl said, slapping the left breast of his blazer, where embroidered wings would go.

"Girls see them, too," one of the fellows chimed in.

Tom nodded, but he still wasn't budging. He enjoyed his current work, decoding and sorting classified messages for the Pacific Fleet.

"Aviation is the new battleship," Carl urged. "It's the future."

He's got a point, Tom thought. Flying was where the United States' military powers lay. Ships were on their way out. Technology was changing. And beyond that, deep down, Tom did appreciate aviation's appeal—the leather jacket, the goggles, the ability to impress women.

"Any red-blooded ensign needs to at least try," Carl said. "If not, there's something wrong with you!"

The others raised their drinks over the center of the table. They looked at Tom, hoping he would raise his own.

Tom still remembered the airsickness vividly. He wanted to say no to his friends but could see the enthusiasm in their eyes. He couldn't let them down.

He raised his glass.

"Okay, I'll put in my chit, too."

CHAPTER 7

SO FAR, SO FAST

Two years later, May 1949
Hattiesburg, Mississippi

Applause shook the auditorium of Eureka High School as Jesse finished his speech. Behind the podium, Jesse stood in the dress uniform of the U.S. Navy—a white jacket with gold buttons and black shoulder boards. He was now twenty-two and a newly commissioned ensign. On his right hand he wore a Eureka High class ring.

Jesse nodded to the crowd and struggled to keep his grin from stretching too wide. In front of him sat rows of teenage Black boys and girls dressed in their finest for the baccalaureate ceremony.

Jesse tucked his white hat under his arm and walked off the stage. He wasn't accustomed to applause, much less from his alma mater. The local newspaper had never announced that he'd earned his navy wings the previous October. After the ceremony, Jesse walked down the school's front steps with the principal,

Nathaniel Burger, a distinguished older light-skinned Black man. Sun radiated over the quiet neighborhood. As Jesse and the principal talked on the sidewalk, families streamed around them, eager to shake Jesse's hand.

Everyone had wanted to know: How had he earned his navy wings? There had been Black pilots before: the all-Black Tuskegee Airmen had done the army proud during World War II. But the navy was known to be more segregated. As of that January, just five of the navy's forty-five thousand officers were Black— and Jesse was one of them. And until Jesse, only whites had flown from carriers.

In his speech at the high school, Jesse had revealed his secret: his flight instructor, Lieutenant Roland Christensen.

During navy flight school Jesse had met Christensen, a former farm boy from Nebraska who'd volunteered to take Jesse— also a former farm boy from Mississippi—as his student after other instructors had refused. Before their first flight, Christensen had told Jesse, "Convince me you have what it takes." He saw Jesse for who he was: a young man with talent and dignity, regardless of race.

A slender young Black woman in a yellow sundress emerged from the auditorium. She approached Jesse and hugged him tightly. "That uniform just gives me shivers," she said. Quiet and graceful, she was twenty-two-year-old Daisy Pearl Brown, Jesse's bride of a year and a half. They had a baby girl together, Pamela Elise, who was five months old. Daisy wore her hair in a bun, pulled up and away from her wide, dark eyes.

Jesse introduced Daisy to Principal Burger.

"You met at Eureka, didn't you?" Principal Burger asked Daisy.

"Yes, sir," Daisy said. She explained that she had been a sophomore when Jesse was a senior. Every day, Daisy and her girlfriends ate lunch near Jesse's woodshop class.

"I still can't get past it," the principal said to himself. "A son of Eureka flying from a carrier!"

Everyone was astonished at how far Jesse had come. For two years he had studied up north at Ohio State. He had chosen to study architectural engineering and paid his way through school by working as a department store janitor some nights and unloading boxcars others.

During his second year at Ohio State, Jesse encountered a recruiting poster on a campus bulletin board. It read: CADETS FOR NAVAL AVIATION TAKE THAT SOMETHING EXTRA . . . HAVE YOU GOT IT? With two years of schooling under his belt, Jesse met the requirements to follow the poster's instruction: APPLY—NEAREST U.S. NAVY RECRUITING STATION.

Leaning forward, Burger had a question just for Daisy. "Has he taken you flying yet?"

"No, sir," Daisy said. "And to be quite honest, I'm not too crazy about Jesse's work—it's awfully dangerous."

"We're working on that," Jesse said, giving Daisy a gentle nudge.

Jesse and Daisy strolled arm in arm through Hattiesburg's Black neighborhood. Hattiesburg had a fresh face of luxury— Art Deco hotels, classical columns on government buildings, marble banks. They passed weeping willow trees, a brick corner store, and an antiques shop.

The couple reached the bus stop on the corner of Pine and Main. There were few cars out and the city was calm.

"Perfect day," Daisy said.

Jesse agreed and kissed her on the cheek.

Some of their best memories had been made around the corner at the Saenger Theatre. They had had to sit in the balcony, in the "colored" section, to watch Clark Gable and Humphrey Bogart movies. Before Daisy was in his life, Jesse first fell in love at the Saenger—with Lena Horne, the famous Black singer who starred in the film *Stormy Weather.*

The stoplight on the corner turned red.

A car full of teenage boys pulled up, windows rolled down. Out of the corner of his eye, Jesse glimpsed the red glow of a cigarette being held by a white hand. The passenger draped his arm out the window and tossed the cigarette butt. Jesse eyed the passengers.

The light turned green, but the car didn't budge. No other vehicle was around.

"Hey, nigger," came a voice from inside the car. "Where ya headed?"

Jesse avoided eye contact. He knew the odds were bad if they wanted to fight—four against one.

"How come you wearing a white man's uniform?"

The light turned red again.

An arm slapped the side of the car. "You hear me, boy? Where'd you steal that uniform?"

Jesse held Daisy's hand tighter.

"Stupid nigger, look at me! I asked you a question."

Jesse looked straight ahead.

"Fine, stay there," said the voice. "Don't move a muscle."

The car peeled away and Jesse followed it with his eyes, remaining tense.

Daisy tried to get her husband to let it go. It was over; they had both endured worse.

Jesse checked his watch and looked up, annoyed—the bus was late. All they needed was a lift across town, to the apartment of Daisy's mother, Addie, who was watching their daughter, Pam.

An engine revved hard and loud behind the couple. The same car was racing back up the road in their direction. Jesse pulled Daisy close. At the corner the car screeched to a stop even though the light was green. Two boys leaned out from the passenger-side windows with fists full of eggs. They threw one egg, then another at Jesse and Daisy, who were too shocked to react. The eggs passed left and right of the couple and exploded against a brick wall in a shower of shells and yolk. Whoops and hollers poured from the car.

More eggs flew through the air. Jesse shielded Daisy with his body, turning his back to the car. An egg flew past Jesse's officer's hat, another splattered the concrete. Daisy trembled against Jesse's shoulder. Another egg flew past Jesse's white shirt and cracked on the bus stop bench. Another zipped past his leg.

A car's horn blared. Jesse lifted his head and saw that another car had pulled up behind the teenagers. Its driver, an older man, was gesturing angrily. One of the boys lowered himself into the car while the other hung out. The teenage driver peeled away.

Jesse watched them leave.

Daisy was sobbing, and Jesse comforted her. "Aww, Tootie, it's over." "Tootie Fruity" was Daisy's nickname, first given to her by her father.

"But they tried to hit us!" Daisy choked out the words.

"Yeah, but they missed." Jesse stroked her back.

A bus screeched to a stop beside them. The door opened.

Jesse removed his hat, walked up the steps, and paid the fares while Daisy waited on the ground. Jesse stepped down and led Daisy to the bus's rear door, where Black passengers boarded. Sometimes a sympathetic driver would tell a Black person that he or she could board from the front—if there were few whites aboard—but not today.

Daisy sat against the window and dried her eyes. She glanced at Jesse and saw that his shoulders were tense. A stern look filled his eyes as he scratched his shirtsleeve with a fingernail. Daisy leaned over and looked closely at his sleeve. A speck of yellow egg yolk had landed on his uniform. She moistened a finger and tried to wipe it off, but the tiny mark stayed.

"I—I can't believe it," Jesse stammered. "Who would want to desecrate the uniform of the United States Navy?"

CHAPTER 8

THE RING

Seven months later, December 2, 1949
Naval Air Station Quonset Point, Rhode Island

A light blue coupe purred along the roadway of the military base. Its engine revved as the driver pulled into the nearly full parking lot beside hangars and a seaside runway. Tom Hudner steered to his favorite spot in the rear corner of the lot. Now twenty-five years old and a lieutenant junior grade, Tom had been stationed at Quonset Point for two months. So far, his role had been flying heavy attack planes called "Skyraiders." He had overcome his airsickness by simply taking the controls. Flying, instead of riding, made all the difference.

Tom stepped out of his car into the chilly December air. He slapped a green tent cap over his wavy brown hair and zipped his brown leather jacket over his black tie and tan shirt. Below his leather jacket, Tom wore green pants and brown shoes. The winter "green" uniform was a pilot's pride and joy, an ensemble that only aviators could wear. All other naval officers wore navy or tan uniforms and black shoes.

Tom flipped up his jacket's black fur collar. The clouds above were heavy with snow. Tom liked the Christmas season. For servicemen, though, a new, uneasy weight blanketed the season of peace. America was at war in a conflict the papers were calling the "Cold War." "Cold" because the bullets weren't yet flying, as they would in a hot war.

The Cold War would turn out to be a fifty-year standoff between the United States and the Soviet Union, involving all of their allies. For now, it was just beginning, with no end in sight.

Just seven months earlier, in May 1949, the first clash had been decided. The struggle was over Berlin, the vanquished city that the Allies had divided after World War II, each taking a zone. In June 1948, America, Britain, and France awoke to find Soviet tanks blockading the roads, railways, and canals into their zones. The ruler of the Soviet Union, Joseph Stalin, was ordering the democratic zones to force the 2.2 million German civilians there to submit to his rule or starve. But America and the democracies devised a way around the Soviet tanks—by flying over them. For eleven months, American and British aircrews flew three hundred thousand runs of food and supplies into Berlin during an operation named the "Berlin Airlift." Ultimately, the Soviets abandoned their roadblocks, but the lasting outcome was clear: the sides of the Cold War had been drawn.

Tom thrust his hands into his pockets and walked toward the hangar, the large building that housed the aircraft. A rush of exhilaration hit him as he headed inside. He was reporting to "Fighting 32"—pilot slang for Fighter Squadron 32 (VF-32).

He had made it to fighters.

★ ★ ★

Tom and his new flight leader, Lieutenant Commander Dick Cevoli, leaned over the railing on the hangar's second floor and looked down at the planes below.

Cevoli was Italian American, with black hair and youthful dark eyes. A grin stretched beneath his long Roman nose. He was thirty and reminded Tom of someone who would make a good baseball coach. Before Tom met Cevoli, he had heard rumors in the officers' club. Apparently, his new flight leader had pulled some jaw-dropping heroics in WWII, although Cevoli himself remained tight-lipped about it.

"Anything I can do to help your transition?" Cevoli asked.

Tom assured Cevoli that everything was fine.

"Everyone brags about his squadron being the best," Cevoli said, "but Fighting 32 really is."

He gestured to the stubby, barrel-shaped planes below. They were F8F Bearcats—speedy hot-rod propeller planes. A white *E* had been painted on the engine cowling of each Bearcat. Every aviator knew that the *E* stood for "excellence." Cevoli explained that '32 had been rated the top squadron in the fleet that year. They would proudly wear the *E* during their yearlong reign.

Cevoli glanced at Tom's right hand, where he spotted a thick gold ring. Anyone in the navy could instantly recognize a Naval Academy class ring. A deep blue stone glimmered on top and *1947* was embossed on the side, the year of Tom's class.

"You know we've got a Negro pilot in '32," Cevoli said as he eyed Tom's ring. "First in the navy."

Tom said he'd read about this pilot in *Naval Aviation News.*

"You'll be flying with me and him," Cevoli added. "He's a good guy." Cevoli explained that the Black pilot was an ensign and, even though Tom outranked him, he had more flight hours than Tom. "If it's just the two of you in the air, he'll lead. That's how we do things here, experience over rank, okay?"

Tom said he was fine with the setup. He had just two months of squadron experience.

Cevoli glanced at Tom's ring again and winced, like something was still bothering him. "Will you be okay taking orders from a Negro pilot?"

Tom knew what he was hinting at. The ring. The Academy.

The Academy was in Annapolis, Maryland, relatively far north, but some still called it "Rebel Country." Maryland was technically a border state during the Civil War, but slavery had been legal there, and when the men of Maryland signed on to fight, most fought for the South. For one hundred years the navy elite had studied at the Academy, white males who were essentially joining the navy for life. Until that June, the Academy had never let a Black student graduate. Just five Black students had been admitted to the school before then, and they had been hazed and harassed.

A bead of sweat formed on Tom's forehead. He wanted to hide the ring so that Cevoli would drop the questions. Instead, he said the first thing that came to mind.

"At my high school we only had one Black student and I was friends with him . . . He was a good guy," Tom said. He glanced away and wanted to pound his own forehead. It was the truth, but it sounded contrived.

Cevoli saw Tom's distress and broke the tension. "Well, that's good. I think you'll get along with this fellow, too—our guy's name is Jesse Brown. And if you don't get along with him, no shame in asking for a transfer," Cevoli added. "We can't have guys flying together if they don't trust one another."

Several nights later

It was dark when Tom walked through the front door of his three-story brick dormitory. The building resembled a roadside hotel, neither fancy nor shabby, and all single pilots at Quonset Point lived there between tours at sea. At the Academy, Tom had been a "Red Mike," the name the cadets gave classmates who were too busy to date.

On his way to his room, he passed a wide-open door. Tom could have sworn he heard a girl giggling and a guy whispering. Women were not allowed in the dormitory. What was going on?

He took a deep breath, lowered his chin, and walked quickly ahead. As he passed the room, he glimpsed a tall young man with black hair kissing a brunette girl.

Oh Lord, Tom thought. He walked faster.

"Hiya!" came a voice from behind him. The black-haired young man was leaning out the door, grinning. With that much confidence, he had to be a pilot.

"Oh, hello," Tom said.

"You're a new guy in '32?" the pilot asked.

Tom said he was.

The pilot stepped from the doorway and approached. He was about six feet tall and lean, with sharp black eyebrows and blue eyes paler than Tom's.

"I'm Marty Goode," the pilot said, shaking Tom's hand. "Not to be confused with my evil cousin, Marty the Bad." He was from Brooklyn and had a strong accent.

"Why, thanks for the warning," Tom said, playing along. "I'll keep an eye out for him."

Marty introduced himself as '32's bull ensign—the ensign in the unit with the most seniority. He was proud of his rank, having joined the navy at age sixteen and worked his way up the enlisted ranks into flying school and an officer's commission.

"Well, I'll see you around," Marty said, "I've got duties to attend to!" He winked and left the way he had come.

Tom walked the other way, shaking his head. In Fighting 32, he was starting from scratch.

CHAPTER 9

THE POND

December 6, 1949
Warwick, Rhode Island

Jesse stepped onto the porch of his white clapboard cottage and glanced around the neighborhood. Frost covered the ground, and early-morning light streamed onto a large, frozen pond across the street. The pond was shaped like an hourglass. This was the first home that he and Daisy rented together, 140 Glen Drive, a cottage built in 1945. Though they were far away from the South, Warwick was really starting to feel like home. Their neighbors had been kind. The ones across the street would invite Jesse and his family over to swim with them in the pond when it was warm. Jesse loved to take dips. He would hold Pam's hand as they waded together.

Beneath his leather flight jacket, Jesse wore green pants and brown shoes. His hair was shaved high and tight up over his ears. Jesse headed toward his car to warm the engine. The car was a sparkling new forest-green 1949 Dodge Wayfarer coupe.

Jesse loved the Wayfarer and had saved for years to afford this, his first car.

Suddenly, the cottage door was flung open. Daisy threw a wool coat over her shoulders and ran down the steps. Jesse looked surprised to see her again. They'd already kissed goodbye inside. Daisy reached Jesse, wrapped her arms around her husband, and held him tightly.

Jesse chuckled and hugged her back.

Daisy kissed Jesse a final time and released her grip. Jesse told her he would see her soon and raised a finger to the sky. Today was a flying day. He continually tried to tell Daisy that flying was fun, but Daisy wasn't convinced. She knew a pilot could meet a swift end in peacetime—let alone in the war that seemed sure to come.

The escalating possibility of war had already become worldwide news. The U.S. and the Soviet Union (today, Russia) had had tense relations for years. And just four months earlier, the Soviets had successfully detonated an atomic bomb on a test site. Now the U.S. wasn't the only one with an atomic bomb. The American military were making plans in case the Soviets launched an atomic sneak attack. The papers called the scenario the "Disaster Attack" and predicted that Soviet bombers would fly over the polar ice cap—down over Greenland and over Alaska and Canada—to atomize cities on both American coasts. The military was hurriedly building radar outposts. These outposts would give early warnings of any enemy bombers that pilots like Jesse would be called to intercept.

Jesse slid into the Wayfarer and shut the door. Daisy remained in the driveway, her arms crossed. Their eyes met through the windshield glass and Jesse lifted his hand from the steering wheel in a small wave. Daisy broke into a grin and waved back. Jesse backed out of the driveway and drove away past the pond.

Inside Hangar 4, Quonset Point

Alone in the locker room, Tom slipped on his flight suit and zipped it up. The room smelled like soap and reminded him of changing for track, football, and lacrosse in high school. He knelt and laced his leather boots.

Today was a training day. The pilots needed to get ready to operate in case the Soviets made a move. Tom found it hard to envision himself lining up a Soviet bomber in his gunsight; just five years earlier, the Soviets had been among the Allies in World War II. In reality, though, the Soviets had been Hitler's ally first. Before WWII began, Hitler and Stalin signed a secret nonaggression pact that allowed German pilots to train on Soviet airfields and German warships to anchor at a Soviet base. Stalin sent oil, rubber, and minerals to Hitler, who supplied the Soviets with tank prototypes and fighter planes. The alliance lasted for nearly two years, until Hitler turned on Stalin and attacked the Soviet Union. Only then did Stalin join the Allied cause.

The locker room door swung open. Tom looked up. Jesse walked in and set his flight bag on the wooden bench that separated them.

"Good morning," Jesse said stiffly. He opened a locker opposite Tom's.

Tom returned the greeting. He knew he was looking at a person who had made aviation history, but he didn't know much else about his new squadron mate. Tom was, however, eager to correct that. He had long forgotten the tough Portuguese boy Manny Cabral but not Manny's lesson—that a man would reveal his character through his actions, not his skin color or background.

"I understand we'll be flying together," Jesse said, looking into his bag. His tone was formal. He removed his boots, then his flight suit.

"I'm Jesse Brown, by the way." Jesse gave an awkward half wave and remained on his side of the bench.

Tom finished tying his boots and stood up.

"Good to meet you, Jesse. I'm Tom Hudner." Tom thrust his open hand across the space between them.

Jesse looked down at Tom's hand, paused, then extended his hand and shook.

Tom pretended not to notice Jesse's reservations and made small talk about the upcoming flight. He paused when he caught Jesse glancing at his Naval Academy ring. Jesse's eyes fixed on the deep blue stone.

Damn it! He's heard stories about the Academy, Tom thought as he slipped his leather jacket over his shoulders. Tom told Jesse he would see him at the preflight briefing, then shut his locker and left the room.

The morning sky was dotted with clouds. In tight formation, Tom's and Jesse's Bearcat planes raced fifty feet above Greenwich Bay. With their square wings extended, the Bearcats had a barrel-like shape that tapered off to a slender tail. Four huge twelve-foot propeller blades whirled like buzz saws from the nose of each plane. Unlike a jet, if a propeller plane flew too close, a pilot could chop off his buddy's wing or tail.

Tom flew behind Jesse in the wingman position, studying Jesse's wing tip as it rose and fell. He snuck a glimpse ahead at Greenwich Bay's leaping waves, then back to Jesse's wing. Flying in tight formation required faith. The wingman always watched his leader's wing tip, and only the leader looked ahead. If both pilots looked ahead, they could collide.

A blurry pole whipped past Tom on the right. Then another flashed by on the left. The poles were actually the masts of fishing boats sailing on the bay; Jesse had taken them down that low. Tom's eyes narrowed with worry. They were flying due north, the wrong direction. All Jesse had said before takeoff was that he needed to make "a quick detour."

The Bearcat's speed was blistering, but Tom fought the urge to look ahead.

Where is he taking me? Tom wondered. They were supposed to fly to Long Island and then navigate from landmark to landmark. These were navigating skills they might someday use in combat. And the idea of going to combat was looming more and more heavily over Tom's head.

High-ranking military officers, the "brass," predicted that the Soviets needed just two more years to be ready for war. And already, the enemy had America outnumbered. The numbers came down to this: Reportedly, the Soviet air force boasted 9,000 planes to America's 3,000. The 2.6-million-man Soviet army dwarfed America's force of 600,000. Only the U.S. Navy's surface fleet of 164 vessels topped the Soviets' 127 ships.

But an American advantage lay within that fleet—15 aircraft carriers and 5,000 navy and Marine Corps combat planes. The Soviets had no carriers, whereas America had built so many that the navy had mothballed a number of still-operable World War II carriers. Overnight, the navy and Marine flyers had become America's competitive advantage.

Now, Tom glimpsed a gray, rocky coastline racing toward him. He knew just where they were, because his hometown lay across the bay. Jesse's plane was roaring low across the shore—in a totally different direction from where he and Tom were supposed to be headed.

What the heck? Tom wondered, still following Jesse. They were supposed to make every minute of training time count, not play games.

Jesse nosed forward and took his plane even lower, nearly scraping the tree branches outside. Tom followed him down, then spotted an ice-covered pond in the center of the peninsula. The pond was shaped like an hourglass and was bordered by cottages and trees. Jesse aimed for it. Tom glanced between Jesse's wing tip and the pond.

Tom scowled. Was Jesse lining up on the pond in order to buzz civilians' heads? "Flat hatting," as buzzing was called, was neither approved nor forbidden. The word was just "Don't get caught." Tom had not gone through the Academy to get booted in a stunt like this, but Jesse was flying lead.

Tom gritted his teeth.

"Get ready to climb!" Jesse told Tom, his voice crackling with enthusiasm.

The silver pond stretched in Tom's windscreen. It looked like Jesse was going to fly them straight into it.

Daisy carried her daughter, Pam, down the wooden steps of the cottage and set the girl's tiny feet on the cold driveway. A year old now, Pam could walk, but unsteadily. She was bundled in a small coat and a beanie. Between the beanie's earflaps was a face with round eyes and chubby cheeks. Daisy knelt and turned Pam back toward the cottage, in the direction of Quonset Point. Far over the tree line she spotted them—two black crosses zooming toward them.

"There's Daddy!" she shouted, pointing.

Pam smiled at the mention of Daddy and blinked at the horizon.

"Here he comes!" Daisy said. "Look!"

Behind the trees, the Bearcats' wings stretched wider. Their whirling propellers purred louder and louder. In a screaming roar the planes blasted over the cottage roof.

Daisy crouched and covered Pam's ears. Tree branches rattled. Daisy turned Pam to follow the Bearcats as the planes raced over the pond. Already far away, the planes pitched up and into a vertical climb. Their canopies glimmered.

"There goes your daddy!" Daisy exclaimed, pointing for Pam.

Pam looked up happily. Daisy took her little hand, and together they waved as the Bearcats shrank toward the clouds.

★ ★ ★

Stick like glue, Tom told himself as the two planes climbed in formation. He kept his eyes locked on Jesse's wing tip.

Jesse looked over to check Tom's position. He was grinning.

"Just saying hi to my girls!" he shouted over the radio.

Tom's scowl lifted. A smile slowly cracked his face. When the clouds disappeared behind them, Jesse leveled out into a sky of pure blue. He turned them south toward the sun, the direction they were supposed to fly.

"Air show's over," Jesse said. "Let's go find the Big Apple."

Tom sat back and relaxed. Jesse looked over and explained on the radio that every time he could, he did a low pass for his wife and little girl.

Tom smiled and nodded. *Why didn't he just say so?*

"Anyone you want to buzz?" Jesse asked as an afterthought. "Now's the chance."

"Nope," Tom replied without hesitation.

Then he gave the opportunity some thought. If he could buzz anyone, he'd buzz his dad's country club when the golfers were there. He and Jesse were probably flying over the club at that moment. Tom imagined his dad's friends would look like a bunch of storks from above as they walked in circles looking for a ball. The grin slipped from Tom's face. He couldn't bring himself to do it, no matter how much fun it would be.

What if someone reported him?

★ ★ ★

On the ground, Tom and Jesse slid from their planes' wings. Both men jumped down, their boots hitting the tarmac. Together they walked toward the hangar. Jesse was still glowing after buzzing his family. He asked Tom if he had a wife or girlfriend.

"Nope," Tom said. "I'm all business, just focusing on my career."

Jesse told Tom that sounded like a good plan. Tom would later realize that Jesse was just being polite. A man could have both, and Jesse was proof.

As they walked, Jesse looked over at his new wingman. "We may have gotten off on the wrong foot this morning," Jesse said. "I apologize." He added, "In flight school I stuck my hand out a lot of times but the other guy kept his at his side."

Tom nodded empathetically. "Well, you don't have to worry about that with me," he said.

Jesse nodded with approval.

Tom caught Jesse looking at his ring again and made a mental note to leave it at home tomorrow.

"Beautiful ring," Jesse said.

Tom stopped writing and looked up, surprised. Jesse was still gazing at the ring's deep blue stone.

"I lost mine swimming in the pond by my house," Jesse said, referring to his high school ring.

Tom told Jesse that he had lost his ring, too, during flight training at Pensacola. The one he was wearing was a replacement, not the original.

"You get used to it being there," Jesse said. "It reminds you of something you can be proud of, huh?"

Tom fought back a grin. He felt the potential to really like this Jesse Brown.

CHAPTER 10

ONE FOR THE VULTURES

Nearly four months later, April 4, 1950
Warwick, Rhode Island

It was morning and Daisy was crying in the cottage's dark bedroom. She was dressed, with makeup on, and was curled up in the fetal position. She knew where Jesse had gone and what he was trying to do, and the thought nearly drove her mad.

After a while, Daisy stood, wiped her eyes, and blew her nose. She snuck down the hallway and cracked the door to the baby's room. Pam was still asleep. At the sight of her child sleeping, Daisy's eyes welled up again with tears. She shut the door to Pam's room, held a hand to her mouth, and hurried to the living room. A thought repeated in her mind: *What will we do if something happens to him?*

Daisy clutched herself and paced in front of the bookshelf. Jesse had given her a book club subscription for her birthday and she had filled the shelves with Emily Post's etiquette books and romantic novels like *Pride and Prejudice*. All Daisy wanted was a happy ending of her own.

Jesse had tried to prepare her for the worst. He often sat her down and reminded her: "On any day that I walk out of this house, there's a possibility that I may not walk back in."

She stepped to the front window and peered through the curtains. Their car sat empty in the driveway. Jesse had taught her to drive on the back roads, and she could manage to drive to the grocery store and back. Yet she felt stranded.

Daisy curled up in a chair near the window and kept glancing outside, as if her longing would bring Jesse home sooner. Dangling from Daisy's neck was a cross. She held it tightly and prayed for her husband's safety.

That afternoon

The aircraft carrier USS *Wright* plowed through the dark, choppy sea. The large warship served as a floating air base, with a full flight deck and more space below for the planes. On the tower of the carrier, Tom Hudner weaved through the pilots and sailors who crowded the observation deck. The overlook was darkly nicknamed "Vulture's Row" because it was the best spot to watch carrier landings—some of which ended in crashes.

Gray clouds hung over the Atlantic Ocean, with cracks of blue sky peeking through in spots. Tom's eyes locked on a sleek dark Corsair that was flying past the ship in the opposite direction. Jesse was at the controls and coming around to land.

Tom's squadron mates shared the railing. Nearby was Ensign Carol Mohring, a lanky twenty-six-year-old with dark hair who'd recently joined the squadron. Carol's folks were Germans who had immigrated to Pennsylvania. He had a cleft chin and sharp eyebrows and often appeared to be frowning.

"How's he doing?" Tom asked Carol.

"He's missed twice," Carol said with the hint of an accent. "Both wave-offs, not even close." Carol spoke matter-of-factly, but with concern. He and Jesse were close friends who carpooled to work together. "He's coming in too hot and high."

Tom knew why Jesse was having difficulties: it was because of the Corsair aircraft.

That winter, the navy had redesigned Fighting 32 from a fighter squadron to a ground attack squadron and replaced their lightweight Bearcats with heavyweight Corsairs. Unlike the Bearcat, the Corsair was combat-tested and capable of hauling tons of bombs and rockets.

Despite a reputation as the navy's iconic fighter plane of WWII, the Corsair had a glaring weakness: its "hog nose." The plane's nose was too long. Besides that, its cockpit—where the pilot sat—was too far back along the plane's body, known as the fuselage. This compromised the pilot's ability to see exactly when he needed it most—during that heart-pounding maneuver that separated naval aviators from every other pilot on earth, the act that Jesse Brown was about to attempt: landing on an aircraft carrier.

Fighting 32 had come aboard the ship for a reason: so the pilots could get their carrier landing certifications in the new Corsairs. To qualify, a pilot needed to land six times on the carrier. Tom had already certified on an earlier cruise, but Jesse was still trying. He had made five landings so far. But the sixth was everything. If he failed on the sixth, he'd be directed back to dry land. Worse yet, his days of flying fighters would be in question.

From the back of Vulture's Row came murmurs of excitement. Dozens of Black sailors in navy pea coats and white hats were leaning across the railing, watching intently. They had come to observe the navy's first Black carrier pilot landing, to see history being made, no different than a man yearning to see Jackie Robinson steal home plate. But the stakes were higher here. No one ever got killed trying to steal a base.

Tom could see Jesse sitting tall in his seat, his canopy back. To the average sailor, everything appeared fine. But Tom knew something the average sailor didn't—Jesse was in trouble. Each time a pilot missed a landing, the panic began to build and subsequent attempts became more hazardous. The Corsair's reputation didn't help Jesse any. It wasn't called the "Ensign Eliminator" and the "Widow Maker" for nothing.

Sailors in brightly colored shirts huddled on the flight deck and shouted into one another's ears. The wind stormed across the deck, rippling their blue dungarees. Their uniforms were color-coded according to their roles: men in yellow steered the planes around the deck; men in red formed the crash crew. Tom saw them glancing at Jesse and knew what they were saying: *Be alert—this guy's shaky!*

The left wing of Jesse's plane slowly tilted toward the sea. He was beginning his U-turn to approach the carrier. The ship's loudspeaker blared, "Clear the deck!" Tom's heartbeat spiked.

The sailors known as deckhands broke apart and ran for cover in the tower.

The deck was empty except for the nine cables across the rear. The cables were essential to carrier aviation. Although the USS *Wright*'s deck stretched nearly seven hundred feet, a pilot used only the back half for landing, a space about the size of a football field. The cables were strung just five inches above the deck. This way, the cables were low enough that a plane's tires could roll over them, yet high enough that a plane's tailhook could snag one and be yanked to a stop. To stand a chance, Jesse would need to set his twelve-thousand-pound machine down at a precise angle and speed.

If he overshot the cables, there were three tall crash barriers across the middle of the ship to stop his plane's propeller and wheels. If Jesse overshot the cables and crash barriers, an ominous final barricade remained: at the front of the deck, Corsairs sat parked and empty, almost asking for a collision.

As Jesse's plane continued its turn, a landing signal officer—the LSO—waved paddles to steer him toward the deck and to signal precisely when to touch down.

Jesse's Corsair curved over the frothy waves, holding steady at 110 miles per hour. Any faster and he'd overshoot the cables. Too slow and he'd stall and wing over, into the waves.

Two hundred yards behind the deck, Jesse broke his turn and snapped his wings level. With his plane's nose high and its tail low, Jesse descended faster and faster toward the cables. He was flying nearly blind, barely able to see a sliver of the deck. That was exactly how an LSO liked it. They expected pure trust in their expertise. *Don't watch the ship!* they were known to tell pilots. *Keep your eyes on me!*

The LSO spread his arms wide like a scarecrow. *You're good!* he was telling Jesse. *Cut the engine and land!*

But something didn't look right to Jesse. He hesitated for a split second and violated the cardinal rule of carrier aviation: *"Cut" means "cut"!*

Instead, he kept flying, approaching the cables.

Only then did Jesse cut the throttle.

In a blur of speed, he dipped the Corsair's nose forward and dived for the deck. At the last second he lifted the nose and dropped the tail to catch a cable. His hook passed over one cable, then another, until they all had slipped away.

The plane's tires slammed the deck. Everyone watching gasped. Puffs of white smoke filled the air. The Corsair sank low onto its landing gear like a coiled spring.

Then it sprang. Upward the plane leapt as its momentum carried it forward, straight toward the crash barriers.

Jesse's engine snarled to life with a roar that shook the deck. Tom's eyes went wide. Rather than roll into the crash barrier as he should have, Jesse was compounding his mistake. He was pouring on full power.

Tom couldn't believe his eyes.

He's trying to take off!

Pilots gasped. Sailors covered their faces.

Jesse's Corsair leapt over the first crash barrier, then the second. He was on course for a bone-crunching collision with the parked Corsairs ahead. Tom, Carol, and the others braced for the sound of crumpling metal.

As the Corsair soared over the final crash barrier, its right tire clipped the wire. The wire spun the Corsair out of control, to the right. Instead of careening into the parked planes, Jesse's plane whistled off the side of the carrier's deck.

Then it dropped out of sight.

Across from the tower, deckhands looked on in horror.

Tom and the others rose from Vulture's Row and leaned across the railing to see forward. The crash crew appeared with axes and fire extinguishers. On the ship's bridge, the captain and his sailors stood and pressed their faces to the windows. There was nothing on the horizon but the churning sea. They waited for the sound of a plane punching into the waves, but it didn't come. The only thing they heard was the wailing wind.

A deckhand climbed cautiously to the deck, then another and another. At the edge of the deck they stopped and looked down, scanning the waves for the wreckage.

All they saw were foaming whitecaps floating on the dark sea.

The men looked up to the horizon. Their eyes narrowed. A mile away flew a dark blue plane just skimming the waves.

The men burst into a massive cheer.

The cheers diminished into laughter and clapping as the Corsair shrank in the distance. After several tense seconds, the plane climbed skyward and slowly began turning.

Jesse Brown was coming back around.

Twenty minutes later, Jesse removed his gear in silence in a ready room below the flight deck. The "ready room" was where the pilots conducted meetings. It looked like a small theater, with an aisle dividing rows of red leather seats. A movie screen in the front could be pulled down, under which was a chalkboard.

The pilots' flight suits hung from pegs on the left wall. Soon, everyone who had flown that day would gather in the room for a debriefing, to hear the LSO read his critique of each landing.

Jesse had completed the six requisite landings and was now fully qualified in the Corsair. But he dreaded what would transpire in the debriefing. A naval aviator was supposed to land correctly the first time—not the fourth—and Jesse knew how the LSO would describe his barrier bounce: "DNKUA."

It was an abbreviation, pilot-speak for "Damn Near Killed Us All."

"There he is!" a voice shouted.

A rush of pilots burst through the doorway. Jesse turned and saw the tall frame and curly black hair of Marty Goode. Marty was Jewish and felt kinship with Jesse because they both had endured prejudice. Marty's gang of junior ensigns followed close behind. Marty threw an arm over Jesse's shoulder to make a pronouncement.

"They say there are two kinds of aviators in the navy," Marty told his gang. "Those who have hit the barrier—and those who will someday hit it. But I think there's a third—Jesse Brown. When he sees a barrier, he jumps it!"

The pilots laughed. Even Jesse had to smirk.

Jesse relaxed his shoulders as Marty and the others pummeled him with their questions. As they replayed his barrier bounce with their hands, Jesse's smile faded. Despite the humor, despite the praise, he understood the reality.

He had damn near killed himself.

CHAPTER 11

A TIME FOR FAITH

The next evening, April 5, 1950
Warwick, Rhode Island

From her seat on the couch, Daisy heard the car pull into the driveway and saw the headlights cut the darkness. She set her book down. A car door shut, then another. Daisy peered through a window and smiled. In the driveway, Jesse was removing his bag from the trunk of Carol Mohring's car. Both men were wearing long blue coats and white officer's hats.

Daisy scooped Pam up as Jesse's keys jingled in the lock. Jesse stepped inside and his eyes turned moist. He hugged his wife and daughter tightly and seemed reluctant to let go. Finally, Jesse remembered that Carol was waiting on the porch, so he took Pam into his arms and stepped aside, inviting Carol in. Carol had visited the family many times. He took off his hat, greeted Daisy, and tousled Pam's hair.

After putting Pam to bed, Jesse sat in the living room with Carol and switched on the radio. A big-band melody drifted into the kitchen, where Daisy was fixing sandwiches. Daisy enjoyed Jesse's taste in music—Glenn Miller, Nat King Cole, and Etta James—but whenever Jesse tried to pull her to her feet, Daisy drew the line. She was convinced she was a terrible dancer.

Daisy overheard bits of conversation as the men discussed Jesse's infamous landing on the deck. She leaned closer and snuck a peek. At one point Jesse sat back, wrapped his hands behind his head in frustration, and said, "If I had done anything right, I would have killed myself."

Daisy's eyes widened.

Carol revealed that once, he had crashed on the carrier USS *Cabot*. He had been coming in to land when he saw the forward deck crowded with planes. He'd lost his nerve, causing his Corsair to skid across the deck.

"I nearly crushed several men," Carol admitted.

Jesse stayed silent. His greatest fear, one he'd confided to his squadron mates, was of dying and leaving Daisy a widow.

"Makes you think of hanging it up, huh?" Jesse said.

Carol nodded.

In the kitchen, Daisy quickly turned back to the sandwiches, her face frozen with shock. She had always comforted herself by thinking, *My husband is different—nothing will happen to him.*

Daisy added cups of coffee to her platter, entered the living room, and set it on the table. Jesse sat up and tried to force a smile. He nibbled at the corner of a sandwich, like he was eating only to please her.

Daisy returned to the kitchen, her eyes heavy with worry.

Four weeks later, May 2, 1950
Quonset Point Naval Air Station

It was a pleasant spring morning. Pilots and their loved ones were gathered on the pier. About a hundred pilots from Fighting 32 and her sister squadrons said their goodbyes. The pilots wore summer uniforms—tan pants, tan jackets with black shoulder boards, and tan hats with black brims. Their girlfriends and wives wore their Sunday best hats and knee-length skirts. The USS *Leyte* loomed high over them all.

In the midst of the crowd, Daisy dabbed her eyes with a handkerchief. Jesse was holding Pam's hand as the little girl twirled circles around him. Carol Mohring hovered nearby. In the middle of a throng of laughing college girls stood Marty Goode and a few pilots.

Jesse tried to cheer Daisy up. He asked what souvenirs she wanted him to bring home for her. In contrast to her fretting, he was bursting at the seams to see the world.

Soon, Fighting 32 would board the *Leyte*. Their new ship would land in the Mediterranean, joining the navy's Sixth Fleet. The unit was nicknamed the "Dancing Fleet."

A period of work and play would follow. The pilots would train over the open seas. They would even launch a mock assault on the sun-drenched island of Crete. But it was the time off in Greece, Italy, France, and Lebanon that made the Dancing Fleet a navy man's dream duty. Stories had traveled back to Quonset Point from earlier cruises—visions of white uniforms, champagne, dances, and romance.

Daisy knew her time with Jesse was running short. Sailors were gathering to unmoor the ship.

The recent headlines had set her emotions on edge. Five days earlier, the papers had revealed the fate of a lost navy plane. A month before, the Privateer reconnaissance plane—nicknamed the "Turbulent Turtle"—had vanished over the Baltic Sea, north of the Soviet Union. When the plane's landing gear had been found, it was riddled with bullet holes. The unarmed navy plane had been shot down, its ten-man crew murdered over international waters. And the perpetrators?

The Soviets.

Daisy asked Jesse if he'd be near the Soviets in the Mediterranean. Jesse assured her that the *Leyte* would be safe. "The worst that can happen is a sunburn from sunbathing with French girls!" he joked. Daisy playfully punched his shoulder.

On the fringe of the crowd, Tom Hudner watched Jesse and the others. His own family hadn't come to see him off. His dad couldn't get away from work, and his younger brothers and sister had school. He couldn't help feeling disappointed, but that didn't mar the excitement and anticipation of going out to sea.

The Soviets' belligerence seemed senseless to Tom, but not surprising. They had been angling for a fight since WWII.

In August 1945—just two weeks after the war's end—Soviet fighters had attacked an American B-29 that was parachuting food and medicine to a POW camp in Korea. Then in September and October they attacked navy planes off the coast of northern China. Their involvement in East Asia was grounded in a desire to spread their own political doctrines, and to undermine America's.

A murmur traveled the crowd, then an officer shouted,

"Okay, let's hop to it." Couples embraced. Children hugged their fathers' waists.

Jesse picked Pam up, kissed her, and set her down. He embraced Daisy as her tears dripped onto his shoulder. She wanted to whisper in his ear: *Jesse Leroy Brown, stop risking your life and stay with us!* In her mind, she and Jesse could live out their days in their cottage near the pond. But she knew saying anything would only spoil Jesse's adventure.

When Jesse let go, Daisy pulled herself together. Her eyes flickered with a thought. She knelt by Jesse's flight bag and pretended to be making sure it was zippered. Swiftly, she slipped a slender book from her coat pocket into his bag without his noticing.

Carol stepped up to Daisy and shook her hand before turning for the ship.

Jesse kissed Daisy once more before forcing himself to break away. He turned back and shouted, "Don't worry, darling, I'll send you a postcard!" Daisy laughed in the midst of her tears. Jesse blew her one last kiss, then turned away and strode up the gangway into the ship. Beside him, Marty Goode was going on about how gorgeous French girls supposedly were. Glancing up at the carrier, Tom felt small. Sailors leaned from the tower above and looked down as the pilots boarded. At the end of the gangway, an officer stood in a blue uniform jacket. The officer held his hand in a frozen salute against the black brim of his white hat. As the pilots passed him, each snapped a salute in response. Jesse, Tom, and Marty did the same, and stepped into a dark passageway that led into the heart of the *Leyte*.

★ ★ ★

For a better view of the carrier's departure, Daisy led Pam closer to the water where the other young wives and pilots' girlfriends milled about. Daisy edged close to Dick Cevoli's wife, Grace. Grace was tall with long brown hair and a slender, gentle face. Several times, Daisy and Jesse had visited the Cevolis' cottage in Shore Acres, an idyllic community south of the base.

Daisy had met Grace and the other young women the summer before, when Jesse brought her to the air group's summer social in the officers' club. Amid the sounds of clinking glasses, the pilots and their wives and girlfriends had lined up to shake hands with the new couple. On the drive home, Daisy had told Jesse how special the others had made her feel. After that, Daisy visited the officers' club once a week with Grace and the other young women.

Chimes sounded and the women began waving up toward the men on the deck, hoping their pilots would appear. Grace Cevoli held her son's tiny hand and helped him wave. Daisy glanced in Grace's direction and realized that the woman wasn't crying, yet Grace had as much to lose as she did. Daisy dried her nose with her handkerchief. She was beginning to understand the duty of a military wife.

Daisy smiled and waved like the others; she would wait for Jesse's letters and hope he was right—*the worst that can happen is a sunburn.*

CHAPTER 12

A DEADLY BUSINESS

Twenty days later, May 22, 1950
Off the southwest coast of Sicily

Tom jumped from the wing of his Corsair and hurried over to Cevoli. Jesse and a pilot named Bill Koenig exited their planes and rushed in the same direction. The men stopped breathlessly at Cevoli's side. They were all wearing cloth flight helmets and silver aviator sunglasses. Each of them had just landed on the deck of the *Leyte* in rapid-fire sequence, twenty seconds apart.

Far in the distance, thin white clouds hovered over the coast of Sicily. A ship known as a destroyer and eighteen other ships surrounded the carrier. Together, these ships formed the Dancing Fleet, the navy's largest active force.

Already the fleet had visited Portugal and Greece, and now it was here in Sicily. Just moments before, the four pilots had been aloft, practicing their aerial gunnery. They had shot at a white banner that was being towed by another plane. The catch was, they couldn't actually see if they had hit the banner—that is, not until the tow plane came down.

As the pilots waited for the tow plane to return, adrenaline surged in their veins. The four men often flew together, and on paper were assigned to "Cevoli's flight." Technically, Cevoli was the flight's best shot, having fired at live planes and ships in World War II. Jesse was second best, with a year's worth of trigger time over Tom. But it was Lieutenant Bill Koenig, the squadron's newest member, who was the most competitive.

Bill Koenig, a short, baby-faced pilot from Iowa, scanned the sky, his pale blue eyes beaming intensity. Today, he was certain, his aim had been on the money. Everyone joked that if there ever was a perfect naval officer, Koenig was the man. His tie was always cinched the tightest, his shoes always the best polished.

"Here he comes!" Tom shouted, pointing to a speck in the sky behind the carrier. Jesse and Koenig and Cevoli leaned forward to see. From the plane's belly hung a thirty-yard banner, fluttering like an advertisement over a beach. Before takeoff, each pilot's bullets had been painted a different color, so they could track their scores.

The white banner was riddled with colored holes. Tom's eyes lit up as the Corsair came into view. Cevoli grinned with the reigning champion's confidence. The men were especially happy not to be towing the banner. Being a tow pilot required nerves of steel. The tow pilot needed to fly straight and level while other pilots swooped in from the side to shoot the banner behind him. If a shooter misjudged the direction of his bullets, the tow pilot could come under fire.

Only Carol Mohring ever volunteered for this job. As the shakiest pilot in the squadron, he seemed eager to make friends, from carpooling with Jesse to towing the banner—anything to get the other pilots to know him as more than the kid with the German accent.

High up in his Corsair, Carol released the hook on his plane's belly. The banner with the colored holes fluttered down like a streamer. It splashed down into the sea and rolled on the waves. "Come on, come on, stay right there!" Koenig said. Tom chuckled at his friend's intensity.

With one scoop sailors lifted the banner from the sea. Tom breathed a sigh of relief. Koenig happily shook a fist. Next, the crew would count the holes by color, then report the results.

The flyboys practiced often for a reason. Their commanders suspected that World War III might be waged in the Mediterranean. The Soviets desperately wanted to gain a "warm water" port there so they could send warships to the Middle East in the event of World War III. The *Leyte* was in the Mediterranean Sea to prevent that from happening.

So far, the strategy was working.

"Clear the deck! Clear the deck!" the *Leyte*'s loudspeaker blared. Tom and the others watched Carol land.

Carol was in the middle of his U-turn and perpendicular to the ship. His left wing was angled downward.

Tom lifted his sunglasses for a better look. The nose of Carol's Corsair seemed to be angled a bit high. Its tail was drooping a bit low.

"His approach is off," Cevoli said. "He needs to speed up."

Tom murmured in agreement. Flying too low and slow was dangerous in a Corsair—but so was the act of acceleration. A pilot needed to level his wings before adding heavy power. Otherwise, the Corsair's powerful engine would surge—and the propeller's massive torque would twist the plane clockwise onto its back.

The LSO stood with his arms at his sides. Carol was still too far away to be directed. His Corsair's left wing dipped farther toward the sea. Then it flicked shakily upward.

"He's stalling!" Jesse shouted with alarm.

Carol's wing dipped again, then rose again. From a distance, Tom heard the Corsair's engine surge, but its wings were far from level.

With a mechanical groan, the Corsair began rolling clockwise as if Carol were attempting a barrel roll above the waves. The Corsair kept groaning and turning, wing over wing, until it was upside down with its landing gear aimed toward the sky.

Tom held his breath.

Jesse stood still.

The plane nosed downward. Its belly flashed in the sunlight, its engine screamed, and the Corsair plunged into the sea. Water burst upward.

Tom raised his hands to his helmet in shock.

The waves settled and the Corsair came into view. It was floating upside down, with two propeller blades jutting from the sea.

Alarmed silence settled on the carrier deck. Suddenly the ship's loudspeaker broke in: "Emergency! Emergency! Plane in the water!" The crash crew raced from the tower. Tom, Jesse, Koenig, and Cevoli ran to the deck.

The plane floated as the waves lapped its wings. When would Carol's waving hand emerge?

The *Leyte*'s helicopter and the destroyer hurriedly approached the wrecked Corsair. But there was no sign of life.

"It's all too late," Tom muttered stunned, shaking his head. Just then, bubbles rose from the Corsair's nose and popped along the surface. The plane seemed to twitch, as if it were coming back to life. Everyone looked on in suspense. Then, in one motion, the nose sank into the translucent sea. Its tail rose slowly until it was standing upright. In a smooth rush, the Corsair slid into the deep. A frothy white circle floated on the waves where the plane had been. Slowly the circle shrank, smaller and smaller until the sea was smooth.

No one said a word. Tom's heartbeat raced with confusion and shock. He and the others timidly avoided Jesse's eyes. They knew how close his friendship with Carol had been. There was no more talk of the banner and scores.

CHAPTER 13

A KNOCK IN THE NIGHT

A month later, June 25, 1950
Off the west coast of Italy

It was just after midnight as the ship drifted at anchor under a half-moon.

On the nearby coast, the city of Livorno, Italy, was wide awake. But on the *Leyte,* the lights began to click off, from the tower down to the deck, until the whole carrier went dark.

Against the shore lights, the *Leyte*'s silhouette stood like a rock in the sea.

Below the ship's deck, a young officer's assistant hurried down the hall of officers' cabins, rapping each wooden door with his fist until a pilot emerged.

Tom thrust his head out from the doorway. His hair was matted and he was wearing a T-shirt and shorts. With all the noise, he seldom slept well on the ship.

"Sir, something big's up," the assistant said. "Skipper wants everyone in the ready room in ten."

"How big?" Tom wiped the sleep from his eyes.

"World War Three just started." The assistant moved on to the next cabin.

Tom wavered on the doorstep, dumbstruck. Conventional wisdom said that it would take two years before the Soviets could attack. Had the military got it wrong?

He threw on his pants, a tan shirt, and a black tie, then bundled his flight jacket around his shoulders. By the time he reached Fighting 32's ready room, it was abuzz with nervous chatter. He dropped into a seat near Koenig and gave his friend an uneasy glance. Neither said much. Everyone was waiting for the skipper, the squadron leader.

Cevoli sat in the ready room's front row, sipping coffee while fending off nervous questions from the younger pilots. Jesse sat silently nearby. Since Carol's death, he had become quieter than usual, withdrawn even, and now he was deep in thought. It was nearly 8 p.m. back in Mississippi, where Daisy and Pam were staying with Daisy's mom.

He didn't have to think long. The skipper entered the room. He looked stern, with a thick jaw and a mustache. The room went silent and the twenty-one pilots jumped to their feet. The skipper stepped front and center. He was Lieutenant Commander Dugald Neill, from Long Island, but the man insisted that his pilots call him "Skipper."

"Here's the skinny," the skipper growled. "The Soviets are mobilizing, so we're mobilizing, too. Is this the big one? Who the hell knows? All they're telling us is 'Code Three, be ready on a moment's notice.'"

The pilots glanced at one another, wondering what exactly that meant.

The skipper gestured to an intel officer, who placed a world map against the blackboard. The intel officer spoke up. "The Reds might be preparing to hop the Bering Strait and charge into Alaska," he said. "Or their armored divisions might be gearing up to race through Germany bound for Paris and up to Denmark and Norway."

The skipper stepped toward the map and added, "*Leyte*'s concern is the eastern Mediterranean. The Reds will move for Turkey after the other attacks are under way. They'll want to cut our oil pipelines in Lebanon and Israel and take the Suez Canal. If they do that, then they'll immobilize the whole of America."

Tom and the other young pilots looked uncertainly at him. *Where is the skipper going with this,* they wondered—*and what does it mean for us?* Cevoli listened closely to the skipper without adding anything. He was the skipper's second-in-command, but he wasn't one to wield strict authority. Some of the squadron's pilots whispered that he was second-in-command in name only, because he spent more time joking and playing backgammon than doing his paperwork.

The skipper nodded to the operations officer, who sat in the front row.

Lieutenant Dick Fowler rose. A six-foot-four Texan, he had a sharp nose, thick chin, and blue eyes. During World War II, Fowler had shot down six Japanese planes by the age of twenty, so whenever he gave a tip or critique, people listened. Fowler was just twenty-six but both the younger and veteran pilots called him "Dad." Everyone in Fighting 32 recognized him as the outfit's best flyer.

In a deep, steady voice, Dad announced that the ship had gone on alert and that the planes were being loaded with ammunition. A third of the squadron was to suit up immediately and man their planes. He read out a list of names. Tom and Jesse were called, along with five others. They were to remain in their planes on deck until 8 a.m. If a mission came down, Dad would brief everyone planeside. Tom and the others became nervous. The squadron didn't fly much at night, and most of the pilots weren't qualified for carrier landings in the dark.

"Don't get too alarmed," Dad said, sensing the tension. "You won't likely be launching tonight or anytime soon, until the ship steams east."

Tom and the others nodded and sat back in their seats. Dad's voice had a calming effect. No one had any questions.

"Okay, boys, have at it," the skipper said.

The pilots jumped to their feet.

Dressed to fly, Tom and Jesse hurried to their planes. Behind them, they could hear waves lapping the *Leyte*.

As Tom sat waiting in his plane in the dark, he considered the war he might be about to wage against the Soviets.

When the Soviet army liberated war-ravaged Eastern Europe, they had promised the people free elections with Hitler gone.

At first, Stalin kept his promise. But when Communist parties in Poland, Hungary, Germany, and Austria lost in the free elections of 1945 and 1946, Stalin set his secret police, the NKVD, in motion. The secret police reopened former Nazi concentration camps—Auschwitz to imprison Poles, and Buchenwald and Sachsenhausen to imprison East Germans. They also built sixteen new camps to hold Hungarians.

Only then did elections start to go Stalin's way. Across occupied Europe, men indoctrinated in Moscow and known as "Little Stalins" were brought to power. From England, former prime minister Winston Churchill watched these troubling developments and famously lamented, "An iron curtain has descended across the continent." That same year, 1950, including the gulags in Russia, the Communist camp system reached its highest occupancy—2.5 million prisoners.

The sun cast an orange glow on the sea at 8 a.m. the next day, when Tom, Jesse, and the others were met with serious news.

War had broken out, all right, but it was contained to the Korean peninsula. The Communist North Koreans had attacked the democratic South Koreans.

Jesse breathed a sigh of relief. At least it wasn't World War III.

Tom himself wasn't initially alarmed by this new Korean war. It sounded like a civil war—north versus south—or a regional dispute. Even if America intervened, the Pacific Fleet could handle the job.

CHAPTER 14

THE DANCING FLEET

A week later, July 3, 1950
Aboard the USS *Leyte* off the French coast

The air crackled with energy. It was early on a Monday morning, and the pilots were off duty. They were headed ashore to Cannes, a city in southeastern France on a legendary strip of beaches called the Riviera.

Tom and Koenig, each wearing blazers over polo shirts, headed to the front of the ship and found themselves in a world of chaos. Record players and radios blared, lockers and trunk lids slammed. Jesse and his fellow ensigns bustled between sinks and their bunks with shaving kits in hand.

This was "Boys' Town," the rowdy bunk room where Marty and the other ensigns lived.

"Hurry! We're going to miss the bikinis!" an ensign shouted. The pilots had heard that French girls were all wearing a scandalous new style of bathing suit.

The skipper brushed between Tom and Koenig and into

Boys' Town. He stopped, stood with his hands on his hips, and glared around the room.

"Don't forget," the skipper said loudly for all to hear, "you're in a foreign city, and you look like foreigners, so stick together." He glanced at Tom and Koenig as he departed, as if to say, *Look after them*.

Some of the ensigns joined Tom and Koenig by the door. One yelled back to his buddies, "Hey, hurry up so we can lie in the sun and get as black as—" The ensign covered his mouth. An awkward silence descended on the room.

Koenig scowled at the offender. Tom shook his head in disbelief. All eyes snapped toward Jesse to see his reaction.

Jesse turned from his bunk and looked around. "Don't wait for me, I'll catch the next boat," he said. "Besides, I've got a head start on my color!"

The cabin erupted with laughter and even Jesse joined in. With relief, the offender grinned an apology to his squadron mate.

Jesse would rather not have had to play along with jokes at his expense. There weren't many people around him who fully understood that, though, and he wasn't sure what else to do but let it slide off him. On the outside, at least.

The Dancing Fleet had sent ships to nearby ports with a plan to reunite after thirteen days—the longest layover of the cruise. The men were headed toward the tropical coastline. Wind rushed through Tom's hair as the boat skipped along the waves. His aviator sunglasses blocked the midmorning glare.

Speedboats raced past Tom and the others, their cockpits

filled with happy young people. The frolicking seemed to sour Koenig's mood. Behind his sunglasses, his face scrunched. "We shouldn't be here," he yelled in Tom's ear over the engine's roar. "There's a war raging and we're pleasure cruising."

Tom nodded. The news from Korea was ominous. After a week of fighting, North Korean Communists had already captured the South Korean capital of Seoul and driven South Korean and American army troops into retreat. The American commander, General Douglas MacArthur, was calling for reinforcements and air support. It wasn't an easy ask. Monsoons had turned the South Korean airfields into swamps.

Tom shared Koenig's frustration. Rumor had it that another carrier had already deployed for Korea, yet the *Leyte* was still here, in Europe. Still, Tom wasn't going to turn down a chance at a break. He leapt from the boat to the dock and slapped his felt fedora onto his head. Jesse, Koenig, and the others donned fedoras, too. Tom looked around him and grinned. *We look like a bunch of gangsters,* he thought.

In Italy, they had all bought hats on the admiral's orders. The admiral wanted his officers to look good.

French dockhands held ropes while the young American sailors and pilots came ashore. Souvenir vendors offered their wares, and tour guides waved pamphlets. Tom squirmed past the vendors and onto the sidewalk. He and Jesse and the others gawked at the Riviera, a place they had seen only on travel posters. White clouds billowed over the city and church bells clanged. Bright white buildings were shaded by gently blowing palm trees. Behind it all stood tall, green, rocky mountains.

The beach curved along a half-moon bay, and white umbrellas dotted the sand. Men and women sunbathed. Others waded into the clear turquoise waters.

Tom smiled at the sight of paradise. The travel posters had boasted, "If you love life, you'll love France," and already he was a believer.

As they crossed the palm-lined boulevard, the pilots stopped to confer. A long line of outdoor restaurants and boutiques awaited them. Sailors with cameras around their necks drifted around other window-shopping tourists. Meanwhile, French locals pushed their way through the gaggles of foreigners.

Tom fished a pamphlet from his pocket, a guide to local culture. Someone said they should visit a casino. Tom wasn't eager to gamble in the morning, nor was Koenig or Jesse. But the others loved the idea. "We've got to be careful where we go with Jesse," Tom quietly reminded the ensign who'd championed the idea. The last thing Tom wanted was some casino with racist rules to insult Jesse or refuse him entry. The ensign reluctantly agreed.

Jesse must have sensed the tension, because he announced that he was going to shop for perfume for Daisy. Koenig had plans of his own. The others headed to the casino, so Tom, Koenig, and Jesse made plans to later take a boat together back to the *Leyte*.

The group broke up and the pilots went their separate ways.

Koenig strolled away in one direction while Jesse set off in the other.

On his own, Tom felt lonesome. He slapped his guide pamphlet against his hand, disappointed and unsure of what to do.

The skipper said to stick together.

CHAPTER 15

THE REUNION

That same morning
Cannes, France

A handful of young Marines in tan uniforms and tent caps stood on the sidewalk behind the beach. The beach was crowded with willowy women lying on striped beach chairs. Behind the sunbathers, waiters emerged from cabanas carrying trays of beverages.

They were more focused on checking out girls than swimming. Spotting a bikini in 1950 was a rare but exciting event.

One young Marine, with red hair and a small, downturned nose, leaned around his buddies. He was twenty-one-year-old Private First Class John Parkinson, but everyone called him "Red."

Red and the others were Fleet Marines, the boys shown in recruiting posters wearing dress blues. They were mostly military rookies, still in training for the role of ground attack. That meant that one day they'd be the ones storming the beaches while pilots like Jesse and Tom would protect them from over-head.

Though they didn't know one another personally, they would depend on one another.

Before joining the Marines, Red had never even seen a beach. When he was seven, his mother left the family's Brooklyn tenement one day and never came home. Red's father worked on the New York waterfront and couldn't care for the boy, so he sent Red to live with family friends at a farm in New York's Catskill Mountains.

Red's adopted family, Uncle Anton and Aunt Anne, were Czech immigrants who raised him to be a farmer, too. When Red turned nineteen, he told them he wanted to see the world before settling down. With their consent, he hitchhiked to the nearest recruiting center and became a Marine.

Red's friend nudged him and gestured toward a woman with dark sunglasses and black hair that curled beneath her ears. She was draping a towel over a beach chair.

"Wow, she looks just like Elizabeth Taylor!" Red said. Taylor was a reigning Hollywood actress.

The other Marines laughed at Red. They said there was no way Elizabeth Taylor would be *alone* on any beach, let alone in Cannes.

Red studied the woman more closely. Headlines called Taylor the most beautiful actress in the world, and the woman on the beach was certainly good-looking.

He took a deep breath and started walking toward her.

★ ★ ★

Sand poured into Red's black shoes. He pretended to be looking for a beach chair. As he walked past, he saw that the woman was wearing a white one-piece with a pink flower pattern. Beneath her sunglasses, she had a pale China-doll face with arching black eyebrows and a nose that turned up at the tip. Red's eyes locked on an unmistakable beauty mark on her right cheek and his heart took off racing.

Holy cow! he thought. *It might really be her!*

Red walked a safe distance, then looked back at his buddies. They raised their hands and shrugged: *Well?*

The last thing Red wanted to do was annoy the woman, and he didn't know what to ask her, anyway. His thoughts flashed back home to his uncle Anton.

How would Uncle Anton handle this? Red wondered. The hardworking Czech, a man with strong Slavic features and muscles like a bull, was his hero. Day after day they'd milked cows and harvested cauliflower, potatoes, and hay, and Uncle Anton had always impressed on him one golden life lesson—*If you're going to do something, then do it right, or don't bother doing it at all.*

Red turned around and doubled back toward the woman. He stopped near her feet.

"Miss Taylor?" he said.

The woman lifted her sunglasses. Underneath were crystal-blue eyes framed by thick black eyelashes. There was no mistaking the eyes of Elizabeth Taylor.

"Why, hello," she said playfully.

Red introduced himself, stammering.

"Why, it's nice to meet you, Red." The star sat up in her chair. "Are you a Marine?"

"Yes, ma'am," he said, sticking out his chest.

"Please, call me Elizabeth," the star said.

She asked Red if he was enjoying Europe. Red told her how at each port he hurried to the train station to go sightseeing—he'd been to Berlin, Switzerland, and even to the top of the Eiffel Tower. Elizabeth asked what he thought of each experience and seemed genuinely interested.

The other Marines came stumbling through the sand, starstruck. They joined Red and introduced themselves to Elizabeth, who seemed genuinely interested in chatting with them, asking them questions about their travels and their work. They were sorry to say goodbye when the time came.

"It was nice to meet you," Elizabeth said in parting. She gave a little wave that made Red smile as he headed off.

Did that really just happen? Red thought in disbelief as he crossed the beach. *What other surprises are in store for us?*

Wealthy guests filled the terrace café of the luxurious Carlton Hotel, but Jesse sat alone.

Between sips from a glass of ginger ale, he scribbled a letter. He'd already written a small pile that he'd sealed in envelopes. Around him, posh travelers chatted in white wicker chairs and sipped flutes of wine. The air smelled of flowers. Music drifted across the terrace.

At seven stories tall, the Carlton was the tallest building in

Cannes. Jesse had discovered the hotel in a *Guide to the Mediterranean* book that Daisy had slipped into his bag before the carrier departed Quonset Point.

The hotel's terrace proved the best place to write letters. A sun canopy provided just enough shade, and a view of the beach lay just across the boulevard.

Jesse had written to Daisy and his family, as usual. Jesse's squadron mates joked that he deserved his own postal code because he sent and received so much mail.

Carol Mohring's death was eating at Jesse. He had watched the plane sink. Carol had been his friend, had known Daisy and Pam. And he knew he had to finally bring himself to break the news to Daisy. Was there any good way to do it?

CHAPTER 16

ONLY IN FRANCE

Four days later, July 7, 1950
Off the coast of Cannes

The morning sun streaked across the *Leyte*'s flight deck and over the parked Corsairs.

Beside the nose of a plane, Tom jotted notes on a clipboard. Marty crouched with a flashlight. Flight operations were on hold while the *Leyte* was at Cannes, but maintenance work continued. Marty called out a string of serial numbers and Tom recorded them. Every pilot in the squadron had a side job; Tom and Marty were "assistant maintenance officers." Their role was to review the mechanics' work and keep tabs on aircraft readiness. Tom took his work seriously. Marty did, too, but his mind was still back ashore. He couldn't wait for them to get back to partying and socializing in Cannes—and he had met a French girl.

"Man, you should have seen her, Tom!" Marty exclaimed as he searched for a serial number. "Blond with green eyes, long legs, a real doll!"

"Sounds nice," Tom murmured.

Marty was going ashore to see her that night and he had invited Tom along. "If you aren't having a fling in this place, there's something wrong with you," Marty added.

Tom grunted. The stay in Cannes was already a third of the way over, but Tom had more pressing concerns—namely, updating the planes' logs.

Just as he had found his work rhythm, the sound of chatter and slapping flip-flops came from across the deck. Tom looked up from his clipboard.

Past the Corsair's wing walked a young woman in a short white sundress, with an officer in dress whites by her side. Tom's and Marty's eyes both went wide. It was Elizabeth Taylor.

Elizabeth spotted Marty and Tom and strolled over.

"Well, what are you doing down there?" she asked Marty. Her sundress was decorated with colorful beads and her handbag was made of white leather.

"Just making sure I don't get a flat tire," Marty said slyly.

Elizabeth flashed a smile. Marty stood, wiped his hands on his pants, and introduced himself.

Tom kept his distance, happy to let Marty do the talking. He had seen one of Elizabeth Taylor's movies and she was stunning.

"Are you mechanics?" Elizabeth asked.

"Us? No," Marty said with a laugh. He explained that they were pilots but checking the planes was part of their job. Tom nodded in agreement as he held the clipboard to his chest.

Elizabeth apologized and added that she couldn't imagine flying one of those planes. Before the officer could steer Elizabeth away for a tour of the whole ship, she invited Marty and Tom to visit a casino with her that night. She told them to bring their friends. Marty said he would be there and Tom agreed, too. The sound of the flip-flops faded as Elizabeth's escort led her away.

Marty looked at Tom with glee. "I guess you'll be meeting my girl now!"

That night, in nearby Monaco

Big-band music floated through the Monte Carlo Casino as Tom slid his chips onto the green velvet of the roulette table.

"Put one here, one here, and one there!" Elizabeth said. Sitting by Tom's left side, she pointed to the table's numbered grid. An orchid was nestled in her black hair and her strapless white dress fit elegantly. Tom happily obeyed. Across the table, Marty grinned at the sight.

Before this night, Tom had never been inside a casino, let alone the world's most famous one, in Monaco, a short train ride from Cannes. The parlor was stately, with high ceilings, ornate chandeliers, and walls embellished with gold.

Tom leaned back, pleased with his gambling partner's advice. Elizabeth knew all the rules.

Around the table, navy pilots and their girls placed their bets. Elizabeth's blue eyes narrowed when an elegant blond woman took her place across the table and cozied up to Marty's side. The pilots all looked her way, and she put her arm around Marty's waist. Her nose was small and sharp, her eyes green and bright. She was Marty's French girlfriend and she'd just stolen the spotlight from Elizabeth Taylor.

Tom looked at Marty, cocked his head in amazement, and thought, *Maybe he's some sort of Casanova after all?*

During a change of dealers, Tom stood to stretch his legs. Marty approached and whispered into his ear, "I feel like I've stepped into the middle of an unspoken competition!" He was talking about the rivalry between his girl and Elizabeth. Tom complimented his friend's eye for beauty. Marty laughed and went to refill his drink.

Tom flipped a chip in his hand as he waited for the game to resume. He was already running low on money and the night was still young.

The next morning

Tom looked up from a desk inside one of the *Leyte*'s hangars. Across from him, Marty hummed as he cross-checked serial numbers with the catalogues.

Tom had never seen Marty this cheerful and knew exactly who his friend was thinking about. The sound of approaching footsteps drew Tom's attention upward. The skipper was coming. Tom began to stand but the skipper stopped him: "As you were."

"Hiya, skipper," Marty said. The skipper nodded in return.

"Boys, we've got a heck of a problem." He told them the mechanics were having trouble starting a plane. There could be water in its gas tank. "Could be sabotage," he added. Tom and Marty glanced at each other worriedly.

The skipper's eyes settled on Marty. "Ensign Goode, I've got a job for you and it's important."

Marty nodded, eager to please.

"I want you to inspect every airplane and fuel tank to figure out if there's water in the gas and how it got there," the skipper said.

Marty's smile disappeared.

"No going ashore until it's done," the skipper added.

Tom could see Marty's mind churning. *Thirty tanks,* Tom thought. It would take Marty forever and the *Leyte* was due to leave Cannes in seven days.

Tom raised his hand, trying to be helpful. "Sir, I can assist Ensign Goode?"

"Nope," the skipper said. "I've got other tasks for you."

Tom nodded and Marty's face fell in despair.

"Carry on," the skipper said, and walked away.

"This is a bad dream," Marty muttered. There was no way for him to call his girlfriend—there were no ship-to-shore phones. He needed to get ashore to see her, to give her his address, at least. His only hope was to work quickly.

With just a few days remaining in Cannes, Marty rushed around the ship carrying glass test tubes to the ship's lab. When the report came back, the news wasn't good. Water was found in the tanks of *all* the aircraft. Marty reported to the skipper's office to explain the situation. He had concluded that the ship had taken on contaminated gas at Livorno.

"Fine work, Ensign Goode," said the skipper from his desk. "Now you can supervise the removal of the contaminated fuel from *all* our planes."

When Marty stepped from the skipper's office, he buried his face in his hands.

★ ★ ★

Several days later, Marty and the sailors and pilots leaned over the railing of the *Leyte,* watching Cannes shrink in the distance. In the morning light, the carrier's wake bubbled a golden V on the sea, like two arms reaching out.

Marty's eyes hung low with despair. He hadn't made it ashore to see his girlfriend again and now the *Leyte* was steaming east to the Greek island of Crete.

CHAPTER 17

THE FRIENDLY INVASION

July 19, 1950
The island of Crete

The Marines braced themselves as the small boat full of troops scraped the sandy bottom of the shallow water. The engine surged, the propeller gurgled. It was early in the morning as the boat pulled up to Crete and the ramp dropped. Amid the crowd, Red Parkinson was cradling an M20 Super Bazooka almost as tall as he was.

Red squinted. Before the men lay a glimpse of heaven— a Mediterranean beach, and beyond it, green fields against a backdrop of scrubby hills.

"Hit the beach!" the boat driver shouted.

"Weapons Company, move out!" an officer yelled, and the Marines surged forward. Red followed the others off the boat and into the water. He wore a full backpack and a carbine slung across his shoulder. Two more bazooka rockets dangled from a bag around his neck, and a pistol, canteen, and knife hung on his hips. Under the weight of it all, he told himself, *Uncle Anton would be proud!*

The brim of his helmet kept sliding over his eyes. *Keep going!* Red's legs grew tired as he scaled a bluff. To his left, he could see the village of Kalives. On the other side he found his five buddies, who had stopped to catch their breath. Now assembled, the boys comprised an antitank platoon. The name said it all: they specialized in destroying the enemy's tanks. Everyone had their assigned roles. In Red's squad, he carried the rocket launcher, while another Marine served as his loader, and another carried extra ammo.

Ahead, beyond the fields, lay their destination: a wide hill. This was where Red and his buddies would set up a roadblock to intercept imaginary Soviet tanks. They needed to garner as much practice as possible in preparation for the real thing.

Two Greek soldiers paced past Red and the others. They wore dark green uniforms and tipped their small brimmed caps in greeting. The Greeks were allies who had come to observe.

"We gotta get moving, or we'll miss the air show!" said one of Red's buddies. The men scaled the hill to get the best view of the *Leyte*'s planes flying over.

The Marines followed footpaths over a creek and through a field. Red carried his bazooka in both hands, evenly distributing its fourteen pounds. The weight made his arms tired, and the muggy heat made him sweat.

A few Marines ahead suddenly veered off the path. Red found them crouched at the edge of a field of melons.

"Hey, Red!" an ammo bearer shouted at him. "You're a farmer. Can we eat 'em?"

Red studied the leaves from where he stood. "Yup, they're watermelons! Get one for me, too!"

The others plucked watermelons from their stems. One of Red's buddies approached him with a melon but stopped when he noticed that Red's hands were full.

"Just shove it in my pack!" Red said with a grin. The Marine laughed and jammed the extra weight inside.

Atop the hill, Red and his buddies stopped and ditched their backpacks on the sandy ground. Red rolled up his sleeves.

One of Red's buddies checked his watch. Thinking aloud, he wondered where the flyboys were.

"Probably overslept in their floating hotel," another man joked, referring to the nicer living arrangements the pilots got on the *Leyte*.

Red tipped his helmet back. His buddies yawned and relaxed. The action in Korea was far from their minds, even as the papers were predicting a longer war, maybe six months, maybe nine.

Though they were supposed to be preparing for the mock airstrike, they all agreed that they were hungry. Someone suggested that it was time for a snack. On the edge of the hill, overlooking the sea, they drew their long Ka-Bar knives and carved into the watermelons.

Red sank his teeth into a slice. *This is the life,* he thought. The Marines enjoyed their feast and the view of the fleet at anchor, a few miles out.

One of Red's buddies lowered the slice of watermelon from his face. "Uh-oh," he mumbled, looking downhill.

Their platoon leader, Corporal Bob Devans, was approaching. Devans was just twenty years old and short, with an upturned nose and sleepy eyes in a square face. He had joined the Marines straight out of high school.

Devans's gaze settled on his men. Red and the five others didn't even try to scamper away or hide the melons. Devans shook his head in frustration.

"Fellas, you know better. Where'd you get 'em?" Devans asked.

"Down by the beach, Bob," a Marine admitted.

"I'd tell you to put 'em back, but it's too late for that," Devans said. He scanned the hilltop and saw that everyone else was in position for the mock attack.

"Keep the melons," Devans said. "Just get back to your positions and at least *act* like there's an enemy coming."

Red and the others scrambled to their positions.

The sound of clanking wheels echoed across the hilltop. Red perked up and glanced toward the fort. His buddies were starting to doze.

"Soviet tank, T-34!" Red shouted, psyching himself up to get to work. He slapped his assistants on their helmets, then raised his bazooka and aimed. The assistants perked up and glanced in the same direction.

Up the road, two small Greek boys were pulling a rickety cart loaded with watermelons. The Marines watched the boys carry melons from their cart to the other Marine squads. Sometimes the boys returned without melons, counting coins in their palms.

The youngsters worked their way down the road to Red and his buddies. They approached, presented their melons, and recited the only English they knew: "Two for dol-la!" They were deeply tanned, with mops of black hair. The youngsters' eyes suddenly went wide, locking on the watermelon rinds scattered around the Marines. Red glanced guiltily at his buddies and asked if anyone had brought any money.

None had.

"We. Don't. Have. Any. Dollars," Red told the youngsters. The boys raised their palms in confusion.

One of Red's assistants hollered for Corporal Devans.

"Oh, you've done it now," Devans said as he approached from behind. He knelt in front of the youngsters, who backpedaled in fear. "Hey, hey, don't be scared," Devans said. He pulled a phrase book from his pocket and jabbered something in Greek. The youngsters laughed. Devans chuckled and looked at his phrase book again. In each port, Red and the others had seen Devans using the local language, like an actor practicing his lines.

Devans turned to his platoon.

"It's official—you ate their livelihood," he said. "They're brothers and that's their farm by the beach." Devans fished a dollar from his pocket and handed it to the youngsters. The boys grinned and returned to their cart.

Devans turned to Red and the others with a parting thought: "You owe me a slice!"

★ ★ ★

Behind the Marines, a droning sound came from overhead. Red and his buddies turned and looked up. At eight thousand feet, four blue crosslike shapes flew in formation, followed by another, and another. More than forty planes were crossing the sky.

"It's the Ks!" a Marine shouted.

"About time," said another.

The Marines could spot the *Leyte*'s planes by the tall white letter *K* on their tails. Tom, Jesse, and Koenig were up there flying Corsairs in Cevoli's flight. Dad Fowler had a flight of his own; so did the skipper and the other squadron leaders from the *Leyte*.

One after another, the Corsairs flew downward at a gentle angle, their bent wings taking shape in the sunlight. Red and his buddies stood up. The planes were aiming for an imaginary target in the fields across the road.

"Bring it in close!" a Marine urged the planes.

The lead Corsair descended. The entire plane seemed to glimmer from nose to tail. It passed high over Red and his buddies with barely a grumble. One by one, the other three Corsairs emulated their leader's mock attack. As each gently swooped overhead, the Marines cheered with a little less enthusiasm. "Come on, bring it in lower!" a Marine shouted at the planes. It was no use. Each Corsair pulled up at the same invisible spot, then flew away. The young men groaned.

"I want my money back," one Marine joked, before they all turned back to their watermelons. High over the island, the formations turned and motored back toward the sea. They had been ordered to avoid flying low over areas populated by civilians or livestock, but the Marines didn't know this.

One young Marine was particularly peeved. He shielded his eyes and spoke for the others.

"That was the worst air show I've ever seen!"

CHAPTER 18

AT FIRST SIGHT

Three weeks later, August 11, 1950
Beirut, Lebanon

The night was young and the party was in full swing at the ritzy St. Georges Yacht Club. Mixed groups of powerful government dignitaries, well-connected young men and women, and naval officers stretched around a pool. The party, hosted by the American ambassador to Lebanon, was to welcome the navy to the capital city, Beirut.

A waiter refilled Tom's and Cevoli's champagne glasses—not for the first time. "I think the ambassador's trying to get us drunk!" Tom said with surprise. Cevoli chuckled and agreed. Neither had ever seen so much champagne being slung around.

An orchestra played within earshot. Palm fronds swayed in the lamplight. Tom and Cevoli strolled around the pool. From the top of his hat to the cuffs of his pants, Tom was dressed all in white. He loved the crisp perfection of the formal uniform. His jacket was punctuated by gold buttons and framed by black shoulder boards; on his chest, his golden aviator wings shone in the light. But the uniform was difficult to keep clean.

Cevoli glanced across the pool. "Look!" he said. "He's dragging Jesse off again!" Tom looked in time to see the ambassador lead Jesse by the arm toward a throng of local dignitaries and their wives. The partygoers swarmed Jesse to shake his hand. The curious expressions on their faces suggested that they had never seen a Black officer, let alone one in dress whites. The men and women leaned forward to hear Jesse's every soft-spoken word. Underneath his politeness, though, Jesse was tired of being seen as a curiosity.

The party still had an hour to run before midnight. For Tom, Jesse, and their squadron mates, the traveling and the parties were becoming tiresome. After being in the South of France, they had kept traveling to Crete, and now Beirut. Next, the Dancing Fleet was scheduled for a last stop in France, and Tom was counting down the days.

Then, out of the corner of his eye, he saw her.

At first he caught a flash of brown hair and a pastel-pink dress and he heard her high heels clattering as she walked past. Tom's eyes followed her. The girl glanced over her shoulder and caught him looking.

Dark eyebrows arched over blue eyes. Her lips were red and her smile beamed all-American friendliness.

Tom felt a rush of light-headedness.

Is she looking at me? he thought.

Tom watched the girl turn away and blend in with a group at the far end of the pool.

Cevoli shook Tom to bring him back to earth. Tom saw his flight leader grinning broadly.

"She's probably with one of them," Tom said, motioning to the group the girl had joined. Cevoli disagreed. He assured Tom that only a single girl would give such a look.

Tom glanced back. The girl laughed and tossed her hair, then shot another glance in his direction.

Cevoli looked down at Tom's flute of champagne. "Drink up!" he said. "That's an order."

Tom chuckled nervously and downed the glass. "Drink mine, too," Cevoli said, handing his glass to Tom, who threw it back in one gulp. "Good, you're fueled."

Tom began to waver. He reminded Cevoli that they would be sailing from Lebanon in two days.

Cevoli leaned close and put a hand on Tom's shoulder. "I shouldn't have to tell you this," he said. "But in our line of work sometimes you only get one chance."

Tom nodded. Here one day, gone the next—every aviator knew the hazards.

Cevoli took both empty glasses from Tom's hands. "Why are you still here?" he asked.

The girl turned and stepped from her group before Tom had reached her. "About time!" she said, laughing. She was certainly American.

Taken aback, Tom grinned. "I saw you from over there,"

he said, and pointed to where Cevoli stood. He told the girl he couldn't help but wonder who she was. A bemused look crossed her face. Tom's was probably the most honest pickup line she had ever heard.

As they talked, Tom discovered that the girl worked for the embassy. She knew all about the Korean War on the diplomatic front, where Britain and India were now calling on the Soviets to stop the North Korean attacks. *Gosh, she's fascinating,* Tom thought.

"Have you seen the lounge yet?" the girl asked at one point. Tom hadn't, so she grabbed him by the hand and pulled him toward the hotel.

In a booth, Tom and the girl sat close together at a table covered with empty champagne flutes. The party was thinning out and the lounge was dark and atmospheric.

The girl studied Tom's face as he smoked a cigarette. Tom pulled the cigarette from his lips and flicked away the ash. He had smoked it down to half its original size.

"Okay, ready for some magic?" he asked.

The girl nodded.

Tom placed the cigarette between his lips and cupped his hands over his mouth. Wisps of smoke rose from the cracks between his fingers. He began making pained expressions with his eyes, as if he were being burned, but he kept his hands clasped over his mouth. Finally, the smoke stopped rising and Tom relaxed. The cigarette was missing from his lips. The girl's eyes followed Tom's hands as he slowly slid them toward her, then fanned them open.

His palms were empty. The cigarette was gone.

The girl's eyes leapt with amazement to Tom's face.

Tom smiled and shrugged. When he refused to tell her how he did it, she punched him playfully on the arm.

"I want to give you something," Tom said. The girl cocked her head and leaned closer.

Tom unfastened his collar and began unbuttoning his jacket, one gold button after another.

The girl sat back in confusion. He slid a hand into his jacket and fiddled inside. From the outside, he grabbed his golden flight wings and pried them from his uniform. The wings were a naval aviator's most valuable possession.

Tom handed his wings to the girl. "For you," he said.

The girl studied the wings in her palm and glanced up, her eyes glimmering. She embraced Tom tightly. When she released him, a dumbstruck grin lined his face.

The girl gazed into Tom's eyes. He gazed into hers.

"This was a lovely night," Tom said. The girl nodded, maintaining eye contact. Tom glanced down at his watch and added, "But I've got a boat to catch." The girl's face dropped. She had expected a kiss.

As Tom gave the girl a hand and led her from the booth, he was sure he had played everything right. They'd made plans for a date the following night, and Tom had already decided: he'd take bigger chances tomorrow.

All navy men were supposed to reach the docks by midnight, and time was running short. Tom stumbled away from the hotel, his hat in his hand and his coat unbuttoned.

Teenage Tom Hudner (seated) with his siblings.

Nineteen-year-old Tom during a visit home from the Naval Academy in 1944.

Daisy holds Pam during a 1949 visit to Hattiesburg.

Jesse and Daisy with Pam at their Rhode Island cottage, summer 1949.

Jesse as an ensign, September 1949.

Marty Goode aboard the *Leyte*.

In February 1950, Jesse rehearses his reading in the Quonset Point chapel. His reading was Romans 12, "A Living Sacrifice."

A *Leyte* LSO signals "Hold steady!"

While training in spring 1950, Marty catches the last cable before the crash barrier.

Fighting 32 during the Mediterranean cruise. Front row, left to right: Key, Hudner, Ferris, Cronin, Cevoli, Neill, Fowler, Jester, Whalen, Koenig, Lane. Back row, left to right: Brown, Sargent, Byron, Stevens, Cotchen, Mohring, Goode, Sheffield, Nelson, Miller, Gelonek.

Leyte deckhands prepare a Corsair for takeoff.

The beach at Cannes during the *Leyte*'s visit.

Elizabeth Taylor, Nicky Hilton, and friends tour the *Leyte* in Cannes.

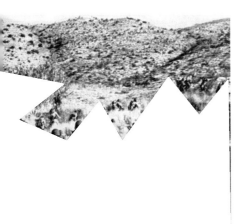

6th Fleet Marines practice an amphibious
landing in the Mediterranean.

Elizabeth Taylor dines with the *Leyte*'s offi

Red Parkinson
(far right) and his
antitank platoon
on Crete.

During maneuvers, a Marine aims an M20 Super Bazooka.

Ed Coderre during a visit home to Rhode Island in 1949.

Enjoying watermelons on Crete. Foreground, left to right: Charlie Kline, Red Parkinson, Bob Devans.

Marines assemble aboard the *Leyte* during the Mediterranean cruise.

Red Parkinson naps as his LST ship passes through the Suez Canal, bound for Korea.

Before Jesse's deployment, he and Daisy drove home through Tennessee, where Daisy snapped this photo.

Days before deploying, Jesse plays with Pam outside Daisy's mother's apartment.

Bill "Wilkie" Wilkinson during flight training.

Wilkie snapped this photo during a practice flight before Korea.

In their cabin aboard the *Leyte*, Jesse pens a letter home while Bill Koenig reads.

On the *Leyte*'s first day at war, her crew watches one of '32's planes launch.

Squadron 32 at the front of the pack, waiting for the takeoff signal.

In the hangar deck, sailors muscle a Corsair onto an elevator.

"Dad" Fowler as a twenty-year-old Hellcat pilot in 1944.

Tom in the cockpit during the Korean cruise.

Dad Fowler launches down the center line. "I always tried to fly like he did," Wilkie would write.

Tom knew that the Shore Patrol, the navy's police, were out rounding up sailors, pilots, and Marines who appeared drunk or in danger of breaking curfew—men like him.

Now you've done it, Tom thought. His shoes slapped the road faster.

Tom saw the docks where the *Leyte*'s boats were bobbing. Unfortunately, the Shore Patrol stood in the way, so he couldn't sneak on. The SPs had formed a human chain to steer drunken sailors and Marines toward the boats to ensure that no one fell in the water. Some of the drunken men were topless, having swapped their shirts for a final drink. Others were wearing souvenirs—kepis, fur shawls—and a few were carrying their buddies. During an earlier shore leave in Athens, a pilot had even brought a goat on a leash back to the docks.

Tom stood as soberly as possible and approached the SPs' human chain.

"Excuse me," he said to an SP.

The SP turned, saw Tom, and said, "Evening, sir, you're just in time." The SP stepped aside.

Tom thanked him and fell in line with the drunken sailors. On the boat back to the *Leyte,* he took a seat in the middle. He sprawled across the damp bench and felt the wood, cool against his cheek. He no longer cared if he smudged his dress whites. Another officer entered the boat, saw Tom, and laughed as he claimed a seat.

"It's not the booze," Tom said, clutching his sore stomach. "I ate a cigarette."

The following afternoon

A puttering noise shook the ceiling. Tom clutched his pounding head and sat up in his bunk, baffled. Without windows, his cabin aboard the *Leyte* was dark and timeless.

Tom glanced at his watch and cursed. Noon had come and gone. It was a Saturday and he had nowhere to go until his date that night, but apprehension still nagged at him. Something was happening on deck.

Tom slid heavily to the floor and winced. His head throbbed. He found his white uniform draped over a chair and went to unpin his golden wings, to transfer them to his tan uniform— but they were missing. Tom slapped himself on his forehead.

What was I thinking?

He knew he could buy replacements back in the States, but that first pair carried irreplaceable meaning.

Tom dressed to go above deck to find out what else he was missing.

Slowly, he climbed the steps to Vulture's Row. "Holy cow," he muttered. Beside the *Leyte,* a few football fields' length away, a massive aircraft carrier lay at anchor. Tom looked to a pilot next to him.

"It's the *Midway*!" a pilot explained. "You missed it, she just came in."

In the water between the two carriers, landing craft were carrying helmeted Marines from the *Midway* to the *Leyte.*

"What's going on?" Tom asked the pilot.

"Our orders just came in," the pilot replied. "We're leaving for the States today, then on to the Far East—you know what that means!" His face lit up with excitement at the prospect of getting into the thick of the Korean War. He explained that the Marines were probably going to Korea, too. The *Midway* had scooped them up from across the fleet and was transferring them to the *Leyte*.

Their cruise travels had officially been cut short. Tom draped his arms over the railing as the thought hit him: *I'm never going to see her again.*

Tom looked toward Beirut. In 1950, before the age of commercial jet travel, Lebanon seemed as far from home as the moon.

Tom's face drooped with self-disgust. He was furious with himself for breaking his own rule. He was a bachelor committed to his career and he knew better than to have chased after that girl. Now his infatuation wilted in the heat of a new reality: he was going to war.

Tom raised his eyes. He glanced toward the shore and up to the St. Georges hotel, where he'd spent the best night of his life with the brunette girl in the pink dress.

CHAPTER 19

ON WAVES TO WAR

The next day, August 13, 1950
The Mediterranean

No longer was it a theory—the Corsairs around Tom would soon be operating in hostile skies. The rear of the ship looked like a yard sale.

Along a side wall, a dozen Marines were inventorying their rifles, bazookas, and other equipment. Red Parkinson followed Corporal Devans as he walked from one boy to the next, scribbling down notes. Each Marine had two seabags to sort, one that would be sent home from Crete and one they would carry to their next destination: Japan.

"Bob, my jungle kit is missing," a Marine said, glancing up. Devans nodded to Red, who scribbled down: *one jungle kit*.

Another fellow's helmet cover was missing. Another had lost his canteen cover. Devans sighed.

"I can't find my Ka-Bar," a Marine reported. Devans shook his head. The knife could be replaced, but that wasn't the point.

At the end of the line, Devans called both antitank platoons together and asked them to take a knee. He squatted in the midst of them. Everyone liked Devans. Rumor had it that he wrote to a girl back home and sent a chunk of every paycheck to his parents, who were struggling financially.

"Fellas, why are we missing more Ka-Bars than anything?" Devans asked.

The others remained silent.

"Where we're going," Devans said, "you're gonna want your knife."

Devans had a last message for the others, this one softer in tone.

"If you get killed over there, your seabags get sent home. Make sure yours is cleaned out of anything you don't want your folks to see."

The boys remained silent.

Red returned to his buddies and found them digging through the personal things in their seabags. Word had traveled throughout the deck. On the floor lay piles of pulp fiction comics and pinup magazines. A few boys unearthed stacks of love letters.

At the bottom of his seabag, Red found a flyer for a French cabaret show. A sheepish grin crossed his face and he quickly crumpled the flyer in his palm to spare Uncle Anton and Aunt Anne any shame.

The Marines carried their stacks of contraband to the rear of the ship and tossed the piles overboard. Somberly, they showered dirty magazines and photographs onto the sea. When Red got his turn at the ropes, he tossed his wadded-up flyer into the breeze and watched it mix with the contraband.

A few Marines lingered at the ropes and looked pensively at the sea, as if they could already feel the chill of Korea, the place that would end their lives or make them grown men. The things that made them boys drifted farther and farther behind the ship until they slipped beneath the rolling waves.

CHAPTER 20

THE LONGEST STEP

Sixteen days later, August 29, 1950
Fall River, Massachusetts

Tom set his seabag on the Persian rug in the entryway of his parents' home. He had one week of leave remaining before the *Leyte* sailed for the Korean War. It was a Tuesday evening, yet it felt like a holiday to Tom. *Ten days.* The skipper had told the squadron to prepare for ten days in America before the *Leyte* would sprint to the Far East.

"My darling!" his mother shouted as she approached from the hall. Mary Hudner's gray hair was curled above her dark eyebrows. A fashionable dress draped her trim figure, and her pearl necklace shone. She led him to the living room and sat down before the fireplace.

As they caught up, Tom told his mother about the Mediterranean and she shared stories about her social scene. Tom's father was away at one of the family's grocery stores.

Suddenly, Mary's eyes sparkled as she remembered something.

She hurried away, reemerged with an envelope, and handed it to Tom. In the upper left corner stood a red shield and the words *Harvard College.*

Tom flipped over the letter and raised an eyebrow when he saw that it had been opened.

"I'm sorry," his mother said. "I just had to see if it was important."

Tom read the letter: "We're awaiting your application as we form our new classes for fall. . . ." His brow furrowed. He had shown early interest in attending Harvard but assumed that the college would have forgotten about him when he never submitted an application. Tom lowered the letter and looked at his mother. "Don't they know I've already got an education?" he said. "Why are they still writing to me?"

Mary smiled. "Well, you were a fine student."

Tom fought back a smile. His grades hadn't been that good. If anything, it was his prep school pedigree that had opened the door to Harvard.

Mary asked Tom if he would consider pursuing a graduate degree at Harvard. She knew her son had fulfilled his two years of service to the navy and could foreseeably seek a discharge.

"Nah," Tom said. "I'm going to make a career of the navy."

Mary looked away with dismay. That meant that her son was due to sail for war.

Tom handed back the letter. "Don't worry, Mother, they'll stop sending them sooner or later."

Two days later, Tom and his father sat in silence at the

dining table. Thomas Senior's gray hair was slicked back and he wore wire-rimmed spectacles and a three-piece suit. Senior had worked hard for his wealth with his own father to build their grocery chain. Tom had also dressed up for dinner, as was the family's custom. He wore a dark suit. The family had just celebrated his twenty-sixth birthday, and now Senior wanted to talk with his son in private. The war was on his mind. That day, the first British unit had arrived in Korea. Troops and medical units were following from eighteen other U.N. nations. The international response was unprecedented: American forces were about to lead the first United Nations army into battle.

"So, how are you feeling about where you're going?" Senior asked, lighting a cigarette.

Tom lowered his pipe. "Well, we have to show the Communists that enough is enough, or their aggression will never stop," he said. "So Korea's as good a place as any."

Senior asked if Tom's buddies felt the same. Tom chuckled and said that one of the pilots had actually transferred out of the squadron recently. Senior's face twisted with distaste.

"He requested transfer to a noncombatant unit," Tom added.

"He chose to be in fighters, didn't he?" Senior asked.

"Yes, sir," Tom said.

"And he raised his hand to protect and defend the American people, didn't he?" Senior added.

Tom nodded. They had all taken the oath. "In his defense," Tom said, "there's lots of ways to serve, and they don't all call for trigger pulling."

Senior nodded. He had been an officer himself during World War I and he regretted being stuck in a staff job while everyone else was deployed. "So you don't exactly need to go to Korea, do you?" Senior asked. "You can call Quonset and transfer out like that other fellow?"

"Yeah, I suppose I could." Tom shrugged. "But none of the other fellows are backing out. We all figure it's dangerous if we just let the North Koreans take the South. If we don't take a stand . . . what message would that send the Soviets?"

Senior looked at Tom and swallowed hard, fighting back emotion. His next words would mean the world to Tom.

"I'm proud of you, son."

A day later, in Mississippi

The sunlight settled over the Hattiesburg projects as Jesse and Daisy sat on the front steps of her mother's apartment. Lamplight leaked from some windows; radio music trickled from others.

Dressed in slacks and a white shirt with short sleeves, Jesse held Daisy's hand, his eyes distant in thought.

Daisy smiled and pretended not to notice. She wore a brightly colored dress, and a floral fragrance drifted from her neck, the perfume that Jesse had sent home from Cannes.

The couple had done most of their dating on the porch, under the eye of Daisy's mother, Addie. Addie was a generous, loving woman, yet strong, too. Her husband had died young, leaving her a thirty-year-old widow with five children. To put food on the table, she worked hard cleaning houses; it meant she had often had to be away from her kids to make enough money to give them a good life. Meanwhile, Daisy, the eldest of the children, had helped raise her younger siblings.

During Daisy's school days, her mother would shoo Jesse off the porch by 10 p.m. But this time, Addie stayed inside. The young couple's time was fleeting. It was Friday evening and on Sunday Jesse had to rejoin his squadron for the cruise to Asia— and to war.

Jesse turned to Daisy and took her hands. His grip was firm, his eyes serious. Jesse had joined the navy—not the airlines—so that he could fly and fight for his country. He had prepared himself for where he was headed.

"Tootie, this isn't easy," Jesse said. "But if something should happen to me over there, I've been thinking, you should go to college and get a degree."

Daisy reeled back, shaking her head. She begged Jesse not to spoil the night. For a while now, though, he'd been trying to broach this subject. Before he'd left for the Mediterranean cruise, he'd even sent her back to Mississippi. He wanted Daisy to be close to her family if something happened to him, not all alone in Warwick, Rhode Island.

Jesse pulled a small notepad from his pocket. He handed it to her. Daisy skimmed the pages with bewilderment.

"Survivors' benefits, Social Security, everything we've talked about," Jesse said. "You'll also find there's a private life insurance policy I took out."

Daisy stopped thumbing through the pages and looked blankly at him. *A private insurance policy?* she thought. *Since when?*

Jesse explained that he had invested in a policy that, if he was killed, would issue a monthly payment for five years. "If something happens, darling, use the money for tuition—even if you go just part-time," he said. "Before five years is over, you'll have your degree and won't need to work in somebody's kitchen."

Daisy stared, her mouth open with shock. Jesse took his wife's hands again, and Daisy shook herself out of her stupor.

"Will you become a teacher, like my mama?" Jesse said. "She'll tell you—it's one of the best professions there is. Will you promise me, darling?"

Daisy knew that this would be Jesse's last deployment—her husband had joined the navy through the reserves in 1947 and had just seven months remaining in his commitment. In March 1951 he'd revert to the reserves and civilian life, and then he'd resume his studies at Ohio State to finish his degree. Daisy looked forward to having him as a husband almost full-time. All she had to do was endure seven more months.

A calmness settled across her face. Daisy squeezed her husband's hands. "I promise," she said. "If anything happens I'll become a teacher."

Jesse's face lifted. "Good." He leaned back with relief. "That way you'd be able to take care of yourself if you can't find another man in five years!"

Daisy laughed and hit Jesse's arm. She loved it when he teased her.

The next morning, the rural airfield of the Palmer's Crossing municipal airport was almost deserted. It was quiet as the Brown family and their neighbors picnicked nearby on the grass. They sat on blankets and sipped sodas. Jesse's mother, Julia, held Pam. In suspenders that stretched over his shirt, John Brown talked with other fathers. Daisy mingled with old friends. Barefoot children chased one another by the forest.

A storm was brewing. A buzzing sound arose in the sky. The families stood up as a red plane appeared above the trees. The plane was a Cessna, a sleek new model for private pilots, with a square wing atop a tapered body.

The Cessna descended toward the runway, but the approach seemed too high, as if the pilot would need to circle around again. The plane's engine suddenly cut to idle. The nose snapped rightward, the left wing dipped, and the plane dropped like a rock. Onlookers gasped and Julia Brown covered her mouth, but Daisy just shook her head: she knew this trick.

Low above the runway, the plane's nose suddenly snapped back to normal and its wings leveled. The Cessna rode down until its front tires and tail wheel kissed the concrete.

The pilot taxied the Cessna near the small crowd. He gunned the engine and swerved the plane around so that the tail was facing the people. The propeller kept whirling. Doors popped open and Fletcher, Lura, and a young friend hopped down to the ground. Lura was now twenty. He was smiling. But Fletcher, now eighteen, wasn't faring as well. His face was frozen in fear. He flopped onto the grass near his family, and his mother, father, and Daisy huddled around him.

"Jesse let me try to land," he panted. "But I was too high

and couldn't get the plane down, so he took over and dropped us from the sky! Called it a 'slip' or something—it scared the hell out of me!" Everyone laughed, especially Daisy.

The pilot's door opened on the left side of the plane and Jesse leaned out, wearing sunglasses and a headset. A friend had loaned him the Cessna. Already, Jesse had given half the community of Lux their first plane ride—including some of the folks from the field who once predicted that he'd never fly an airplane.

As Jesse leaned out of the door, he shouted, "Daisy!" She shook her head and pointed to someone else. One of her friends gently elbowed her and another nudged her forward. Finally, Daisy threw up her hands in defeat. She ran to the plane and hopped in, and Jesse took off.

Fifteen minutes later, the plane taxied back to the concrete patch and its engine cut to silence. The Brown family and their neighbors flocked to the plane. Together, Jesse and Daisy emerged from beneath the wing, and the crowd broke into applause that went on and on, as if no one wanted it to end.

A day later, Sunday, September 3

Jesse leaned across the steering wheel and peered through the thick rain as he drove along the Mississippi roadway. The roads were slick and rain slapped against the green Dodge Wayfarer's hood.

It was midmorning and the storm had turned the world gray. From the passenger seat, Daisy held Jesse's uniform jacket across her lap as her eyes focused on the car ahead, the one her husband was following. Two red taillights beamed in the gloom.

In the rear window of the car ahead, a small hand emerged over the seat back. Then another hand. Pam's face popped into view. She waved.

"Ooooh! She's up again, she sees us!" Daisy said over the pattering rain.

"Hiya, baby!" Jesse said, and waved.

In the car ahead, Jesse's mother, Julia, was taking Pam to an aunt's house, so Daisy could focus on seeing her husband off to war.

Jesse was catching a flight in time to ferry his plane aboard the *Leyte* the next morning.

A road sign for Meridian flashed past Jesse's window and his smile faded. He knew that the turn he had to make to get to the airport was nearing. Jesse waved faster at Pam and blew his daughter kisses. Daisy saw tears sneaking down his cheeks.

Through the rain, Jesse and Daisy watched Julia's car stay straight on the road to Meridian. From his side window, Jesse waved at Pam. His car was angling away in the other direction, toward the airport. The baby's face turned to follow him, her eyes welling with confusion.

From the passenger seat, Jesse's mother blew him a kiss before a misty patch of woods came between the two cars.

Jesse focused his eyes forward and wiped them dry.

★ ★ ★

As rain fell on the terminal, Jesse parked the Wayfarer at the Birmingham airport. Daisy checked her watch. It was just after noon; they had made it with time to spare.

Daisy and Jesse took hold of each other. Jesse stroked his wife's hair. "I could sit here forever and never find the words to describe how much I love you," he said.

Daisy's eyes turned wet as she met her husband's stare.

Jesse spoke again. "No man ever loved a woman more than I love you."

Daisy broke into tears on Jesse's shoulder and soon felt his tears on the back of her neck.

Twenty minutes later, maybe more, Daisy lifted her head from Jesse's shoulder and wiped her eyes. *An aviator has enough worries at work, he doesn't need any more at home!* she thought. She apologized for the waterworks. "I'm crying because I'll miss you," she said, "not because I can't handle myself."

Jesse nodded.

"What I'm saying is," Daisy added, "you do what you need to do over there, love, and don't worry about me—I'll be here when you get home."

Jesse smiled, wrapped an arm over Daisy, and pulled her close. "When I get home, we're going on our honeymoon," he said. "I'm taking you to the Bahamas and we're going to have the time of our lives."

They held each other until Jesse's boarding time had arrived.

Jesse and Daisy shared a last kiss.

Jesse slipped his uniform jacket over his shoulders and climbed from the car. He slapped his officer's hat on his head and tossed his seabag over a shoulder. As he hustled toward the terminal, he glanced back at his wife through the rain. At the terminal doorway, he gazed one last time, then walked inside.

CHAPTER 21

THE LAST NIGHT IN AMERICA

Two weeks later, September 18, 1950
San Diego, California

Tom and Koenig sat in the cocktail lounge of a California hotel. Cups of coffee stood on the table between them. This was their last night on American soil, for a while at least.

Tom looked up. "Look what the cat dragged in," he whispered. Koenig scrunched up his newspaper and glanced between the lobby's yellow pillars. Eight young pilots in tan uniforms were sauntering in. They were the squadron's ensigns. Without a word, Tom and Koenig shrank in their seats. Both knew what would happen if the ensigns spotted two "old" lieutenants trying to enjoy an uneventful night—the young pilots would try to pressure them into drinking. In Tom's mind, there was a time for that, but it wasn't now. The *Leyte* was casting off for Korea the next afternoon. On their last night in America, all Tom and Koenig wanted was some peace and quiet.

"Hey, Hud! Bill!" an ensign shouted, and waved from the entrance to the lounge.

They'd been spotted.

Tom rose in his seat as he and Koenig greeted the boys. Six new pilots had recently joined the squadron, bringing the unit to a war-ready strength of twenty-four flyers.

"Dad's hosting a martini muster over at the bar," an ensign said. "You need to join us!" Another young pilot announced their objective—to try to out-drink Dad.

Koenig told the ensigns that he and Tom would have to pass on the invite. The ensigns mockingly groaned.

Tom looked up and saw Dad Fowler and Jesse enter the lobby and head for the barroom. *Jesse's bar hopping?* Tom thought. *Now I've seen it all!*

The young pilots broke from Tom and Koenig and flocked to Dad's side.

Tom returned to his pipe and Koenig to his newspaper. The headlines were all about the war. One stated that the First Marine Division had just landed behind enemy lines at the port of Inchon, halfway up Korea's western coast. Already, the Marines were moving to liberate Seoul and cutting off North Korean supply lines to choke the enemy's assault in the south. Reporters speculated that the Marines' bold landing could turn the tide of the war.

Inside the dimly lit barroom, sailors, couples, and businessmen sat along the bar and filled curved booths, drinking beer and cocktails. Rhumba music piped in from the ceiling.

At the head of a long wooden table, Dad sat and told jokes with Jesse at his side. Dad had appointed Jesse as his assistant operations officer, and the job fell to Jesse to review the pilots' flight logs. The two became fast friends. Both were Southern gentlemen; Dad came from rural roots outside Houston. During high school he'd been captain of the debate club and worked as a carpenter's assistant for his father, who taught him a guiding principle: *The color of a man's skin makes no more difference than the color of his eyes.*

A waiter went from pilot to pilot, scribbling drink orders onto a pad. Dad told the waiter to make his drink a double and encouraged the others to do the same. He was trying to build a bond with the young ensigns, one they would need in combat.

The waiter approached Jesse last. Sometimes Jesse would order a gin and tonic, then jokingly add, "Just hold the gin!" But before Jesse could place his order, the waiter walked away. Jesse glanced to see if the man had realized his mistake and would come doubling back. He didn't.

"Excuse me!" Dad said loudly. The waiter turned on his heels. Dad pointed to Jesse. "You missed this gentleman's order."

The ensigns' chattering wound down.

The waiter approached and leaned in toward Dad's ear. In a low voice he said, "Sir, I apologize, but we don't serve Negroes."

Jesse glanced away. Dad held up his hand to stop the waiter from leaving. "How about an exception?" he said, keeping his cool.

The waiter whispered something about "hotel policy." The ensigns mumbled in disgust. This was California, not the Jim Crow South. Black folks could sit anywhere on the bus and in movie theaters, the ensigns had assumed, so why not here? But California was in fact still segregated, just under a seemingly welcoming veneer. In fact, the YMCA allowed Black folks to swim only on Thursdays, and most bowling alleys excluded them outright. The National Guard was still segregated, and restaurants and bars could legally refuse Black patrons. They never posted WHITES ONLY signs—but they stopped Black folks at the door. As Jesse knew all too well, Black folks were met with racism across America, not just in the South.

Dad's jaw tightened and he scowled at the waiter. "You're either going to serve him, or you aren't going to serve any of us."

Jesse stood. "No need for trouble," he said. "I'll see you fellas back at the ship." He quickly walked toward the door.

Dad curled his fists.

The waiter's voice turned shaky. "Sir, I apologize, but we'll happily serve the rest of your party."

Dad abruptly stood, nearly flipping over his chair, and announced to the table: "We're outta here! Let's go, boys. Up, up, up!" He was six foot four and the shoulder boards of his uniform made his frame seem even bigger. The waiter stumbled back.

The pilots snapped to their feet and grabbed their jackets. Throughout the bar, other patrons peered over at them. Dad stormed up to the bar, where the waiter was whispering to a bartender.

Dad addressed the wide-eyed bar patrons.

"Tomorrow, that young man is leaving to fight the Reds," he said, gesturing toward the lobby to which Jesse had fled. "And these people won't even pour him a drink!"

The bar patrons—sailors among them—turned to the bartender with angry eyes. The bartender shrugged. "Mister, we already explained our policy."

"Oh, stuff it!" Dad growled. Dad unclenched his fists, turned, and walked away. He didn't want to risk winding up in jail and having the *Leyte* sail without him.

In the lobby, the ensigns fell in behind Dad.

"This is the only time I've ever regretted wearing the uniform of the U.S. Navy," he muttered, "because it keeps me from going back there, jumping the bar, and kicking that guy's ass."

From his seat in the lounge, Tom had seen Jesse stride through the lobby. His friend's eyes were locked forward. His hands were buried in his pockets. And he was heading for the revolving front door alone. *That can't be good,* Tom had thought.

Not a minute later, Dad and his pilots followed.

"What the heck?" Tom muttered. Koenig lowered his newspaper.

One of the ensigns broke from the group to alert Tom and Koenig. "They wouldn't serve Jesse!" he said.

Tom shook his head in disbelief. *He can fight for his country but can't order a drink?*

Koenig's face turned red and he glanced around wildly in search of a manager, eager to leap to Jesse's defense.

Tom stood. "Let's get the hell out of here."

"With pleasure," Koenig said, tossing his paper aside.

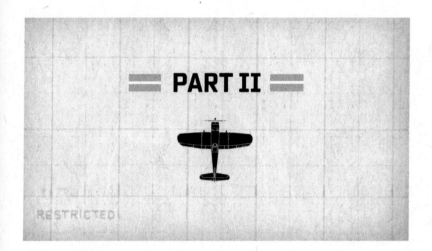

PART II

RESTRICTED

CHAPTER 22

THE BEAST IN THE GORGE

Nearly two weeks later, October 1, 1950
The front lines, South Korea

Red Parkinson knelt on the rural Korean road. A wide mountain gorge towered above him. The Marines had been marching forward in a column. But in the rugged terrain north of Seoul, South Korea's capital, the column had been stopped.

Corporal Devans paced behind his platoon, his eyes locked forward. The North Korean troops had planted box mines to delay them, and it was working. The mines were wooden boxes containing eighteen pounds of explosives—and the Marine column wouldn't be able to move ahead until they were certain the coast was clear of them. As Red and his peers inched ahead, riflemen patrolled nearby. Corsair planes occasionally raced above the gorge. The air crackled with tension.

Red slid the blade of a bayonet into the rocky soil, probing for mines. His hand trembled as he sank it in deeper and fished around. *Nothing.* Red slid the blade out and sat back on his heels. *Whew!* Dressed in pale green fatigues and camouflaged helmets, sixty other Marines were also digging with their bayonets nearby.

Red glanced up from his work and scanned ahead. He felt vulnerable, having stashed his bazooka and pack beside the road. The midday sun warmed his back while the cool breeze chilled his sweat. Beyond the men lay fresh, green pastures. War had spared nature, but not the South Korean settlements beside the road. Here and there lay white pagodas with shattered blue roofs and footbridges that had been smashed earlier when the North Koreans invaded.

Red shuffled and stabbed the earth again. His bayonet hit something hard. His eyes widened. He wiggled the blade and dug down with his fingers. Out popped a rock. Red wiped his brow with relief.

After steaming from Crete to Korea, Red and the other Fleet Marines had joined the First Marine Division during the fighting for Seoul.

That was nine days ago.

Since then, the twenty-two thousand Marines had liberated Seoul. This action had thrown the North Koreans into retreat. Friendly forces were now driving the enemy from the south. As soon as the Communists were pushed back above the thirty-eighth parallel—the prewar border—everyone expected the war to end. With the border just twenty miles to the north, Red didn't mind the idea of coming home soon, as long as he came home with some good stories to tell Uncle Anton.

Behind Red, a voice began quoting a Bible verse. PFC Charlie Kline was talking to himself as he probed the soil. He was tall, with sandy blond hair and blue eyes. He was a fired-up Baptist from Philadelphia who loved to sing "Go Tell It on the Mountain."

"Being right with the Lord is necessary for protection in this life and the next!" Charlie proclaimed. "Ain't that right, brother John?"

Red averted his eyes. "Uh, yup," he muttered.

Charlie was one of the most all-American guys Red had ever met and, at that moment, one of the most annoying. Since landing in Korea, Charlie had been harping about "being right with the Lord." At first, Red had told Charlie to give it up, but Charlie only became more persistent. So Red had decided it was easier just to agree. Red knew his friend meant well.

Tat tat tat! Burrrip!

Flashes of gunfire zipped between the trees. Whooshing sounds fell from above, followed by explosions cracking beside the road. Soil burst into the air. Red and Charlie wrapped their arms over their heads.

"Mortars!" Devans shouted, sprinting for cover from the explosive shells. "Get off the road!"

Another mortar dropped in, then another. Red seized his Super Bazooka and dived into a ditch with Charlie and Devans. Over the gunfire and explosions came a growling noise from the road up ahead. The mortars stopped falling. *Is that,* Red wondered, *the sound of squeaking wheels?*

"Tank!" a faraway Marine shouted. "Tank, incoming!"

A hundred yards away the machine turned the corner, and

Red's eyes went wide. "Jesus help us," Charlie whispered as it rolled toward them. The tank was green like a dragon, and the hole at the end of its cannon looked like a lone eye. It was a Soviet-built T-34 tank, the first one Red had ever seen in person.

The tank clanked past the Marines without firing a shot. A machine gun protruded from the front of the tank's body and swiveled as its gunner scanned for targets.

It was now only ninety yards away from Red, Charlie, and Devans.

Frozen in place, Red watched the T-34 churn closer. Charlie's chin trembled. The tank was well within the Marine lines.

More than a hundred Marines surrounded the machine, but only one was in a position to stop it. Only a bazooka man could slay the T-34, the best Soviet battle tank of WWII, one that Stalin had given the North Koreans. Red's face twisted as a realization struck him. The only bazooka man in position was him.

Tat tat tat!

"Get down!" Devans shouted. Red and the others flattened against the base of the ditch as bullets snapped overhead.

Tat tat tat!

Red could see that the enemy tank was focusing on a target. Its machine gun fired toward a pasture to the left, where a lanky Marine was running uphill. Bullets bit the earth around him, nipping at his heels.

That's Bill Morin! Red realized. Morin was from upstate New York, like Red. He was a party Marine who loved scotch. Everybody loved him.

"Take cover!" men shouted at Morin. "Get down, you idiot!"

Morin dived behind a clump of small trees. Bullets snapped the branches overhead and kicked up the soil around him.

With a roar, the enemy tank belched black smoke and wheeled in place to face the pasture where Morin was cowering. Gunfire burst from its machine gun's muzzle. Morin was trapped.

You can save him! Red thought.

Red hoisted the Super Bazooka onto his shoulder. "Load me up!" he shouted to Charlie over the tank's gunfire. Charlie grabbed a rocket from his pack and shinnied up to Red.

Red fixed his eyes on the tank. It was an ideal target profile.

Stay put! Red thought.

Charlie slid the eight-pound rocket into the bazooka tube and connected an electrical wire to the rocket. Once he'd let Red know the bazooka was armed, he dived out of the way.

Alone, Red leapt to his feet and scrambled up onto the road. In one motion he slid to a knee, lifted the bazooka, and braced the tube on his right shoulder. Red peered through the circular gunsight. He clenched his breath. Then, he aimed the gun's crosshairs right onto the tank's rear, over an auxiliary fuel drum on its side. Behind the drum stood armor that shielded the machine's fuel tank and engine.

Now!

Red squeezed the trigger. A coil behind the trigger produced a spark. The spark raced up the grip and into the rocket. The rocket's propellant ignited with a *whoosh,* and the projectile shot from the bazooka's mouth in a flaming bolt of orange.

Crack!

The shell punched into the twenty-six-ton tank. It shuddered on its tracks. A split second passed.

KABOOM!

The tank's hatches burst open suddenly. Black smoke streamed from the hatches and flames boiled over the engine compartment.

A shock wave blasted Red onto his back. Lying there, he saw the North Korean tank commander writhe out of the turret, his blue uniform and padded helmet engulfed in flame. The tanker fell to the ground. None of the other crewmen emerged.

Red set his bazooka down and took in the sight. Behind him, his buddies were cheering and whistling.

Did Morin make it? Red wondered. He glanced toward the hillside. Morin stood and dusted himself off. He looked over at Red. "What the hell took you so long?" he shouted. A grin stretched across Red's dusty face. Morin waved and gathered up his gear.

Charlie approached and shook Red by the shoulder. "Hallelujah! Be right with the Lord and *he* will protect you!"

Red smirked and placed a hand on Charlie's shoulder. "Shucks, Charlie. I thought an eight-pound rocket was protectin' me."

Charlie shook his finger. "Steered by the Lord!"

Red laughed.

"Attaboy!" a Marine said, coming over to slap Red on the back. "Nice shot!" said another. An officer paused to say that he would recommend Red for a medal. The men steered around the burning tank and marched with fresh vigor. The advance resumed, thanks to the enemy tank: the road was obviously clear of mines if the enemy tank had safely traveled it.

Red remained in the road, his gaze settled on the dead North Korean tank commander, whose body had shrunk into the dirt.

Red had aimed at a machine, but he had killed maybe five men in the process. It was shocking and unsettling to him, and he wasn't quite sure how to process it.

Better them than Morin, he thought. Still, he wondered, why in war did saving one life often mean taking another?

CHAPTER 23

INTO THE FOG

Two days later, October 3, 1950
Near Tokyo Bay, Japan

Fog floated from the hills, blanketing the harbor where the *Leyte* was at anchor. Below deck, Tom passed through the officers' dining room with his dress coat draped over an arm. The dining room was elegant, with a carved wood ceiling and white tablecloths. A few officers sipped coffee. They were likely debating the topic of the times: Should the U.S. commander, General MacArthur, allow U.S. and U.N. forces to follow the North Korean army across the border and crush them once and for all? Most Americans were unaware, however, that Soviet and Chinese diplomats had just issued a warning—if U.S. forces did cross the border, China planned to attack because of what they called America's "frenzied and ruthless imperialistic aggression."

Past the chatting officers, at the end of the dining hall, Tom parted a green curtain and stepped into a small back room. More than twenty pilots crowded the space. At a table, Jesse and

Cevoli were playing backgammon. Another pilot kept a record player spinning, while others passed a coffeepot around to refill their mugs. A teletype machine's green TV screen flickered with the weather and shipboard announcements.

This was "ready room forward," and it was '32's new hangout. Tom slid into a seat next to Cevoli and Jesse. Nearby, six pilots were putting on jackets and life preservers in preparation to fly. They were older, saltier-looking men, some of the Marine Corps' first helicopter pilots: men trained to fly the Sikorsky HO3S, used for rescuing downed airmen.

The chopper pilots remained tight-lipped as they suited up. They and the fighter pilots had shared the ready room since Norfolk, yet they seldom intermingled. The younger fighter pilots were the problem. They assumed that any man stuck flying a flimsy helicopter had to be beneath them, a flight school dropout. Sensing the disdain, the chopper pilots generally ignored the fighter pilots.

The two groups maintained their sullen distance—all except two pilots. Between tosses of dice, Jesse exchanged quips with First Lieutenant Charlie Ward, a stocky chopper pilot with red, grinning cheeks. Ward was a former salesman from Troy, Alabama.

"Heya, Mississippi, do you remember . . . ," Charlie would say, then ramble something in a drawl so thick the others would wrinkle their noses.

But Jesse would understand every word. "You said it, Alabama," he would reply.

The two had met during the journey over, when Ward was warning the fighter pilots about helicopter rescue capabilities.

"If you gotta crash, do it at sea level," Ward had said, half jokingly. "If you crash in the mountains, I ain't coming for you!"

Afterward, Jesse and Ward had struck up a friendship, and Jesse had discovered that Ward and another chopper pilot had actually flown Corsairs during WWII. Now Ward was about to enter his second war. He and the other chopper pilots were due to join Observation Squadron 6 (VMO-6), their unit in Korea.

"Have you fellas popped a head outside?" Tom asked the chopper pilots. "You can stir the soup out there, the fog's so thick."

Several of the men stopped dressing and turned toward Tom. Their thoughts were written on their faces. *Another fighter jock trying to teach us how to fly?* Only when they saw the genuine concern on Tom's face did they relax.

"Nah, that won't stop us," a chopper pilot said. "We'll just go under it." His buddies nodded.

More than one fighter pilot raised an eyebrow.

"I'll admit, I don't know the meaning of the word *fear*," Charlie Ward said, thumping his chest. "Not because I'm brave," Ward continued, "but because I jus' don't understand big words!"

Ward was used to making people laugh. At parties he'd strum a ukulele and sing profane Irish ditties. But beneath the bravado, he was wary of the primitive machine he was tasked with flying. Ward was married with children and had already crashed one helicopter. He knew that his new mount was underpowered and almost too flimsy to fly on a windy day—let alone if someone was shooting at him.

One by one, chopper pilots filtered from the ready room.

"Hey—take it easy, Mississippi!" Ward said, slapping Jesse on the shoulder.

"Be safe, Alabama," Jesse replied.

Tom shook his head in disbelief. The chopper pilots were really going to try to take off.

"See ya later, fellas!" Ward said over his shoulder as he brushed through the curtain.

I sure hope not, Tom thought.

He had nothing against Charlie Ward—he just hoped he would never need the man's services. If Tom had gone on deck to watch the helicopters fly away between the fog and waves, he'd have seen that Ward was wrong about himself: he *was* brave, even borderline wild.

And one day those traits would matter. They would meet again, Tom Hudner and Charlie Ward, in a place where only a wild man would go.

CHAPTER 24

THIS IS IT

Several nights later, early October 1950
The Sea of Japan

The *Leyte* steamed through the darkness. A sliver of moon hung in the sky, the only light to be seen. The *Leyte*'s crew ran her all blacked out to hide from enemy submarines.

On either side of the *Leyte,* the outlines of countless ships could be seen. The *Leyte* now belonged to the Seventh Fleet, one of the largest flotillas assembled since WWII.

Together, the ships steamed northward, toward the waters of North Korea.

Several days later, October 10, 1950

On the horizon, the carrier *Philippine Sea* cruised alongside the *Leyte*. Somewhere beyond the horizon lay North Korea's eastern coastline. The fleet was now one hundred miles above the border, known as the "thirty-eighth parallel"; they were officially deep in enemy waters. Now, within striking range of North Korea, the *Leyte* had entered the war.

Earlier that week, America and its allies had started crossing that same border to pursue the North Koreans. And yet, despite their threats to get involved, the Chinese army had remained on the sidelines. For now.

Aboard the *Leyte,* the men huddled in the dining room. It had been transformed into a theater. Every few days, the *Leyte* pilots watched movies they themselves had filmed in the air.

When mechanics began moving in small groups toward the rear of the dining room, Tom asked one of the sailors what had happened.

"A damaged Corsair is coming down, sir," the sailor said. "Number three elevator." The sailor hurried away, eager to see the first battle-damaged plane.

Tom followed the exodus through the string of hangars, his eyes wide with alarm. His friends were on that flight— Jesse and Koenig, and the new guy, Wilkie. At the rear of the deck Tom joined the sailors in glancing anxiously at a square platform in the ceiling. The contraption was the plane elevator, a means of delivering aircraft to and from the flight deck. Chains clinked and the elevator began descending. Sunlight poured in and water showered from the elevator. A Corsair sat at the platform's center, dripping wet. Tom studied the sky through the opening in the flight deck. There wasn't a rain cloud in sight. Tom glanced back at the dripping plane. *What the heck?*

The elevator settled into the floor and the men crowded closer. "Good grief," Tom murmured. Black holes spanned the Corsair's left wing and deep dents marked the engine cover, as if fists had punched the plane. The large white number 203 on the nose was pitted and scraped. Corsair 203 didn't belong to one pilot or another; everyone alternated planes.

Tom ducked under the nose to check the other wing. It, too, was full of holes. He began a mental checklist. *We're gonna need two new wings.* Tom shook his head. It was awfully soon to be dipping into the spare parts. As he ran his hand along the punctures in the wing, his eyes narrowed.

A gooey brown substance bled from the holes. Tom swiped a finger and examined it. "It's mud, all right," he announced. The deckhands murmured, unsure how mud could wind up in an airplane.

The bullhorn interrupted their thoughts. "Now hear this!" a sailor's voice bellowed. "Now hear this! A message from the skipper of Fighting 32." This was the new routine—after each combat mission, the flight leader would report the results to the ship's crew.

A pause followed as the microphone changed hands. "This is Lieutenant Commander D. T. Neill, skipper of Fighting 32," the gruff voice announced.

The skipper explained that he had led '32's patrol over Wonsan Harbor that morning. "We had good hunting, although pickings were slim," he said. "We knocked out some shore batteries and trucks on some islands."

Tom nodded to himself. The mission was important. The First Marine Division was due to land at Wonsan Harbor to open a new front on Korea's east coast, as they had in the west. But until the navy softened up the harbor's defenses, the Marines weren't going anywhere.

"Overall, we encountered little resistance," the skipper added. "Just one plane banged up and no one hurt—a mighty good start."

Now Tom was really curious. He had seen the damaged plane and wondered: *Who took the first lumps?*

The film projector's beam cut through the darkness and onto the blank screen. Shadows crossed the screen as officers took their seats, hands laden with coffee or soda. Pilots filled up the first two rows. Tom sat with Jesse and Koenig.

In the rear of the dining room, sailors loaded film onto a projector's reels. The dining room had been transformed into a theater.

"Gentlemen, we have a treat for you tonight," an intelligence officer announced. "You're about to see a smattering of gun camera film from today's missions, courtesy of Fightin' 31, Fightin' 32, and Fightin' 33!" Whistles and clapping arose from the audience; Tom leaned forward in his seat. He hadn't flown on the mission that day, but his friends had and he was eager to see what had happened.

The screen filled with life. In blotchy color, the camera flew over a stretch of rugged seaside hills. It was the island in Wonsan Harbor on North Korea's southeastern coast, seen from treetop height. Wonsan Harbor was an important strategic point where the Marines were trying to open a new front on Korea's east coast, just as they had in the west.

The screen flickered as the next film clip appeared from

a new camera angle. Rough waves flowed toward the viewer. Whoever was filming was racing toward a watchtower on a beach. Marty Goode's wingman elbowed him. The scenery was instantly familiar to them; they were the ones who had shot the footage on a recent flight.

The camera shook as the plane's guns fired. Orange bolts arced toward the watchtower on-screen, and sparks flickered. The audience cheered. Just before the plane could collide with the tower, the camera lifted and filmed the blue sky as the pilot climbed over the target.

A grin stretched across Marty's face as he whispered to his wingman, "Remember when you asked Dad, 'What are all those flashes?'" The wingman nodded. "'Why, someone's shooting at you,'" Marty said, imitating Dad's deadpan reply.

The screen flickered again. The camera dived toward a rocky cave. An enemy cannon jutted out from it. Koenig's face lifted. "Jesse, it's your cave!" he said. Jesse's eyes perked at the sight of his film. He remembered that day well.

The cave's mouth grew wider in the film's frame as Jesse's plane dived closer. Enemy soldiers appeared in the distance. In a bright flash, a rocket streaked from his plane's wing. As the rocket plowed toward the cave's mouth, the audience leaned forward to see the impact. Then, suddenly, the camera flicked upward and filmed the sky. The audience groaned. They wanted to see the explosion.

"Did you hit it?" a pilot called out. "Any secondaries?"

"He sure did!" Koenig said. He told the men around him how flames had leapt from the burning cave. Jesse just shrugged and smiled. Several seats over, Dad nodded with approval—Jesse's technique had been sound.

After the gun camera viewing, the nightly movie rolled.

Through the light that spilled from the projector's beam, Tom saw his buddies: some hazing one another, some fixated on the big screen. He had spent countless hours imagining this, their first day at war, and he had expected something scarier and bloodier. Deep down, Tom wanted to become a veteran of a "real" war, one that mattered, like World War II.

A thought crossed his mind, followed by a pang of guilt.

This is it?

CHAPTER 25

TRUST

Nine days later, October 19, 1950
Near Songjin, North Korea

At first the valley was gentle and calm. The dawn's warm light spread across the trees, revealing yellow, red, and brown autumn leaves. Mist floated through the mountain peaks.

From the south came a sound, soft like the buzz of a mosquito but lower in pitch. Then the sound grew louder.

On a dirt road, a young Korean boy and girl pulled their goats by the reins. The children stopped when they heard the sound and turned in its direction.

Farther up the road, an elderly farmer repaired a fence in his field. He heard the sound, lowered his tool, and looked to the south. The sound was still growing, though the morning sky remained empty.

Still farther up the road, several middle-aged women carried baskets across a stone bridge. They also paused and turned. The sound was clear now, a roaring, throaty buzz.

At the opening to the valley, they appeared—eight Corsairs silhouetted against the morning sky. The planes flew low, lower than the telephone poles. A bomb hung from each plane's belly.

The children covered their ears and scurried to the roadside as the lead plane burst past. From the plane's cockpit, a white face in a helmet peered out. One after another, the planes roared over the valley.

They ripped past the farmer, who shrank but held his ground. In his lifetime he had likely seen Japanese occupiers, then Soviet "liberators," then homegrown Communist soldiers, and now the men in blue planes, whoever they were.

The women on the bridge lowered their baskets and crouched. In a flash, all eight Corsairs raced over them.

Without firing a shot, the blue planes thundered up the road.

At the controls of Corsair number 200, the seventh plane in line, Tom Hudner cringed. He had seen the North Korean people below, their faces frozen in confusion or fear. *They must hate us,* Tom thought. He wished he could tell them that flying low was the best way to hunt for targets while also avoiding anti-aircraft fire.

A week earlier, the port city of Wonsan had been liberated. The city of Hamhung was next. That was where the South Korean army had discovered the bodies of seven hundred political prisoners executed by the North Koreans. Now, the U.N. forces were pushing the North Koreans up the eastern coast, killing and capturing them along the way. To support the advance, the *Leyte* and another carrier called *Philippine Sea* had traveled north to operate off the coast of Songjin, a city behind enemy lines.

Tom's eyes rose with concern to a rearview mirror. His face relaxed. *Good, he's still there,* he thought. One hundred yards behind him, Marty Goode flew low over the terrain. Marty was last in line, the flight's "Tail-End Charlie." Tom could see he was sitting tall in his seat. Tom was Marty's leader for the hop today. That was because Cevoli and Jesse had the day off and Koenig was flying in the plane ahead as wingman to a senior pilot.

Dad was flying with Bill "Wilkie" Wilkinson as his wingman. Beneath Wilkie's helmet and goggles was a slender face with blue eyes. "Wilkie" was a twenty-two-year-old rookie who had gone straight from Yale University to navy flight school and who had gotten married mere weeks before the *Leyte* sailed. Everyone in the squadron knew that the young man had as much flight time as a veteran. As a boy, Wilkie had soloed at sixteen after working nights in a grocery store to pay for flying lessons.

Marty, on the other hand, seemed like more of a wild card. Tom wished Marty were flying in front of him so that he could keep an eye on him. Tom knew Marty as the young, unpredictable ensign who boasted about being a ladies' man and making trouble. But he wasn't sure he could rely on Marty to keep in formation with the flight.

Tom looked away from Marty suddenly, his eyes narrowing. An orange light was blinking at the bottom of a mountain. It looked like a bonfire, growing larger and larger. "What the heck?" Tom muttered.

In a blur, a glowing sphere arced over Tom's plane and past

his tail. *Zip!* Tom flinched in his seat. *Zip!* Another one curved over his wings. Tom's head whipped from side to side to see the golf ball–sized pyrotechnic projectiles. *Tracers!*

Someone was shooting at him. Tom had flown five combat missions so far. This was the first time he'd ever taken anti-aircraft fire.

Zip!

Another orange sphere whipped over Tom's wing. *Is anyone else seeing this?* he wondered. He glanced in a mirror to check on Marty. Marty was shifting in his seat as shells whipped around him.

Tom pulled his microphone close to his mouth but stopped short of speaking. He knew the skipper's rules: *Don't clog the airwaves! Speak only when urgent.*

Tom's eyes shifted forward. Dad wasn't panicking, nor was his wingman, Wilkie, nor was Koenig or any of the others. Everyone was flying in eerie silence.

Tom shrank in his seat. The enemy gun was nearing, brighter than ever. It was becoming unnerving. He could hold his tongue no longer.

"Lead, this is 200!" he said. "We're taking fire back here!"

"Copy that, 200," Dad said calmly. "You may take evasive action if you so desire." His voice sounded unimpressed.

Tom gritted his teeth.

If he began weaving now, he'd reveal his fear. Aviators were taught not to panic because it was unsafe—and worse, "unprofessional."

Through the windscreen, Tom watched Dad fly past the gun

without taking a hit. The other Corsairs followed. At the end of the valley, Dad broke radio silence.

"Target spotted, twelve o'clock," he said.

Tom strained his eyes, trying to see what Dad had spotted through the mountains and low-hanging clouds. Ahead, the land twisted into a rocky gorge between mountains. In the gorge stood a bridge.

The planes followed Dad, one by one. Dad dipped his right wing twice, the signal for the flight to get into their attack formation. Dad held his position as three pilots nestled beside and behind his right wing, forming a diagonal line in the sky. The second formation assembled next, behind the first. Koenig settled beside his leader, and Tom settled beside Koenig. Tom glanced past his right wing and saw that Marty had parked himself tight. The assembly was complete.

The bridge Dad had spotted was an important target. The bridge was how North Korean troops traveled and got new supplies, how they kept their army running. Its destruction would surely be a huge blow to the enemy.

Dad peeled off from the formation to kick off the attack, disappearing from sight. Five seconds later, his wingman followed. Then came the next pilot in line, then the next. In fifteen seconds the first formation was gone.

Tom's formation leader raised his fist and made two pumps. *Prepare to attack!* Tom flicked up a switch to activate his guns and bomb. He braced himself.

By now, Dad and his formation were already dropping their bombs. Tom heard the pilots spotting one another's results. "Did mine hit?" Dad asked. "No sir, just missed," Wilkie replied. Deflated voices reported more failures: "No dice!" "Close one!" "No go!" The first formation had struck out.

It was the second formation's turn. After five seconds, Koenig turned to Tom, tapped his helmet, and peeled away. Tom was next. His breath quickened as he silently counted off. Tom turned to Marty and saw the young ensign's blue eyes blinking nervously. When the count reached five, Tom patted his helmet, and Marty rapidly nodded.

Tom grabbed the control stick to the left and pulled back. In a violent rush, his Corsair peeled leftward—then aimed in a sharp dive toward the mountains. For a moment, the world rotated clockwise in the windscreen; sky and clouds turned to trees and leaves.

Five thousand feet below, gray smoke wafted across the bridge. Koenig's Corsair was diving sharply. After dropping his bomb, he pulled up from his dive. Another bomb failed to strike the target. "Near miss, Bill," Dad called out.

Open air lay between the bridge and Tom's plane. Tom squinted through the gunsight. With precision, he aimed the gunsight's crosshairs at the bridge. When his aim looked just right, Tom stopped steering.

Hold her steady! he thought.

He flew at 320 miles per hour, 330, 340.

Tom's ears popped. *Keep the wings even! Fight the crosswind!* The needle in the altimeter spun backward.

He flew at 4,500 feet, 4,000, 3,500.

The bridge swelled in the shaking crosshairs.

Tom was at 3,000 feet . . . 2,500.

Now!

Tom mashed the red bomb release button with his thumb.

Clunk! The bomb released.

Climb! Tom thought. He had to put distance between himself and the explosion. He hauled back on the stick and slammed the throttle forward. Gravity sucked his cheeks back and pulled him into his seat.

Behind Tom, the bomb exploded. *Thump.* The Corsair soared up from the valley.

"Tom, you missed," came Dad's voice over the radio.

"Damn it!" Tom said.

Tom turned and glimpsed Marty's Corsair gliding straight from a dive. Tom watched for the explosion from Marty's bomb. Nothing happened.

"Marty, you didn't drop at all," Dad reported.

The bridge—their prized target—remained untouched.

"Join up, and let's head for home," Dad said. He sounded annoyed at himself. The results were an embarrassment to the squadron.

Behind the others, Marty climbed to catch up. His black eyebrows were furrowed in frustration. The pylon beneath his plane's belly had malfunctioned and still gripped his bomb. Mechanical malfunction or not, he couldn't land aboard the carrier with a hung bomb.

Marty's face twisted as he reached to disarm the bomb. With the flick of a switch he could deactivate the bomb, then release it. He hesitated. If he dumped the bomb, the others might assume he'd messed up—or worse, he'd panicked. Marty wanted to look good for his buddies, and Dad in particular.

Dad was the best pilot in the squadron and maybe on the entire ship. Others would line Vulture's Row just to watch him land because he came in so smoothly, without a twitch of his landing gear, all the way to the deck.

More than anyone, Marty wanted to win Dad's approval—especially because it wasn't easy to get. Now, as Marty flew with a live bomb beneath his feet, he had yet to realize that Dad's hard-nosed manner was a veteran's way of leading, a way to let the young pilot know that he still had room to improve and further to go. And that Dad fully believed in his ability to do so.

Marty sat back in his seat.

"This is 217 to Lead," he said into his microphone. "I'd like to make another run on the target."

Dad was silent for a moment; then he said, "Okay, go ahead."

Marty's Corsair rocketed up past the others and toward the clouds, then dived back toward the bridge.

Tom kept his eyes fixed on his wingman. Marty had really set himself up. If his bomb released and missed, he'd look worse than if he hadn't tried at all.

Tom saw Marty's Corsair get smaller as it plummeted toward the bridge. The bomb fell from its belly and punched into the smoke around the bridge. The Corsair pitched upward as the bomb flashed and crackled. A swirl of white dust arose: the dust of shattered concrete.

As the dust settled, the space where the bridge was reappeared. Its stone pillars still stood—but without a concrete ceiling to connect them. Slabs of bridge lay collapsed in the stream. Marty had scored a direct hit.

A grin stretched across Tom's face. After several more orbits, Marty slid into formation on his wing. When he caught Marty's eye, Tom smiled and flashed a thumbs-up. Marty cracked a grin himself. He nodded to Tom, then returned his focus to flying.

Dad wheeled the flight eastward and the sea appeared on the horizon. For several minutes, the pilots flew in silence, until Dad's voice crackled over the radio.

"Nice job, Marty."

Three simple words.

"Thanks, sir," Marty replied. He tried not to sound too excited. Coming from Dad, those words were possibly the highest compliment he had ever received.

Tom glanced over his right shoulder and saw Marty concentrating on maintaining close formation. Tom turned forward again and didn't glance back until the end of the flight.

He knew Marty would be there.

CHAPTER 26

HE MIGHT BE A FLYER

That evening, after the bridge attack

The officers dug into dinner in the *Leyte*'s dining room. Black stewards lowered silver trays of food in front of them. Though the navy claimed to be desegregated, the division of labor was still along racial lines—and the lower-rung, service roles were most often given to Black sailors. They wore clean, high-collared jackets and their hair was closely cropped. Silverware clinked and savory smells filled the air as the mostly white officers ate. As usual, Tom sat across from Jesse and Koenig. The men wore tan pants and shirts open at the collars. Conversations buzzed as officers planned their return to civilization. In a week, the *Leyte* was leaving for six days of R&R in Japan.

Marty ate with vigor. He had received plenty of backslapping after the mission. His destruction of the bridge had been recorded as a squadron victory. Even the usually solemn skipper had said to him: "You know, someday you may make a naval aviator."

The day's most triumphant moment actually came just before supper. The pilots had been relaxing in their ready rooms when the teletype machines blinked: "Enemy capital, Pyongyang, fallen to U.S. Army First Cavalry Division. U.N. Forces now occupying." The pilots had cheered at the news. A glance at the map revealed that the boys on the ground had the enemy cornered in North Korea's mountainous northwest. All that remained was to push the Communists out of the country—just seventy-five more miles. Four days earlier, in a meeting with President Harry Truman, General MacArthur had even predicted a timeline for the war's end: "I believe that formal resistance will end throughout North and South Korea by Thanksgiving."

Tom picked at his plate. Even if things were looking good for the American forces, in his mind, he could still envision the glowing spheres whipping past his canopy. *What if the gunner had fired a split second earlier?* he thought. A harsh reality jabbed at him—even if he did everything right, one shot could change everything.

At first, only Jesse and Koenig noticed.

Something was amiss in the dining room.

As the stewards held plates of food in front of Jesse, they remained tense and tight-lipped. Jesse quietly scooped his portions. Normally, the stewards were chatty. "Good hunting today, Ensign Brown?" they'd ask. Or, "I watched you take off this morning!" Jesse was their personal hero, and not just because he was the only Black carrier pilot. Whenever he passed through the dining room in his flight gear, he always greeted them as they folded napkins and polished silverware. The steward who cleaned Jesse's cabin had told the others how Jesse always made his own bed, did his own dusting, and left him with little work to do. The stewards knew his full name, Jesse Leroy Brown, and behind the scenes they affectionately called him "Jesse L."

But now, something had changed. The stewards hurriedly moved from Jesse to the next man. Jesse's eyes followed them and his face pleaded—*What did I do wrong?*

With the main course concluded, the stewards removed dirty plates and filled the officers' coffee cups. As they served dessert, they continued to avoid Jesse's eyes. Some even fought to keep from grinning.

Confusion filled Jesse's face. Koenig lowered his cup to the table. "What the heck is going on?" he asked. Jesse shook his head.

A group of stewards drifted from the kitchen and congregated by the back wall, followed by cooks in T-shirts and aprons. Their eyes settled on Jesse. The kitchen door swung wide and a steward emerged carrying a small cake on a tray. Some of the officers' heads turned. When the steward reached Jesse's table, Tom saw an unlit candle on the yellow sponge cake.

Jesse's eyes grew wide and Koenig relaxed in his seat. Tom grinned. *Last week was Jesse's birthday!* he remembered. The ship's paper had run a blurb announcing that Jesse had turned twenty-four on October 13.

The steward leaned in and lowered the cake in front of Jesse, who shook his head in disbelief.

"Hey, Jesse," Cevoli shouted from down the table. "How did you swing a cake and party with a hundred and fifty guests? There's a war on, you know!" Jesse and the others laughed.

The chief steward approached Jesse with a small box in his hands. He was an older Black man with a small mustache. His jacket's left sleeve had three red V-shaped chevrons and the white eagle of a petty officer first class. The stewards and cooks stepped from the back wall, eager to see.

"Ensign Brown," the petty officer said, "me and the boys chipped in and got you a little something." He handed Jesse the box. Jesse grinned and surveyed the faces of the kitchen staff. They were smiling, now free to show their excitement. Jesse removed the packaging and flipped open the box top. Nestled inside was a steel watch with a white face and a tiny silver crown for a logo.

A Rolex.

Jesse's jaw hung open.

"Holy cow!" Koenig murmured.

Along the table, officers leaned in. The watch had a black leather band and a silver winding stem. *That's a chunk of change!* Tom thought.

Jesse slid the Rolex over his left wrist and fastened the snap. He held the watch up to catch the light and marveled at its glimmer.

"Thank you for lifting us up," the petty officer said to Jesse. "Now, on this ship, when a Black man passes you in the hallway, you never know, he might be just a cook—or he might be a flyer."

Jesse looked at them all, from the petty officer to the line cook. "Thank you all so very much," he said. "I hope I never let you down."

"No, thank you, Ensign Brown," a steward replied. The others murmured in agreement. "Enjoy it, sir," said another. "God bless." One by one the cooks and stewards broke from the gaggle with a nod or a wave and returned to their duties.

A steward remained behind. He leaned forward with a lighter and lit the candle on the cake. The flame's tiny light flickered on Jesse's cheeks.

In a bashful voice, Koenig broke into song: *"Happy birthday to you . . ."* Tom and the officers joined in, and the steward sang, too. Jesse grinned as the chorus of warm voices reached a crescendo.

As the song ended, applause arose. "Thanks so much, guys," Jesse said. He thanked the steward and waved to the officers up and down the table. "Thank you all."

With everyone watching, Jesse leaned forward and blew out the candle.

CHAPTER 27

HOME

Sixteen days later, November 4, 1950
Sasebo, in southwestern Japan

The sun was setting behind craggy mountains. Tom, Cevoli, Jesse, Marty, Wilkie, and other pilots found themselves on Black Market Alley, Sasebo's most energetic street. Colorful signs with Japanese lettering decorated the neighboring storefronts. Sailors milled about, jovial, loud, tipsy. Japanese vendors hawked lacquer boxes and silk pajamas. Smoke rose from grills, and the air smelled of sizzling meat and plum wine.

This was their last night in Japan before the *Leyte* sailed in the morning. Although the ship's destination remained unannounced, Tom and the others had their suspicions. They had last heard that the army and Marines were mopping up in Korea, and even running out of targets. And when the *Leyte* had anchored in Sasebo, spare parts and new Corsairs were supposed to be waiting—but the docks were empty. When Tom inquired, he discovered that his requests for spares had been denied, the delivery of new planes canceled. The facts steered Tom and the others to the same conclusion: *We're heading home.*

Together, the pilots peered through store windows, eager to knock out their Christmas shopping early. The Korean War was short—and they'd survived.

Tom absorbed the sights around him as old women passed by in wooden clogs. Sailors sat on stools while Japanese artists painted their portraits. Other sailors tried to sweet-talk Japanese women, only to be rejected.

Tom and the others each ducked into shops to explore.

Beneath a jewelry store's high ceiling and dangling lights, Jesse examined a string of pearls. Then he trickled them back into their case. He had decided to save his money for the diamond ring he intended to buy for Daisy. Since hearing the rumors that the *Leyte* would be making a beeline for home, Jesse had felt happy. The first thing he planned to do was to buy the ring and then present it when he and Daisy were vacationing in the Bahamas.

As Jesse stepped back into the street, a jeep honked in the distance. A whistle sounded from one direction, then from another. All at once, flocks of Shore Patrol sailors—the navy's police—emerged from the crowds. The SPs went from building to building, stopping American servicemen in the street and shouting messages into their ears. The servicemen nodded; even the drunk ones straightened up.

The Shore Patrol sailors worked their way closer to Jesse. Jesse had always tried to avoid them. During flight training, they had often shown prejudice toward him, trailing him and

Daisy from street to street in Pensacola, not quite believing that a Black man was an off-duty pilot cadet.

Two uniformed SPs hustled toward him.

"Sir, liberty is suspended," one said. "Everyone needs to head back to their ships ASAP—something big is happening."

Jesse asked if something was wrong.

"Shit's hitting the fan in Korea," the SP said. "That's all they're telling us, sir." The SPs hurried off to the next navy men.

Jesse's face fell. He'd just written to Daisy to tell her that he might be coming home.

A full-scale roundup was under way. Along the street, SPs pried sailors from movie theaters and steak dinners. Tom and Cevoli emerged from a shop, each man wearing newly purchased binoculars around his neck. Tom's eyes swept the street with alarm.

Even before the SPs reached him, the whistles told Tom what every fighting man dreaded.

Home was going to have to wait.

CHAPTER 28

THE FIRST BATTLE OF WORLD WAR III

Two days later, November 6, 1950
Northeastern North Korea

At the floor of a valley, Marine artillery pieces sent shells rocketing toward the clouds. Flashes exploded against the hilltop. *Crack! Crack! Crack!* Plumes of smoke rose into the gray afternoon sky. The top of the hill was charred black.

Five thousand Marines watched the fireworks from the valley floor, near the village of Sudong. They were the lead element of the First Marine Division. Korean refugees walking past the Marines stopped to watch, too.

Before this, the Marines had been making good progress marching north. Their orders were to push the North Koreans over the Chinese border—just eighty miles away—and go no farther.

Then, the massive hill appeared in their path, blocking their way through the mountains. The hill stood 891 meters above sea level, so men called it "891."

From atop 891, a formidable force had fired down on the Marines and stopped the column in its tracks.

Now, the Marines fired back.

Red Parkinson took a few steps from his buddies and unslung his carbine. His eyes settled across the road, where North Korean refugees were resting.

A man standing near the refugees caught Red's eye. The man wore a peasant's long coat, but he had strayed from the group. He strolled over to a cluster of Marine trucks along the roadside. Marines were unloading boxes to set up a supply depot. The man in the coat lightly waved a finger, as if counting the trucks.

Red's eyes narrowed. "Charlie, take a look at this," he muttered. Charlie Kline stepped to Red's side. The man seemed to be scribbling something down.

Red said, "He's taking notes."

"He's awful curious," Charlie said.

Red lowered his carbine and shouted, "Hey, you!" The man glanced over his shoulder and slipped something into his pocket.

Red started toward him, and the man took off running.

"Halt!" Red shouted.

But the man kept sprinting through a field.

Red raised his rifle and took aim.

Bam! Red fired, and smoke rose from the carbine's barrel. The man lost his footing, steadied himself, and kept running.

"Out of the way, Red!" said another Marine. He calmly

leveled his M1 Garand rifle on the running man. *Bang!* The man flopped to the ground.

The Marines hustled toward the fallen man. Devans crouched and rolled the body over. Red saw that the dead man was Asian, probably in his twenties. Devans scratched his chin.

Charlie glanced at Red with a raised eyebrow. Devans flapped the young man's long coat open. Beneath was a second layer, a quilted white jacket that was brown on the inside. Red had heard of this attire. He felt a knot form in his gut.

Devans fished through the man's pockets and retrieved a notepad. Red peered over Devans's shoulder as he thumbed through pages filled with drawings.

"Well, I'll be," Devans said. "He's got our positions marked up and down the road!"

The Marines muttered in alarm.

"He's no refugee," Devans said, shaking his head. "He's not North Korean, either. Take a look at that jacket."

All eyes settled on the white jacket. Then their eyes followed the sounds of gunfire back to the hill known as 891, where something ominous was brewing. One man spat and another nervously fished for a cigarette. Something about the dead man's attire told them that the fighting wouldn't be over by Thanksgiving, as General MacArthur had boasted.

The North Koreans were no longer fighting alone.

CHAPTER 29

THE SKY WILL BE BLACK

Twelve days later, November 18, 1950
Aboard the USS *Leyte*

The ready room was quiet and the pilots of Fighting 32 were fidgety. All that remained was one last briefing. It was 8:00 a.m. and the pilots—just six of them—were about to make the world's most dangerous commute.

Tom had been chosen to fly. With his leather jacket stretched over his seat back, he leaned forward to study a crinkly map on the wall. His eyes locked on a blue line that snaked up the side of Korea and divided North Korea from China.

The Yalu River. That name gave him the chills. He took a drag from his pipe to try to cool his nerves.

Tom and the others snapped to their feet when the skipper entered. The man motioned for his pilots to sit and stepped front and center.

The brass had identified twelve Chinese divisions in Korea—at least a hundred thousand enemy soldiers, the skipper reported. No one was sure if the Chinese had entered the war to stay—or just to help their fellow Communists escape. The reason didn't matter. Colonel Litzenberg, the Seventh Marines' commander, had said it: The results of these battles would "reverberate around the world"—and send a message to Stalin himself.

Yet, after one week of combat, the Chinese army had mysteriously disappeared into the mountains.

Tom shook his head in disbelief. "Just because the Chinese aren't engaging doesn't mean they're gone," the skipper pointed out. "Our night fighters are reporting headlights coming *into* Korea—not out." He explained what that could likely mean: that the Chinese were bringing in fresh troops and supplies to keep their army strong.

Across the river was the key to the Chinese route into Korea: the Yalu bridges.

The skipper nodded to a sailor in the rear who was manning a slide projector. The lights dimmed. Tom and Jesse readied their notepads. Cevoli rocked in his chair ambivalently; he'd take notes on his palm.

"Today, the strike package is paying a visit to the twins," the skipper said.

Click.

An aerial photo of twin bridges on the Yalu appeared on the screen. The bridge to the south held a highway, and the other one held railroad tracks. Both bridges had been damaged enough to halt traffic, but neither had fallen.

The skipper explained that the enemy was repairing the bridges under darkness and soon both would be back in operation. Tom wanted to groan. Supposedly the Chinese had five hundred thousand troops on their side of the river just waiting for a lift across and the North Koreans had six thousand trucks on their side, eager to serve. Only the damaged bridges were preventing them from teaming up.

No target held greater importance in all the war. And yet no target had been more difficult to reach. That was because American pilots were forbidden to cross the river and violate Chinese air space, so they had to fly up or down the river and attack the bridges at their narrowest parts.

"Today, we're going after the highway bridge," the skipper continued. "But this time we're going in ahead to suppress the flak—we'll leave the bridge-busting to the Skyraiders."

The pilots nodded approvingly. Skyraiders were heavy attack planes, almost like flying tanks—perfect for the job of destroying the bridge.

The skipper explained that '32 would lead the formations to the target, with '33 following and the Skyraiders trailing them. He nodded to the projectionist.

Click.

A photo appeared of Sinuiju, a city on the Korean side of the bridges. Sinuiju now served as the acting North Korean capital for the regime in retreat.

The skipper explained that there were plenty of antiaircraft guns in Sinuiju—the most in all of Korea. He added that '32 would go in first, to combat as many antiaircraft guns as possible, and to clear the path for the Skyraiders to safely make their attacks on the bridge.

Tom glanced nervously at his buddies. Jesse didn't blink from the image on the screen. Veteran pilots who'd been to Sinuiju swore that the antiaircraft flak was as bad as anything in WWII.

Click.

The next photo showed three red circles over the city grid, near the bridge. Each circle was numbered and represented three Soviet-built 85mm cannons grouped together in what was called a battery.

The skipper said that the pilots would each be assigned a battery to strike. "Considering the current level of ruin, Intel believes the area is civilian-free," the skipper added. The men were relieved. It meant that they wouldn't run the risk of harming local Korean people.

The lights flicked on. Tom closed his notepad.

"Today's gonna be rough," the skipper warned. "They know we're coming, they know from which direction. The sky will be black and we're just gonna have to plow through it." His eyes filled with determination. "Let's give the Skyraiders some clear skies, and let's tumble a damned bridge already!"

Tom, Jesse, and the others nodded. Wilkie, who would be flying with them that day, wasn't feeling as confident. When he'd heard their target would be flak suppression in Sinuiju city, he'd felt pure dread. Earlier, he'd written to his parents: "It's all been fun so far, as we've just hit buildings, vehicles, etc. Hope I don't have to kill men, as I'm not looking forward to that part at all, but someone has to do it, I guess. Just hope I'm not the one, as I can't see this killing crap at all. Just ain't built that way, I guess."

Now Wilkie was lost in thought, his blue eyes distant. There was no way to bomb a flak gun without killing the men operating it.

Two hours later, at twenty thousand feet over North Korea

Tall in his seat, the skipper looked to Tom. He held his finger like a gun and pointed: *Target sighted!*

Between breaths from his oxygen mask, Tom peered ahead. The midday sunlight seemed to magnify every scratch in the windscreen. In the distance, he saw mountains standing above the blue Yalu River. Cities lined both banks—and between the cities were the notorious bridges.

The Corsairs swept over the outskirts of Sinuiju, the city on the Korean side. The neighborhoods looked clean and hospitable. But as the formation neared the bridges, the city turned scorched and shadowy. Ten days earlier, an American B-29 raid had burned and destroyed sixty percent of the city below.

Tom's eyes lifted. Across the river, on the Chinese side, was an industrial city. Smoke rose from its factories and paper mills. There were warehouses full of the food and ammo that kept Chinese armies functioning in North Korea. And there was also manpower: five hundred thousand fresh Chinese troops ready to fight.

Tom kept scanning the fields on the Chinese side. Reportedly, antiaircraft guns dotted the fields. For weeks, the North Koreans had been moving their guns into China, to keep them safe. From there, they could fire on American planes, but the Americans couldn't legally fire back. The U.S. military was careful not to escalate any conflicts with China, and for complicated reasons. The Chinese had signed a mutual defense treaty with Stalin back in 1949 that stated that an attack on either would spark a war with both. Before the first bridge strike, naval admiral C. Turner Joy reminded his pilots: "Our government has decided that we cannot violate the air space over Manchuria (northeastern China) or attack on Manchurian territory regardless of the provocation. If such attacks were made, the world might be thrown into the holocaust of a third world war."

And yet, Tom couldn't fathom how the Chinese army could look the nations of the world in the eyes and deny that they were involved in the Korean War.

A black puff of smoke burst below Tom's plane. Then another. Black puffs began soiling the sky. Each was an exploding flak shell. The hairs on Tom's neck stood up. The gunners were laying their flak right in the Skyraiders' flight path. Tom glanced in his rearview mirror. The formation of Skyraiders looked like dots on the horizon, lower than the Corsairs. They were just minutes behind.

The skipper pumped his fist—*Prepare to attack!* Tom lowered his goggles. He armed his guns and bomb. Beneath the Corsair's belly hung an olive-painted bomb with a message in chalk, scribbled by a deckhand. It said something like *With love, from the USS* Leyte.

The bomb was special, a proximity bomb. A silver cylinder

protruded from its nose, and within the cylinder was a radio fuse that would emit a sound wave and trigger the weapon just above the ground. The consequences of hitting the target—or missing—would all be his.

The thick cloud of gun smoke passed beneath the Corsairs. To reach their targets, the pilots would have to dive through that abyss. Tom's breathing became heavy. He peered through the cloud and saw the highway bridge's humps rising from the river like a sea serpent. Bomb craters pocked the streets just inland from the river. Tom's eyes narrowed. His target area was coming into view.

The skipper reached his target first. "Commencing flak suppression!" he announced. A split second later, his plane peeled into a dive.

Tom held his course toward the bridge with Jesse and Wilkie following close behind. Several seconds of flight would place him parallel with his target. Tom blinked nervously. Sweating, he tilted the control stick and peeled away. Tom allowed the Corsair's nose to fall into an eye-watering dive. Wind cut through gaps in the canopy seal and he felt the plane running with him, its weight on his back. The speed mounted—320 miles per hour became 330, then 340.

Below, Tom saw the skipper and his wingman diving side by side toward the black cloud before they plunged into the abyss. Darkness surrounded Tom's plane as it punched into the abyss next. Shells flashed like lightning. *Ka-boom! Ka-boom!* Nineteen pounds of jagged steel leapt from each explosion. Tom shrank in his seat and held his breath. The smell of burned gunpowder filled the cockpit. Shock waves rocked the Corsair's wings, tossing Tom against his shoulder straps. *Come on, old girl!* Tom urged his plane.

The black cloud passed, and the Corsair popped abruptly into the clear. The city now filled Tom's windscreen. He sucked oxygen from his mask and snapped his eyes back to his target. The altimeter needle spun backward as the Corsair dived through 12,000 feet, 11,000, 10,000.

Orange tracers rose from the city, arcing toward the Corsair. *Zip, zip, zip!*

Tom winced. Glancing to the right, he tracked the fire to its source. "Holy hell!" he muttered. The fields on the Chinese side of the river were ablaze with flashes of gunfire.

Below, Tom glimpsed the skipper and his wingman peeling right to escape the city. Their bombs exploded behind them. Tom hit the radio button and stammered, "You—you hit something!" No reply came—the skipper was flying for his life.

Tom's own Corsair rocketed down through 9,000 feet, 8,000, 7,000. He could still see the flashing of the flak cannons, their fifteen-foot-long barrels aiming at the planes in the sky.

Ka-boom!

In unison, the cannons fired. Shock waves blasted from their muzzles and dust rippled across the street. Spinning shells as wide as baseballs rocketed up toward Tom Hudner.

Crack! Crack! Crack!

As the shells exploded behind him, Tom no longer flinched. A gleam of certainty filled his eyes. His finger tightened on the trigger. The altimeter needle spun backward as the Corsair dived through 6,000 feet, 5,000, 4,000. His target was within reach.

Now! Tom squeezed the trigger. With an ear-shattering roar, all six of the Corsair's machine guns fired away like jackhammers. Ferocious streams of orange tracers blasted from the wings.

Tom squinted at his target against the blinding light. With metallic rage, the bullets pierced and thudded and ricocheted into anyone and anything.

Drop! With his thumb, Tom mashed the red button atop the stick. Beneath the Corsair's belly, the proximity bomb clicked loose. The plane lifted from its dive as the bomb whistled down.

Blackness squeezed Tom's vision. He sipped air from his mask and muscled the Corsair's control stick back. The wings groaned and creaked, threatening to rip away. Just above the charred rooftops, the Corsair leveled out.

Behind Tom, a flash burst—*Ka-boom!* Twenty-five yards above his target, Tom's bomb had exploded. It sprayed a cone of hot metal down onto the gun battery. Shock waves rippled. High above, Jesse's voice crackled: "Looks like a hit, Tom!"

Tom shook the vision back into his eyes. The Corsair was flying fast and low. Tom tore his oxygen mask from his helmet and breathed in fresh air. Relief filled his face.

Behind him, another enemy gun battery was silent.

Meanwhile, seven thousand feet above, fifty feet separated Wilkie's and Jesse's Corsairs as they dived through the web of fire. Wilkie squinted through his gunsight. "Crap!" he muttered. He could see the bridge to the right but couldn't spot their target.

Wilkie glanced left and saw Jesse's face fixed forward. Behind his goggles, his eyes were steady. He must have spied their target, because the muzzles on his Corsair's wings erupted with gunfire.

The Corsairs plummeted through 6,000 feet, then 5,000, then 4,000. Wilkie hovered his thumb over the bomb release button. Jesse's words were still fresh in his mind: "Just drop when I drop and you'll get through just fine." As the city came into focus, Wilkie's eyes flashed with horror. Just above his aim point he spotted a walled compound. Within the walls, civilians were scattering. Small civilians.

Children.

"Oh, shit!" Wilkie muttered. Down to 3,500 feet, 3,000 feet. The compound resembled a school—and it lay just a few streets above his aim point, in his flight path, not in Jesse's. Wilkie began breathing heavily. If his aim was off, he'd hit the school.

The bomb-ravaged city came into view as Wilkie flew lower to the ground. Still, the rubble obscured Wilkie's target: the cannons. Wilkie could see the children clearly. Some were scattering—some looked frozen in their tracks.

The bomb released from Jesse's plane. That meant it was Wilkie's turn to drop his.

Wilkie couldn't do it. It was too risky with the children there. He shifted his thumb away from the bomb release button and hauled back on the control stick. With the bomb still slung tight, the Corsair swooped from its dive so low it rattled the roof tiles.

Ka-boom!

Jesse's bomb exploded behind Wilkie. A split second later,

Wilkie flew over the school and saw the Korean children looking up, unharmed. Wilkie tore his oxygen mask from his face and breathed deeply. He checked his rearview mirror. Jesse had placed his bomb precisely. None of the children were hurt.

Wilkie throttled forward to catch up to Jesse, who was darting toward the river. Enemy gunners were tracking them both. The smell of the burned city below was pungent.

Then Wilkie remembered: his bomb. He had nearly forgotten it was still attached. He flicked a switch to deactivate the radio fuse before the bomb self-detonated. His face clenched with frustration. He couldn't dump the bomb just anywhere, not with civilians living in the rubble.

Wilkie glanced behind him and caught a glimpse of the Skyraider aircraft. They were nearly over the bridge, seemingly safe.

Wilkie nestled into formation on Jesse's right wing. Jesse glanced over at Wilkie, his eyes lowering to the bomb, still attached. Jesse's eyebrows rose with surprise. He grinned and shook his head as if to say, *What can you do?* Mechanical malfunctions were often the cause of hung bombs. Wilkie forced a tight-lipped smile—he'd explain later.

High above, the skipper and the others were assembling.

Wilkie followed Jesse into a climb to re-form.

As he flew, Wilkie kept an eye on his altimeter needle. When the needle wound above 2,500 feet, he took a deep breath and hoped the skipper wasn't watching. With his thumb, Wilkie mashed the bomb release button. The bomb jettisoned, fell, and splashed into the waves. His record was intact—he hadn't killed a soul. Still, he shook his head in frustration.

The Corsairs had done their job—the flak cloud over Sinuiju had thinned from black to a pale shade of gray. Now ten Skyraiders could be seen motoring through it. The specks were the navy's flying tanks. The plane was anything but graceful—its nose seemed too small, its canopy too far forward, its body too wide—but it could pack a punch. And each one was carrying a thousand-pound bomb and a two-thousand-pounder.

Tom breathed steadily. Anxiously, his eyes tracked the Skyraiders as they attacked the bridge. From afar, it resembled a prop or a tiny toy. Minuscule splashes leapt from the river. The first two bombs had hit only water.

"Near misses!" a pilot reported.

It's okay, Tom thought. *They're just getting started.*

More splashes jumped from the river. The radio crackled with disappointment.

"No dice!"

"Damn close!"

A flash of light burst from the middle of the bridge and smoke billowed.

"A hit! It's a hit!" a pilot announced.

Bombs kept falling, the river kept splashing. A new flash burst and fresh smoke rose.

"On the money!" a pilot shouted.

One after another, the Skyraiders ran for the Yellow Sea. More specks appeared on the eastern horizon. Skyraiders from the carrier *Valley Forge* had come to pummel the other "twin," the railroad bridge. But all eyes were turned toward the highway bridge.

Behind the Skyraiders, the smoke settled. One part of the bridge leaned into the Yalu, shattered. Nearer to shore, another part sat sunken on the river's bottom. The Skyraider leader radioed all *Leyte* planes: "A-1 job, boys."

Tom couldn't restrain his grin.

They left the Yalu smoking.

CHAPTER 30

A CHILL IN THE NIGHT

That afternoon, after the bridge strike
Aboard the USS *Leyte*

Word of the bridge's destruction traveled across the ship. So did the news that the *Valley Forge* Skyraiders had damaged the railway bridge. The strike had been successful.

Inside the ready room, Jesse, Tom, and Wilkie were freshly showered and had donned clean uniforms after the long day. Conversation swirled around the three of them. Their buddies pumped them for details about the bridge strike. On the fringes, Cevoli and Marty eagerly followed the conversation.

Word of the bridge mission would soon travel the world. First the American commander, General Douglas MacArthur, would review the strike photos, then President Truman in Washington. The carrier pilots had possibly prevented five hundred thousand Chinese troops from entering Korea and might have helped win the war.

A pilot turned to Tom, Wilkie, and Jesse. "It's not fair," the pilot joked. "You're going to all get medals, too!"

Tom dismissed the idea—he wasn't one for medals to begin with. Tom was the pilot who wouldn't sew the squadron patch onto his leather jacket because it would be "showing off."

"Nah, I doubt you'll get anything," said another pilot. "The skipper doesn't believe in medals."

The circle turned quiet. It was true. After almost two months of combat, the skipper hadn't nominated anyone for an award.

Later that night, the cabin was dark but for a single lamp that hung over Jesse's desk. Jesse was keeping the lights low because Koenig was trying to fall asleep. Gonglike sounds echoed as steam pipes clanged. The floor hummed from the ship's propellers.

Jesse cleared his desk of any letters and clutter. He wrote to Daisy almost nightly and told her about his missions but never admitted that the enemy had actually shot at him.

Since Sasebo, Jesse had added to his nightly routine. He'd begun a long-distance college course in international law—but he wasn't studying. He was a subscriber to *Architectural Forum* magazine—but he wasn't reading. He opened a drawer and removed a wide pad and some pencils and rulers. He flipped the pad open.

In the center of the paper, he had begun to draw a house. Only the first floor had taken shape so far. He'd drawn windows and a front door that led onto a porch with an awning over it.

Jesse leaned over the desk, focused his eyes, and used the

rulers to steady his pencil as he drew. He and Daisy had spent days planning the house together. They called it their "dream home."

The dream home was simple. A single story. Painted red, Daisy's favorite color. They had agreed to build it whenever the opportunity arose. Jesse had barely four months remaining in his active duty commitment. In March, he'd revert to the reserves and resume his studies to become an architectural engineer, who selects the building materials for an architect. Afterward, he would build the dream house.

That night, like others, Koenig saw Jesse sketching. Jesse smiled to himself when he drew a line perfectly. He erased vigorously if an angle wasn't perfect. He stared deep into the drawing, as if he could see the house filling with color and coming to life, as if he could see the front door swinging open and Daisy and Pam standing there.

With every passing night, Jesse sketched faster, as if the drawing were his ticket home.

Several days later

In the darkness, lanterns sat on the snow as far as the eye could see. The flame from each lantern flickered against the frigid night, spreading just enough light to see by.

A white shape lumbered along the path of light. *Crunch, crunch, crunch.* The shape was a man wrapped in a quilted white jacket and pants. His chin was lowered and his face was bundled by the earflaps of a winter cap. Tanned skin showed around his eyes.

He was a Chinese soldier. Close behind him marched his fellow soldiers in a silent, seemingly endless parade. Some had submachine guns around their necks. Others had rifles slung over their backs, or bags of grenades across their shoulders. Beneath their feet, the Yalu River was frozen solid and easy enough for them to cross by foot. Under darkness, the troops marched across the ice and straight into North Korea.

The bridges that the navy had destroyed had been rendered meaningless. A man who called himself "Feng Xi" had goaded the Chinese into the Korean War. Feng Xi was Stalin's diplomatic code name. Fully aware that the Chinese still suffered from the wounds of World War II, Stalin preyed upon their worst fears. He told the Chinese leader, Mao Zedong, that the Americans would transform Korea into a "bridgehead" through which Japan could once again invade China. To prevent this outcome, Stalin urged the Chinese to commit five or six divisions to battle in Korea. Mao pledged nine.

The soldiers' breath hung in the subzero air. On each man's back were a backpack and bedroll and across his chest hung a bag of rice. Slipperlike canvas shoes covered the men's feet. The ice creaked and groaned beneath them.

For some Chinese soldiers, this was just another march in a lifetime of war. Some had once been rural peasants, drafted to fight the Japanese in World War II and then their own countrymen from 1947 to 1949 in the Chinese Civil War. For many, there was no honorable discharge—none except for injuries or death.

By then, more than three hundred thousand Chinese soldiers had snuck into Korea, far more than the one hundred thousand that American commanders had imagined. The brass had consistently underestimated the Chinese. They'd failed to realize that the first Chinese attack had been only a test. Now armed with knowledge of American tactics, thousands more fresh Chinese soldiers crossed the Yalu. Soon, they'd join their comrades. In rugged mountain terrain, in bitter winter conditions, they would attempt to destroy all the American forces in North Korea.

Several days later, November 26, 1950

At the back of the ready room, Jesse and the pilots of Fighting 32 were about to become American celebrities. *Life* magazine had decided to run a photo-essay about Jesse. At the time, *Life* was one of America's biggest magazines, seen by half of all American adults in any week. The article would be released in a few weeks and would be shipped coast to coast. The magazine simply needed some photos of Jesse and quotes by him. The ship's photographer would handle the assignment.

Everyone in '32 was thrilled for Jesse—except Jesse himself. The *Leyte*'s PR officer made small talk with Jesse to loosen him up for the photo shoot, but Jesse wasn't biting. "Isn't it too soon to be celebrating?" he asked. "Shouldn't we wait until we're out of this mess?"

The PR officer brushed off Jesse's concerns. "It's perfect, you'll be famous by the time you get home!"

Embarrassed, Jesse turned away.

The "mess" that Jesse referenced had begun two days earlier.

In northwestern Korea, the U.N. forces had left their defensive positions and resumed their drive to the Yalu, giving the Chinese the opportunity they had been waiting for. From the mountains, the enemy had attacked. Now the U.S. Eighth Army—four full divisions—was stopped in its tracks after covering just fifteen miles, and South Korean divisions were disintegrating on the flanks.

The lights and camera were ready. The PR officer asked Jesse and Cevoli to pause their game, look up, and smile. They did.

Pop, flash!

The officer asked Jesse to wear his leather jacket, so the folks back home would know he was an aviator. Jesse sighed and reached for his jacket.

A month earlier, after the first mission, a sailor from the PR department had interviewed Jesse for a press release. "There's nothing special about me," Jesse had insisted. "I'm just another pilot."

"Okay, look excited," the officer said now as the camera was raised.

Cevoli grinned and Jesse forced a smile.

Pop, flash!

The officer urged Jesse to show more animation. "Your wife will see these photos," he said, "and someday your grandkids!"

Cevoli shook Jesse by the shoulder to loosen him up. "Hey— this is good PR for the navy," he said.

"Okay, okay." Jesse scooped up the dice, shook them in his fist, and flashed a wide grin.

Pop, flash!

"Great!" the PR officer said. He flipped open his pad and began to interview Jesse. When the officer asked if there had been any prejudice aboard ship, all eyes turned toward Jesse, curious to hear his answer.

"There hasn't been one instance," Jesse said.

The officer nodded, impressed. "So what's your secret?"

Jesse thought for a second. "I never try to force myself on people. If they're going to be friendly, then they will be pretty soon."

The officer chuckled. Cevoli and the others nodded—it was true. A journalist would later read Jesse's answers and publish his conclusion: "The key to Jesse's popularity was his assumption that no race problem existed and, as a result, none did."

The PR officer closed his pad and turned to Jesse with a last request. "Can you suit up like you're going to fly?"

Jesse took a deep breath and went to retrieve his gear. When he came back, he had on a helmet and goggles, a green flight suit, and a yellow life vest. He wore a pistol on his side. The sky was calm and cold. Jesse followed the officer and cameramen across the deck.

The photo shoot wound its way up to the tower and onto a high deck at the front. With the parked Corsairs below, the photographer directed Jesse to stare ahead, into the wind. As Jesse gazed toward the horizon, he couldn't relax. His face was uneasy, his eyes tense, his mouth tight.

He tried. He knew the camera was on him. But at that moment, far beyond sight, the western half of Korea was embroiled in battle, and in the eastern half the Marines were marching deeper into the frozen mountains.

As if he sensed the danger beyond the horizon, Jesse couldn't bring himself to even fake a smile.

Pop, flash!

CHAPTER 31

A TASTE OF THE DIRT

A day later, November 27, 1950
Wonsan Airfield, North Korea

Through the late-day gloom, a line of Corsairs taxied along the airfield by the sea. The flight had just returned from a strike in northwest Korea when a blizzard set in over the *Leyte*. Since the men were unable to land on the ship, Cevoli had steered the sixteen Corsairs—eight from '32 and eight from '33—to the Marine air base at Wonsan. Tom's, Jesse's, and the others' Corsairs rolled in after him and cut their engines. To their right lay Wonsan Harbor; to their left, a chain of scrubby hills overlooked the field.

Sweaty and tired, Tom had never been happier to reach land.

The airfield resembled a POW camp. Grimy wooden barracks stood side by side.

A young Marine ground crewman hustled to the plane to see if Tom needed assistance. The Marine wore a hooded parka and a helmet with a camouflage cover. A carbine dangled from his shoulder. *What the heck?* Tom thought. The Marine was dressed for battle.

In the distance, Tom could hear the staccato bursts of gunfire. His eyes filled with worry. *Did we land in the wrong place?* Wonsan was supposed to be ninety miles behind the front.

"Sir, you may want to come down," the Marine shouted to Tom. "You're presenting an awfully big target!"

Tom dismounted hurriedly.

"What's happening out there?" he asked.

"The Reds are making a play for the field," the Marine said. It seemed that a contingent of North Korean fighters and Chinese troops were attacking. He explained that the army's Third Infantry Division was holding them back, but barely. Tom shot him a questioning look. The Marine was suggesting that this could be the start of a new Red offensive.

Tom jogged over to find Jesse, Cevoli, Koenig, and a handful of Marines crowded around Jesse's plane's tail. During the earlier strike, a flak burst had hit Jesse's rudder, partially stripping the fabric skin. The right side of the white letter *K* now dangled in ribbons.

"Think you can still make the deck?" Tom asked Jesse with concern. The damage could hinder a carrier landing.

"Sure," Jesse said as he tugged and tested the remaining fabric. "I made it this far without a rudder."

Marty approached the group. "Any of you fellas get shot at coming in?"

Several pilots nodded.

Cevoli told the Marines around him that if the weather didn't soon improve by the *Leyte,* the flight would need to spend the night here. The pilots glanced uneasily at one another. The temperature was falling, and many of them had already flipped up their collars against the cold.

A Marine approached the group. "Sirs, if anyone wants chow, they're serving supper early." He gestured to a green tent where Marines and infantrymen waited in line.

Marty, Cevoli, and a few others said they were hungry and headed for the chow line.

"I'll stay near the tower and wait for word from the ship," Jesse said. Tom said he was staying, too. *It's a bit hairy to be wandering off,* he thought. Koenig was of the same mind.

Tom and Jesse glanced at each other with unease.

The chow line was long and slow, and no one seemed worried about snipers. Marty and the others waited with exhausted Marines and army soldiers. The infantrymen wore battered helmets, and their uniforms were soiled and muddy.

The line shifted forward. Cooks in winter jackets stood behind tables. As each man reached the cooks, he held out a mess tin. One cook ladled mashed potatoes inside, another drizzled gravy, and a third forked up a juicy steak and dropped it into the tin.

Marty turned to a Marine. "You fellas always eat like this? I think I joined the wrong branch!"

The Marine grinned. "No, sir, this is a treat for us, too. The cooks figure if we get overrun tonight, we're not leaving anything good for the Reds."

Marty glanced down at his feet, embarrassed at his question.

He collected a plate and utensils and was about to reach the cooks when a Marine air traffic controller appeared. The controller hurried to Marty and the other pilots. "You can launch!" he said. "*Leyte* just called—they found a window in the storm!"

Marty set down his plate and tried to restrain his grin. "Hey, just take a steak with you!" a young soldier suggested. Marty politely declined and his face turned sheepish. He knew that unlike these men, a bottle of brandy, a hot shower, and a meal were awaiting him. That was just one of the differences between the men fighting on the ground and the pilots who stayed on the carrier.

Adrenaline pumping, Marty and the others sprinted for their planes.

In the cockpit, Tom set the throttle forward and flipped switches to bring the engine to life. *Come on, old girl, kick over!* he thought. He had never felt more eager to reach the sky.

Tom glanced left and saw Cevoli's propeller cranking to life. To the right he saw Jesse, his propeller already humming. Jesse's face looked uneasy, and Tom felt it, too. Darkness was falling and his heart pounded to escape this place—yet he felt reluctant to be running. His Corsair and the others could help defend the field and the men on it, but they had been ordered away to safety.

A symphony of motor noise shook the frigid air—all sixteen Corsairs were ready to roll. Cevoli's plane lurched forward.

Tom checked his wing tips. Beyond the left wing stood the

Marine who had urged him to dismount. The Marine saw Tom looking and raised a hand in farewell. Tom nodded in reply. He wanted to open the canopy and shout, "We'll be back!" But he couldn't be certain of that.

Tom released the brakes and let the Corsair roll. He swung onto the taxiway and left his fellow Americans behind, to face whatever was out there, lurking in the dark.

CHAPTER 32

WHEN THE DEER COME RUNNING

That same night, around 9 p.m.
Ninety miles farther north, at the Chosin Reservoir

Beneath a full moon, Red and Charlie shivered, huddled together on the floor of a frozen valley. They were among the ground Marines that Tom, Jesse, and Marty knew were struggling out there, vulnerable to enemy attacks overnight. Here in the northern reaches of Korea, it was twenty below zero.

The duo wore knit hats, hoods over their hats, and helmets over their hoods. Still, the cold crept down their necks.

Thirty other Marine shelters stood in the field, but not a soul stirred. This was the encampment for sixty Marines, a third of Weapons Company. The 188-man company had been divided into three detachments, and the other two had been dispersed to support units on the hills.

All told, the division had sent 9,500 Marines into the valley. Now they camped on hills in every direction except to the east, where the shacks of Yudam-ni village stood near the Chosin Reservoir.

Red unzipped his parka and cringed as the cold raced in. He reached a gloved hand inside and yanked out a can of fruit cocktail, then hurriedly zipped back up.

Charlie had given Red the fruit cocktail—the prized item from his C-rations—as a birthday present. In return, Red had given Charlie a tin of cocoa, because it was Charlie's birthday, too. By some twist of fate, both had been born on the same day, and now Red had turned twenty-two and Charlie twenty-one.

Red pawed open the can's lid. He drew his Ka-Bar knife and speared a chunk of fruit. He chewed with contentment and offered some to Charlie.

"All yours," Charlie murmured beneath his collar.

As Red ate, he gazed at a gap between two hills. The hill on the left stood a massive 1,403 meters above sea level. It was occupied by Marines, who had named it "1403." To the right, across the two-hundred-yard gap, the other hill was small and vacant.

The gap between the hills was an important place: it was the gateway to the northern no-man's-land, a place of endless mountains. A road ran through this gap, and if the enemy appeared, Red and his detachment were to serve as a roadblock. Sixty miles beyond it lay the Chinese border.

Charlie clutched his carbine against his chest. Red held his M1 Garand close. That morning, as they had entered the valley, they had observed herds of deer bolting from the woods. Their radios began picking up the sounds of people speaking in

Chinese. Then the Marines captured several Chinese deserters, who confessed, "Two of our armies now surround you."

Boots crunched against the frozen grass. Red tensed and spotted a short silhouette approaching. The figure was bundled in a long parka. *Who the heck would be out for a stroll in this?* Red wondered. The figure stopped and crouched beside him.

The cleft chin, upturned nose, and sleepy eyes of Sergeant Devans came into view. He had recently been promoted to sergeant, while Red had been made a corporal.

"You fellas staying warm?" Devans's voice quivered from the cold. Ice encrusted his shoulders and helmet cover. He was checking on the dozen men of his two heavy weapons platoons.

"Jesus, Bob," Red said. "Quit playing mother hen and get to cover!"

Devans grinned. "You're drinking regularly?" His breath cast small clouds.

"Yessir," Charlie mumbled.

Red nodded reluctantly—he hated the order to drink; he didn't feel the urge and hated having to urinate in such cold. But the Marines had been warned to avoid dehydration.

Devans's eyes turned serious. "It's no birthday without a cake, fellas, so let's make up for it when we get home?"

Charlie happily agreed, whereas Red simply played along; he had no illusions about seeing American soil anytime soon. Of the homesick Marines in the antitank platoons, Devans had been pining for home more than anyone, recently. Red knew why his sergeant was in a hurry to get back to Wilkes-Barre, Pennsylvania. Her name was Audrey Johns, and she was his former high school classmate. The two had then dated until Devans shipped off to join the Marines, his lifelong dream. On the ship to Korea, he had confided to a Marine from the same hometown: if he survived, he would return home in his dress blues to win Audrey back, even if that meant leaving the Corps for good.

Devans stood slowly, ice crackling on his parka. "One of you should be sleeping. The other, stay vigilant."

Red and Charlie nodded.

Devans buried his hands in his pockets and hobbled down the line to check on the others.

Red readied his knife to dip it into his fruit cocktail but stopped. His brow furrowed. "Damn it!" he said. The fruit was frozen solid.

Charlie lifted his face from his parka like a turtle from its shell. "Could be worse, brother John." He motioned to the left with his head, toward 1403.

High on Hill 1403, dark shapes climbed in the cold. They were the boys from How Company, a different Marine unit, who were hauling the last of their supplies to the crest. Red, Charlie, and their detachment were temporarily assigned to How Company as heavy weapons support. Word had it that the temperature was even lower on the hilltop where How Company was stationed. It was so cold, in fact, that Marines couldn't even take their boots off to go to sleep at night, for fear the boots would freeze and be impossible to put back on. Some were even afraid to close their eyes, as there were rumors going around that a person's eyelids could freeze shut. Night was when the Reds often struck—because they knew that was precisely when the Americans didn't have their long-range rifles and airpower as protection.

Red looked away from the hill and shook his head. "Poor mucks," he muttered.

CHAPTER 33

BACKS TO THE WALL

Meanwhile, on the valley floor

Red threw his bazooka over his shoulder, gripped his rifle, and ran from the encampment with Charlie, Devans, and the other men of the heavy weapons detachment. The Marines had left just about everything behind, besides their parkas and sleeping bags. They ran past dead Chinese soldiers, who lay on the road between the hills. The White Jackets had never expected the detachment's roadblock.

Beyond the rise of Hill 1403, Red could hear screams piercing the air. A wave of Chinese troops were charging How Company, their bayonets shining in the moonlight. The sounds of weaponry had given way to desperate hand-to-hand combat. The Chinese had launched a massive assault from almost every direction around the valley, and this was just the start of it.

The moon shone brightly overhead as Red and his comrades sprinted ahead. Soon enough, about a hundred yards away from the encampment, they reached a frozen creek. The creek snaked across the valley, surrounded by trees. Red slid down the bank and stopped short of the iced-over water. Charlie, Devans, and the others followed.

A new battle line was forming. The sixty Marines spread themselves across ninety yards, everyone crouching low. Devans called his platoons together. The twelve men gathered around. "Okay, let's hope they didn't see us regroup," Devans said in a hush. "This is the end of the line. If they get past us and take HQ, the whole valley may fall."

Oh, great, Red thought. Nearly 9,500 Marines were relying on them.

Devans gave the platoons a firm set of instructions: place one man on watch, and make sure everyone else remains silent and hidden until the enemy returns.

The men glanced nervously at one another. Devans noticed.

"Remember, fellas," he added comfortingly, looking around the circle. "We're Marines. If we stick together, we can't be beaten." Red and the others nodded and straightened up a bit at the encouragement.

Before Devans could depart, Charlie grabbed his arm. "Sarge, I left my rocket launcher out there." He gestured to the encampment. "Can I go get it quick?"

Devans shook his head in disbelief.

"I thought one of the other fellas had it," Charlie explained. Red scoffed at him.

"You're not going out there, Charlie," Devans said. "Too risky."

Charlie nodded reluctantly.

Red took first watch. He could hear gunfire still crackling around the valley. On 1403, explosions revealed ghostly figures darting across the crest. They were likely Chinese soldiers, although Red couldn't be certain. At last report, How Company had been driven off the summit. For now, all he could do was wait.

Four hours later, snow kept filtering down through the trees, collecting on the men's shoulders and helmets. Red watched it settle onto the icy creek. At his side, Charlie dozed, and Devans struggled to keep his eyes open. Along the bank, fifteen Marines remained on watch, their chins tucked against the wind.

Another nearby Marine raised his head suddenly. Red's eyebrows lifted. Something was amiss out there. Men began shaking their buddies. Up and down the line, Marines reached for rifles. Devans rose to a knee. Red nudged Charlie.

A tall Marine hustled down the line, gripping his rifle. His face was tight and tough; his black hair was gray on the sides. He was Gunnery Sergeant Alvin Sawyer. The gunny, who hailed from the backwoods of Kentucky, was forty-eight years old and a WWII veteran.

At each cluster of men, he whispered in a thick Kentuckian accent, "They're a-comin'! Stay low!" The gunny stopped at Devans. "Bob, keep your boys down," he whispered, "and fire on my call."

"Yessir," Devans said as the gunny moved on. Red and Charlie glanced nervously at each other.

Red lowered his M1. To his left, Charlie and Devans steadied their carbines. Two machine-gun squads laid their guns on tripods and took aim. All eyes settled on their abandoned encampment.

About a hundred White Jackets were circling the very tents that the Marines had been in earlier. Red shrank lower against the earth. Charlie's teeth chattered.

In a frenzy, the White Jackets charged the encampment. The Marines could see it all from afar. Flashes blinked through the falling snow as the White Jackets sprayed burp guns and bayoneted the Marines' canvas shelters. But when they lifted up the fallen shelters, they exclaimed with surprise. The Marines weren't there.

Since no one was around, some began ransacking the Marines' backpacks.

"My bazooka!" Charlie whispered, looking on from afar. Red shook his head in exasperation. Other Marines hoped the enemy wouldn't steal the war loot that they themselves had collected on their travels.

They saw a Chinese officer look up and shout an order. His men turned outward and raised their weapons. Red could feel their eyes searching for him.

"Don't look!" Devans hissed. Red scrunched his eyes tight.

Star shells—flares that dangled from parachutes and showered bluish light onto the earth—popped in blinding flashes over the encampment. Red slowly opened his eyes. Bluish-white light beamed down, revealing two hundred White Jackets, all momentarily blinded. Around them, the falling snow sparkled.

"Fire!" the gunny bellowed.

Red took aim but couldn't pull the trigger. His eyes widened with alarm. His finger wouldn't curl. *It's frozen stiff!* he thought. He figured out another way. He took aim and jerked the trigger back with an outstretched finger. The M1 cracked and spat flame. Red jerked the trigger again and again.

The two Marine machine guns raked the encampment. Bullets punched enemy troops backward. White Jackets fell, dropping their weapons. Tracers thudded into dead bodies and sizzled. Red and others slowed their firing to watch. A group of White Jackets dived for cover, but tracers followed them and zipped through the fabric, leaving smoking holes.

Charlie elbowed Red. Up the line, a machine gunner was singing a hit song between bursts—*"If I knew you were coming I'd've baked a cake!"* Some of the men around him laughed.

"Cease fire!" the gunny shouted over the din. After a few long seconds, the Marine line turned black and silent. Red shook the ringing from his ears.

Star shells swayed and revealed mounds of dead enemy soldiers. Some of the wounded chanted prayers. One by one, they went silent.

Red and the others listened and stared as the last light fizzled.

A half hour later, the moon was gone. Hill 1403 had turned quiet. Word had come that How Company had been ordered off. Everyone in the creek bed knew it—the White Jackets could now turn their full fury against them.

★ ★ ★

Minutes passed without a hint of the enemy. The snow trickled down like sand in an hourglass. Mesmerized, Red, Charlie, and Devans gazed at the field ahead. The encampment had seemed to vanish in the darkness.

Gunny Sawyer moved down the line, keeping low. He stopped at Devans. "Bob, I need you to send a few men out to reconnoiter." His beady eyes were impatient. "Tell 'em to go far enough to catch a whiff of the enemy, then get on back there."

Devans nodded dutifully.

Once the gunny had stepped out of earshot, Red spoke up: "That's a terrible damned idea!" Reconnoitering meant scouting out an area to see if it was safe. But nowhere in front of them could possibly be safe, and Red and the others knew it.

Devans hesitated, almost as if he was going to nod in agreement, but instead he grabbed his carbine and flicked the safety off.

Red raised an eyebrow. "Where do you think you're going?"

"I'm not about to order someone else out there," Devans murmured, shouldering his carbine. He turned to Charlie and asked, "Want to come with me—maybe find that rocket launcher of yours?"

A grin cracked Charlie's face. "Would I!"

Charlie slapped Red on the shoulder and followed Devans out into the field.

Fifteen minutes passed. Far away in the darkness came the patter of feet, the soft sounds of men running on the fresh snow.

Devans's shout pierced the darkness: "Here they come!" Up and down the line, Marines raised their rifles and machine guns.

In the field ahead, two forms took shape against the snow. Red recognized Charlie's husky silhouette sprinting toward the line, followed by Devans's smaller shape farther behind. "They're hot on our heels!" Charlie screamed.

We're surrounded, Red thought in despair.

A bugle blared. Then another bugle wailed the same tune. Then another and another as a dozen horns bled a haunting symphony.

A chorus of a thousand voices arose in Chinese: *"Sha! Sha! Sha!"* Kill, kill, kill! Cymbals began clanging and whistles began shrilling. The noise blended into a terrifying cacophony. More voices. The enemy stampede seemed to shake the frozen earth.

Charlie reached the Marine line and dived forward, rolling down into the creek bed. Red helped him to his feet. But his jaw sagged at the sight before him. About thirty yards from the line, Devans was running sloppily, obviously winded. He glanced over his shoulder. "They're a hundred yards out!" Devans shouted forward. "Call for illumination!" The snow spun around him.

"Okay, get back here!" Red shouted.

A Marine bellowed for illumination rounds so that they would be able to see better in the darkness. Charlie took his place at Red's side, panting. "Come on, Sarge!" Charlie cried to Devans, his voice shaking. A chorus of Marines' voices urged Devans onward. Devans was slipping and stumbling between glances at the enemy behind him. He shouted, "Hold your fire! Let them come in closer!"

"Get out of there, Bob!" Red screamed.

Devans stopped looking back and bolted for the line.

Whoosh! Whoosh! Star shells burst above the encampment, causing Red to squint. The bluish light spotlighted Devans in midstride, his carbine in one hand, the other holding down his helmet. Behind him charged a horde of White Jackets in an arrow formation, their feet stirring a cloud of snow.

Crack!

Devans's head snapped forward in a spray of blood. His helmet flew off, his arms fell limp, and the young sergeant tumbled into Red's arms.

Red sank to the ground under his sergeant's weight. "No! No!" Red shouted as he cradled Devans's body. The Marine line around them came alive with fire. "Bob?" Red shook his friend. "Come on, Bob!" But Devans's eyes remained fixed. Blood poured down Red's sleeves and over his parka. "No, God, no!" Red cradled his friend tighter.

Charlie glanced with terror between Devans and the onrushing enemy. Two Marines broke from the line and pried Devans from Red's grip. Red stood and tried to resist, but Charlie held him back. Blood covered Red's parka. His eyes bulged with horror as the Marines laid the young sergeant beside the creek and kept moving. Charlie turned Red back toward the bank—the enemy troops were nearly upon them.

"There's n-nothing you can do!" Charlie stammered. "He's with the Lord."

Red's eyes narrowed with rage at the mention of God. He grabbed Charlie and hurled him to the ground. Charlie looked up in shock. Red glared at him, then turned back to his rifle. Fifty yards away, White Jackets were falling like dominos, dropped by Marine bullets. Charlie returned to his firing position without a word.

Red lowered his sights on a White Jacket and fired. He snapped off round after round, cursing ragefully. Charlie glanced over with fearful eyes.

Fifty yards away, some enemy soldiers stopped charging forward and took cover behind their dead. But most kept going. More and more packs of White Jackets were wrapping around the Marine line. Over the gunfire, a Marine shouted, "They're flanking us!"

A cry came from the right: "They're in the line!"

Red and Charlie lifted their eyes from their gunsights and turned toward the sounds of trouble. More White Jackets were splashing down the creek and stumbling to shore, their padded pants and canvas shoes drenched. Marines sprinted straight toward them. One bayoneted a White Jacket against the creek bed. Another jabbed his rifle butt and sent a White Jacket tumbling into the icy water. Charlie and others waded into the fracas, firing from the hip. A Marine named "Big Daddy" Wiggins, one of the few Black Marines in the outfit, swung his rifle like a bat, knocking White Jackets into the creek and against the bank.

Still another pack of White Jackets charged. Red fired until his rifle went empty. Then he drew his .45 pistol and dashed toward a White Jacket who had wrapped his hands around a Marine's neck. Red blasted the enemy soldier off the Marine.

Meanwhile, more White Jackets leapt from the bank. Red fired as they landed and sent several sprawling.

Atop the bank, a White Jacket officer appeared, an empty burp gun hanging from his neck. He jumped onto Red's back and wrapped his arms around Red's face, clawing at his eyes. Red's helmet went flying, and he dropped his pistol. The officer bit down on Red's right ear, straight through the cartilage. Red howled and flipped the officer from his back.

Clutching his bleeding ear, Red staggered to face the officer. The officer leapt to his feet and drew a short sword. Red simultaneously slid his knife from its sheath. The officer snarled and thrust his sword. Red sidestepped as the blade darted past his chest, then swung his knife wildly and sliced the officer at the waist, cutting across the man's stomach through his jacket and belt. The officer's pants fell to his knees. He pedaled back, entangled.

Red lowered his knife and was preparing to stab when a shot rang out from behind. A bullet zipped over Red's shoulder and knocked the officer backward into the creek. The officer floated, motionless. Red wheeled and glanced up. Against the bank, a helmetless Marine held a smoking carbine. Red nodded in thanks. The helmetless Marine turned back toward the field. Beside him, the machine-gun crew lifted their weapon up the bank and swung it forward.

The gunner pulled the bolt and hammered away.

Red lowered his rifle to the snow. Dead White Jackets lay scattered before him. His eyes scanned the field for any enemy still moving. After thirty furious minutes of fighting, it seemed like the surviving White Jackets had crept away into the dark. Sporadic bullets snapped the trees overhead, but the attack was over, for now.

Red turned away from the bank, his chest heaving. What he saw horrified him. A gut-shot Marine wailed and thrashed while a medic tried to inject him with morphine. Another boy moaned against the bank, dying from a chest wound. Red couldn't see Charlie anywhere. The wounded and dead were being collected over by the road juncture, but Red couldn't yet leave his post to look for him.

From what Red could see, about two-thirds of the detachment—forty men—remained standing. Two Marines dragged a wounded man, his arms draped over their shoulders. Red stepped toward them and glanced under the wounded man's helmet and hood.

"Charlie?"

Teeth clenched in pain, a young soldier shook his head: "No." His buddies carried him away.

Another hour of darkness remained, enough time for the enemy to attack again. Up and down the line, battered Marines returned to their positions.

The gunny moved down the line. At each cluster of men he exhorted, "Go down fightin'—don't let 'em take you alive." During World War II, the gunny had endured the horrors of a POW camp. The gunny paused at Red. "No surrender, son," he added before moving on. Red nodded, his throat tightening.

Alone now in the shadows, Red traced his gloved fingers over his bloody right ear. He grimaced and began to remove a glove but then stopped and reeled back in horror. He held up his gloves. Devans's blood encrusted them. Red glanced down and realized that his arms and chest were crimson, too. Furiously, he pawed at his chest to scrape away the bloody crust. He turned to the bank, scooped up handfuls of soil, and rubbed the earth along his arms like sandpaper. He scrubbed harder and harder, but the crimson remained. Mere hours before, it had been his birthday, his friends by his side. Now Charlie was missing, and Devans lay with his head on the creek stones, eyes unblinking.

Tears welled in Red's eyes. He covered his ears, but the wailing of the wounded and the gunfire's snapping still reached him. He felt cold; his shoulders shook. Tears began leaking. Red sank to his knees. He gripped the sides of his face and began to choke up. He had never prayed before, but now he tried. "God, don't let me die, not here." He glanced upward, his cheeks streaked with tears. "I just want to see the sun come up one more time, just give me another day!" Red slumped against the bank and buried his face in his arms.

A blue glow hung over the frozen creek. It was 6 a.m., and the sky over the reservoir was turning pink beneath dark clouds. In the distance, at Yudam-ni Valley, Marines were starting trucks, jeeps, and tractors to warm the engines.

A hand shook Red and he opened his eyes. The face of a bazooka ammo bearer came into view. "Red, we're moving out on the double," he said. Red lifted his head and blinked. Around him, Marines were stirring. Meanwhile, two or three hundred White Jackets lay dead in the fields.

Marines fell into a column behind Gunny Sawyer. The detachment had been ordered to reinforce a unit on the west side of the valley. It was time to pick up and go.

But first, an important task. One by one, the surviving bazooka men gathered around Devans's body. One spread a sleeping bag on the ground. Together, several hands lifted their sergeant onto the bag and tucked him in. Red stumbled closer to see his friend's face for the last time. *Why him?* Red thought. *Bob was a better guy than me.* A Marine slowly zippered up the bag until Devans's eyes vanished.

The men flanked Devans's lifeless body.

The column began moving down the creek toward a field.

Four of Devans's men lifted him high as they marched. They had been told their dead would be retrieved later, but the bazooka men weren't about to take a chance.

In step, the Marines carried their sergeant toward the light.

Red found himself torn between the emotions of losing Devans and not being able to find Charlie. He moved rearward along the procession, looking intently at each man he passed. Tired eyes looked blankly back, but none belonged to Charlie Kline. He asked the others in the procession if they'd seen Charlie. "Yup," one replied. "He was helping the wounded." The man gestured back toward the road. Red sighed with relief. At the tail of the column, two Marines backpedaled between nervous glances at the creek. Red kept pace with the rearguard Marines and asked about Charlie.

"Yup, he stayed back." One nodded toward the creek. "Said he needed to get his rocket launcher, then he'd catch up."

Red shook his head in exasperation. He unslung his rifle and set off toward the creek to find Charlie. Time was of the essence. The White Jackets would surely swoop into the abandoned area once they saw that the Marines had left.

Red hadn't gone far when another Marine grabbed him by the shoulder. "No way, Red, you're not going back there."

Red shook the man's hand away. "Charlie's going to get himself killed!"

"Should we send someone looking for you next?" the Marine challenged. "Then someone else after that?"

Red glanced at the thin column of Marines that was slowly leaving them behind. His face twisted. If the White Jackets attacked now, his buddies wouldn't stand a chance.

Red shouldered his rifle and followed the Marine back to the column.

Exhausted and numb, the bazooka men struggled to carry Devans. The turn of events seemed unreal to Red. Eating watermelons on Crete, meeting Liz Taylor on the beach—any good memory seemed to belong to another lifetime.

Ahead of Red, a Marine glanced at Hill 1403. "Oh, Lord," he muttered, his eyes locked. Other Marines turned toward the hill. Red did, too. His eyes went wide, his jaw dropped. Of all the hills in the Marine defensive ring, only 1403 had fallen. The morning glow revealed its conquerors.

White Jackets filled the hilltop. They stood on the crest, visible against the dark clouds. The Chinese soldiers numbered in the hundreds, maybe the thousands. Red tightened his grip on the sleeping bag and felt a surge of defiance.

Why don't you come down and finish this? he wanted to shout up to them.

What are you waiting for?

CHAPTER 34

THE LOST LEGION

Five days later, December 3, 1950
Aboard the USS *Leyte*

The skipper spread a map on a table. Tom, Jesse, and the rest of the squadron crowded closer. It was 7 a.m. Breakfast was being served nearby, and they could smell coffee and pancakes. The pilots of Fighting 32, however, had bigger concerns than their empty stomachs.

Tom's eyes drifted to the map, to a body of water shaped like an inkblot and the words *Chosin Reservoir*—precisely where Red and his detachment were. The Marines there had been surrounded for six nights. The papers back home were now comparing the relentless fighting to the Battle of the Bulge in World War II, which had been a ruthless and deadly battle between German and American armies.

"Well, gents," the skipper said, his voice buoyant, "I've got good news—the Marines made it through the night." Tom, Jesse, and the others were relieved.

"They're still hanging by their fingernails," the skipper added. "That's all we know."

The pilots nodded.

"We're not going to sit around and wait," the skipper continued.

Tom's eyes leapt with hope. Everyone wanted to defend the Marines at Chosin, to fulfill their role as ground attack pilots and protect the Marines below. Today was '32's turn, and he was on the roster. It would be their biggest mission since the Yalu bridge raids. The *Leyte* would be putting up twenty-four planes—if the weather didn't spoil it. A massive snowstorm was blanketing eastern Korea. Conditions were so bad that the four Corsairs of '32's dawn flight had already diverted another strike far from the Chosin.

"Cevoli." The skipper turned to his second-in-command. "Your six-ship will launch for the Chosin as planned, at 0840."

Cevoli nodded.

"If Cevoli gets through to the Chosin," the skipper continued, "then Fowler's four-ship will follow in the afternoon . . ."

Dad Fowler nodded begrudgingly.

"Dang it!" Wilkie muttered, and Fowler's other pilots grumbled. Their flight was scheduled to launch at 2 p.m. Everyone knew the weather could worsen by then, making it more difficult to fly.

The skipper rattled off map coordinates, call signs, radio channels. He reviewed the changes to the roster. "Hudner, you're with Brown today," the skipper said. Jesse glanced at Tom and gave a nod. Tom smiled. Jesse's usual wingman, Koenig, had flown a recon mission the day before and had the day off.

The skipper glanced at his notes, his brow furrowed. He had neither target photos nor a strike pattern to plot. The *Leyte* was sending planes to the Chosin on blind faith; the fighting had gotten that desperate.

The skipper turned to Dad: "Anything to add?"

Dad glanced around the table. "You can't attack ground troops without having a lot of crap flung at you, so I'd suggest we all review the escape and evasion brief."

The pilots nodded. Escape and evasion procedures were to be followed if a pilot was shot down. Everyone knew that the odds of that were mounting.

"Okay, you have your mission," the skipper said. He tapped the map of the Chosin.

"Get there!"

Dressed to fly, Tom sat to review the list of escape and evasion procedures, although he knew it by heart. Behind him, others checked their pistols and gear.

Tom slid his finger down the list that explained how to signal a downed pilot:

- Pilot has been seen: Fly low over pilot, rocking wings.
- Proceed in direction indicated: Drop wheels and fly in direction in which pilot should move.
- Use the right hand orbit to indicate that a rescue will be attempted . . . a left hand orbit to indicate that no rescue attempt is possible.

The skipper and Dad had refreshed the procedures in November after the *Leyte* lost a Skyraider pilot named Roland Batson. Batson had been shot down during a bridge strike and had belly-landed in a cornfield behind enemy lines. Dad's flight had seen the downed pilot waving up at them but couldn't communicate with him. They couldn't tell Batson that a rescue helicopter wasn't coming, that it was already too late in the day. They couldn't coordinate where he should hide for the night.

No one had given up on Batson, however. For days, the *Leyte* sent search planes. But it had been too late. Batson was never seen again.

After the failed searches, a young pilot had asked the skipper, "Why didn't someone just land and pick Batson up the first time? It was just a cornfield!"

A hush fell over the ready room. "If tomorrow or the next day you see Batson," the skipper had replied, "even if he's waving up from a field of clover—you leave him there! It's bad enough to lose one pilot. We can't lose two. And if any of you try to land and pick someone up, I'll court-martial your ass." They had heard the skipper's warning loud and clear: a downed pilot was to be left where he was.

Tom set the clipboard aside and reached for his helmet. A man could prepare only so much for the unthinkable.

Meanwhile, at the Chosin Reservoir

Snow drifted over the entrance to Yudam-ni Valley. Flurries settled onto piles of rocks. They settled onto the low bunkers. They settled onto the bodies of the dead.

A wisp of breath rose from a rock pile. Mittens clawed up, then arms pried themselves free, then a helmeted head popped through. Delirious, Red Parkinson brushed the snow from his helmet. His face was pale and dirty. His eyes were heavy with sleep. Patchy red stubble marked his cheeks, and his nostrils were encrusted with mucus.

Red slid from his snow-covered sleeping bag, careful not to wake the young Marine who dozed beside him. The Marine was seventeen-year-old Jack Danaher, a bazooka gunner and one of about forty survivors remaining in the detachment. The youngster's hair was dark, and his nose was short and pointy. His back was turned to Red as he rested. On this sixth day of the enemy's siege, every minute of sleep was precious.

Red squinted against the flurries. Stormy gray clouds stretched in every direction, so low that they swallowed some hilltops. Red's face sank. *With weather like this, forget any air support,* he thought. No way planes could fly in such overcast skies. He gazed up the slope, past the corpses of White Jacket soldiers.

The Marine battle lines lay halfway up the hill. A Chinese regiment—more than two thousand men—had been up there the night before. But no Chinese soldier stirred. Red's eyes lifted with hope: *Maybe they're gone?* Two days earlier, he and a tired force of three hundred Marines had attacked this hill—named 1542—but had failed to win the crest. Instead, they had been forced to hunker down, to maintain a toehold.

Downhill, an endless column of Marines and vehicles filled a road. The column was bound for the ramshackle American base at Hagaru, fourteen miles away. Red watched the column with longing eyes as it disappeared around a bend. He wished he were down there, leaving with them; riding or walking, it didn't matter.

On 1542, Red and the tired three hundred other Marines weren't going anywhere anytime soon. They were the gate-keepers, with orders to hold the hill and shield the column until the remaining nine thousand surviving Marines had passed.

Red grabbed his rifle and crawled out from behind his fight-ing position. Burst cans of food littered the snow. The cold had ruptured the rations they had, so Red and his buddies were now reduced to eating crackers, frozen grape jelly, and Tootsie Rolls.

Red stopped at a pile of rocks behind the others. "Gunny?" he whispered. "Don't shoot—it's Red."

"Yeah?" came a muffled voice.

Red leaned over the rocks. Gunny Sawyer lay on his back in his bag, his helmet tipped over his face as he savored every second of sleep.

"Is it okay if I go look for Charlie?" Red asked. Charlie Kline hadn't been seen since the creek bed.

"You're wastin' your time, son," the gunny muttered. "He's dead in a ditch or being marched to a camp in Manchuria."

Red bit his lip. "God as my witness, I'll come back," he promised.

The gunny studied Red's face. Others had snuck from 1542 and vanished into the column of Marines who were allowed to leave. The temptation to desert was higher than ever. The gunny lowered his helmet. "Okay, Red, I believe ya."

Red slung his rifle and crawled away.

★ ★ ★

Red ambled toward the base of 1542. On the Marines' maps, the road was labeled the "MSR"—Main Supply Route. Despite the name, supplies weren't flowing these days, because of Chinese roadblocks. The column was still creeping along the MSR. Tired, wounded Marines slogged through grimy snow, yet each still carried a weapon. Able-bodied men were ahead of the column, fighting to clear the way for the rest of them.

With every step Red's pants crinkled, and he winced. Ice lined the inside of his pants legs and chafed his skin. Like many Marines, during the depths of night, Red had taken to urinating inside his pants. It had been too frigid for anything else.

Through the flurries, Red searched the haggard faces for Charlie's. Beneath their helmets and hoods, the Marines looked old, even the young ones. Dark bags hung under their eyes. Their chins were tucked against the cold and their achy bodies were bent.

"Wake up, you lugs!" a sergeant shouted. "You can sleep when you're dead!"

Red leaned from side to side for a better view, but the faces around him were caked in dirt and camouflaged by beard stubble. A few eyed Red's bloodstained parka blankly.

Trucks and jeeps rolled by. Marines who had been injured lay on the hoods, strapped to stretchers. Red watched their worried faces as they came past. A perilous journey awaited them through frozen hills.

More trucks passed by with stiff bundles lashed to their bumpers. Red's eyes narrowed at the bundles. His jaw quivered. *They're dead Marines.* The Marines had suffered more than four hundred men killed in Yudam-ni and were bringing out all they could. Such horrors had become commonplace across North Korea. Back home, Americans had heard of these Marines who were facing annihilation in northern Korea, and now the papers had given them a title: the "Lost Legion."

Red caught a flash of crimson beneath a truck's tailgate: an icicle of blood. He glanced into the truck's bed and his eyes went wide. Wounded men lay in three levels, separated by wooden boards. Marine engineers had created the additional floors to haul nearly seventeen hundred casualties. *Charlie could be in any of these trucks,* Red thought.

Horns honked. Brakes squealed. The column stopped, then started. "Keep moving!" An officer waved the vehicles onward. "Keep moving!"

Red felt the urge to remove his helmet and thought of Devans. He and the bazooka platoons had delivered their sergeant's body to headquarters but had received no assurances as to where he'd be buried—or *if.*

Red backpedaled from the road—he had seen enough.

Gunny's right, Red finally concluded. *Charlie's long gone.*

Red crawled back into his fighting position, his chest heaving from the climb. He found Jack, the young bazooka gunner, awake and shivering.

"Did you hear?" Jack's voice was high, his eyes filled with alarm.

Red shook his head.

"The entire Chinese army's comin' for us!" Jack blurted.

Red's face twisted. "Where'd you hear that crap?"

Jack said the fellows in the next hole had heard it from the men beside them. Red shook his head. *That has to be nonsense, doesn't it?* he thought in disbelief. Still, he couldn't deny that he was spooked.

He glanced down the line to trace the source of the rumor.

Once again, he left his position.

Keeping low, Red darted to the bunker and ducked inside. Red was surprised to find the gunny there, crouched behind a Marine officer with binoculars. At the officer's side, a radioman clutched a map.

"What now?" The gunny looked perturbed to see Red.

"The boys are talking." Red shivered. "Is it true? The entire Chinese army's coming?"

The gunny glanced at the officer, and the officer lowered his binoculars and turned toward Red. "We don't know their numbers," the officer said, "but there's sizeable Chinese activity up and down the MSR—a whole mess of 'em."

He was implying that the Chinese were moving to attack the column. Red gulped. *Chinese attacking in daylight?* he thought. *This never happens.*

The clouds seemed to be thickening and growing more ominous. Red glanced at the stormy sky above the crest. His eyes welled up with concern. "Sir," he said, "do you think our flyboys will get through this weather?"

The officer was not just any officer, he was a forward air controller. A FAC, as men like him were called, was a Marine pilot who called in airstrikes. The FAC aimed his binoculars at the gray sky. "Doubtful. Even the birds are walking today."

Red glanced down, stunned. Ever since the creek bed, he'd clung to Devans's words: *If we stick together, we can't be beaten.*

Around him, the others remained quiet as snow settled on their shoulders. They were the Lost Legion and they knew it.

Soon after, around 9 a.m. aboard the USS *Leyte*

With a roar, Jesse's Corsair began its takeoff roll down the *Leyte*'s wooden flight deck. Tom glanced past his own whirling propeller just in time to see Jesse's Corsair leap from the deck. All three wheels of Jesse's plane were in line with the horizon, by the book. Jesse banked rightward and climbed into a frosty blue sky where twelve Corsairs were assembling.

The *Leyte* was steaming forward with all eight boilers burning and 150,000 horsepower churning. Waves brushed the carrier below. Behind Tom's tail, the sounds of Corsairs' and Skyraiders' engines blended into one blasting drone. His heartbeat raced. The forward deck was clear—he was next. He gave the instrument panel a last scan. *Oil pressure, normal! RPMs, steady!*

Tom's eyes lifted—*Here we go!* The collar of his jacket—once black—was turning reddish at the edges with passing time and exposure to saltwater spray. Tom was becoming a veteran, even if he didn't notice it. He eased off the brakes and the Corsair's tires rolled slowly. A drop tank and a napalm bomb shuddered beneath its belly, and eight rockets shook beneath the wings.

Rev it up! Tom pushed the throttle forward. The Corsair's engine growled and the propeller spun faster. From nose to tail, the Corsair vibrated. Tom released the brakes and pushed the throttle. Furious noise filled the cockpit. The Corsair's 2,250 horsepower surged.

At eighty miles per hour, the Corsair sprinted. *Whoosh!* The deck passed beneath the tires and Tom felt his stomach lift. Blue stretched around him and white-capped waves slid beneath his wings.

When the needle in the airspeed indicator ticked above 150 miles per hour, Tom banked to the right and pulled into a climbing turn to find Jesse.

The three squadrons—twenty-four *Leyte* planes altogether—climbed in formation through five thousand feet, on their way higher.

Ahead, he saw ten Corsairs climbing across the sky, all '33 birds led by the *Leyte*'s air group commander. Tom peered leftward through his canopy. His eyes fixed on Jesse's wing tip. Side by side, the two planes soared upward. Just beyond Jesse's plane flew Cevoli and his wingman.

As the planes punched through ten thousand feet, Tom snapped his rubber oxygen mask to his helmet. The Corsair began feeding him air.

At fifteen thousand feet, the planes of the lead squadron stopped climbing and lowered their noses toward the horizon. Cevoli's flight leveled off, too. Jesse glanced over to Tom, glad to see his wingman in place. The sun shone brightly on Jesse's plane; every rivet glimmered.

Tom's eyes snuck to his rearview mirror. Behind him, the silhouettes of two Corsairs bobbed against the morning sun. They were '32 birds, with white-tipped spinners. Beneath them motored eight Skyraiders, planes from '35, the same boys who had busted the Yalu bridge.

Static crackled from Tom's earphones. The flight was cruising under radio silence. An hour away lay the Chosin, buried somewhere beneath the clouds. Tom took in the sight of the twenty-three other planes around him. He had never seen so many white *K*s against blue tails. Beneath his mask, he beamed with pride.

CHAPTER 35

BURNING THE WOODS

An hour later, around 10 a.m.
On Hill 1542 at the Chosin Reservoir

From the safety of his fighting position, Red looked worriedly at the Main Supply Route down below. At the base of the hill, the column had stopped in its tracks on the MSR. Trucks and jeeps idled; their drivers leaned out to peer around their windshields. For fifteen minutes, Chinese mortar shells had rained down on them. The enemy must have been short on mortars now, though, because the shells were falling sporadically and inaccurately.

But even the near misses were trouble. As long as the shells kept falling, the column wasn't going anywhere. A whooshing sound fell from above. Red ducked. A dark streak zipped down and slammed beside the road. *Crack!* An orange explosion burst. Then came a shock wave of black smoke.

Red raised his head to see if anyone had been hit. Jack elbowed him and pointed.

"It's true," Jack muttered.

Red's eyes settled on the neighboring ridgeline and his face tightened.

In plain view, a stream of White Jackets were snaking over the ridge. Chinese soldiers balanced rifles on their shoulders as they waded through the snow. Others dragged Soviet machine guns on wheels.

Jack clutched his rifle close. "They're flanking us," he whispered.

"No, they're headin' for the column," Red muttered, nodding toward the line of trucks and jeeps. Then he turned to the neighboring Marines. "You fellas seeing this?" he shouted.

"Yeah, we're tracking 'em," came a reply. They already had their weapons aimed; all they needed was the order to fire.

"Hey!" Red called to a nearby sergeant.

The sergeant raised his eyes.

"Can we fire?" Red asked.

"Are you crazy?" the sergeant said. "If you shoot, you'll stir 'em up!"

Red glanced uphill at the crest. It was true: if the Marines fired now, they'd bear the wrath of the two thousand Chinese soldiers above. Yet the enemy kept streaming toward the column. The column was practically defenseless. Sitting ducks.

Red raised his rifle and took aim. He still believed Devans's promise: *If we stick together, we can't be beaten.* Red's gloved finger tightened on the trigger.

Crack! Someone beat him to the first shot. Another rifle barked nearby, then another. Red blasted away, too, and the smell of gunpowder filled the air. Everyone was firing—machine gunners, army soldiers, even some inexperienced replacement soldiers.

On the neighboring ridge, the enemy stumbled back uphill and fumbled to drag their machine guns with them.

Red glanced behind him, hoping to see the Marine column escaping on the MSR, but the column still idled in place.

Seven miles ahead, near the front of the column, Marines were crouched and taking cover. Halfway through their journey, the Chinese army had struck. Now the Marine column—that long line of tanks, jeeps, and men—was stopped on the high ground between two valleys. Bullets pinged against metal, and tires popped and hissed. Some men rolled out from the vehicles. Others steered their buddies away from the enemy fire. Bandaged and bleeding, the wounded who could still walk crumpled into a ditch beside the road, beneath a barren hill. Those who had already been badly wounded never left their trucks. Beneath wooden ceilings they flinched and prayed as bullets raked the side rails.

Furious enemy fire came from the right, where muzzles flashed across a snowy ridgeline. Five hundred White Jackets were up there, shielded by rocks and rises. From a patch of woods, more Chinese troops poured onto the ridge. In packs, they plowed ahead and expanded their lines.

As the Marines returned fire, it became clearer and clearer that they were desperate for reinforcement. Nothing could help them except the pilots.

Shielded by a jeep, a colonel pulled his FAC officer close and told him to call for air support.

The FAC glanced at the low, stormy clouds and knew that air

support was unlikely, but he snatched the radio handset anyhow. What else could he do to protect these men? His radioman dialed in the American base at Hagaru. If any aircraft were nearby, the base's dispatcher would know.

"This is Dark Horse 14," the FAC announced himself. "We need close air support—it's damned urgent!"

He looked to the heavens and waited for a reply.

High above the clouds, frustration creased Tom's brow as he orbited behind Jesse. Ten thousand feet below, storm clouds blanketed the earth, stretching in every direction.

Several planes ahead, Cevoli led the squadron orbit. The other two squadrons circled in separate patches of sky, everyone searching for a "window" to the ground. The storm over the Chosin seemed impenetrable. The column below had called for air support, but for now the pilots were powerless to lend aid. They hadn't glimpsed the landscape below since leaving the ship.

Tom shook his head. Not one mountain peeked through the blanket. The land below could be upstate New York in winter or San Francisco in the fog, it all looked the same. One thing was certain: a blind dive through the clouds would be suicidal over mountainous North Korea.

Tom had set the radio so that he could listen to two channels at once—the Guard Channel for emergencies and the Squadron Channel to communicate with Cevoli. Suddenly the radio squawked to life.

"Lead, I'm coming up."

Tom's eyebrows rose. The voice sounded familiar. It spoke again. "That's Fusen Reservoir, sir. I can make out the shape."

That sounds like Marty! Tom thought. Then just as quickly, *It can't be.* Marty had launched at dawn with the flight sent to the other side of Korea.

"Roger that. Join up," a second voice said. That voice sounded a lot like Lieutenant Frank Cronin, the leader of the dawn flight.

Tom's face twisted. He wondered if he was somehow picking up chatter from nearly two hundred miles away. He checked the seal of his oxygen mask and took a deep breath. *Am I going nuts?* he wondered.

"P.A.N.! P.A.N.! P.A.N.!"

The second voice had returned, this time across the Guard Channel for all to hear. Tom tuned his ears. "P.A.N." meant: *Pay Attention Now!*

The voice announced his call sign and said, "Calling all planes, there's a break in the weather over the Chosin Reservoir— we'll hold position over the spot, just home in on us." Finally, an opening in the clouds had been found for them to fly through.

Beneath his mask, Tom grinned as he recognized Frank Cronin's call sign. He wasn't going nuts after all—he *had* been hearing Marty's voice earlier.

Tom scanned the sky and saw them. Marty Goode and the dawn flight were orbiting ahead. Their original target had been obscured by the same bad weather, so instead of returning to the carrier, they'd come here, looking for the Chosin. And they'd found it. One by one, they dived and disappeared into the hole they'd located in the clouds. Now, Cevoli led the way toward the clearing in the clouds. He rocked his wings to tell his flight, *Form up!* Tom assembled beside Jesse. Jesse caught up to Cevoli and the trailing Corsairs tucked close. Cevoli gave chase and the Skyraider planes fell in behind them. Sure enough, a small dark patch appeared like an island in the sea of clouds.

"Okay, boys," Cevoli radioed with excitement. "Let's go downstairs!" Cevoli banked leftward and his wingman dived beside him.

Tom was next. He flicked on the navigation lights. Far below, through a tubelike hole in the storm, they saw the Chosin Reservoir.

Jesse glanced over, his eyes calm. He nodded to Tom, then snapped his head forward, and his Corsair peeled leftward. Tom followed him down.

Side by side, Tom and Jesse dived through the tube in the storm. Tom kept his eyes fixed on the green light that glowed in Jesse's wing tip. Jesse's Corsair vanished, then reappeared. The green light rocked in the turbulence. Tom held his breath—the dark cloud seemed endless.

Tom remembered that the first time he had flown with Jesse, he had worried that Jesse was about to lead him into a flock of seagulls, or a ship's mast, or get them reported for risky flying. But now Tom knew better. He could see Jesse's eyes fixed forward, steady and certain. Now, after nearly a year together, Tom would follow him to the ends of the earth.

Jesse and Tom passed through the clouds and emerged in a silvery world of frozen ice and snowy hills. A smile cracked Tom's lips. They had found the Chosin Reservoir.

The rest of the planes were waiting for them. Ahead of Tom and Jesse, Cevoli's plane began signaling—*Trail formation!* Cevoli's wingman dropped back and swerved behind his tail. Tom cut back on the power and slid in behind Jesse.

The radio squawked—a Marine dispatcher was calling from the base: "That was some piloting . . . Way to get through that ceiling. Good, we've got targets stacked up." He rattled off a target and set of coordinates for each flight. Calls for help were coming in from around the reservoir.

Tom nodded with satisfaction. Cevoli steered the remaining planes toward a gap in the hills where the icy reservoir met Yudam-ni.

Meanwhile, on Hill 1542, Red hugged the slope as bullets splintered the rocks around him. "Lord help us!" Red muttered. He felt paralyzed. Spurts of green tracers zipped overhead, so close that he swore he could reach up and snatch one. They had succeeded in drawing the enemy's fury away from the column, but now the enemy were unleashing a hail of gunfire on *them*. No one wanted to die like this.

One by one, the green tracers lifted. Bullets stopped hitting the rocks, but gunfire still sounded.

What was going on? Red raised his head and peeked uphill. The White Jackets were no longer firing at them—they were firing into the sky.

Whoosh!

A dark blur roared over Red and the Marines on the ground. Thunderous gunfire shattered the air. Red hit the dirt. Hot shell casings tumbled from above and thudded into the snow, sizzling.

On the *Leyte*'s second day at war, Marty (far left) and others review maps in the ready room before a strike.

Captain Sisson (left) and the skipper display captured enemy flags that the skipper brought back after his emergency landing at Wonsan.

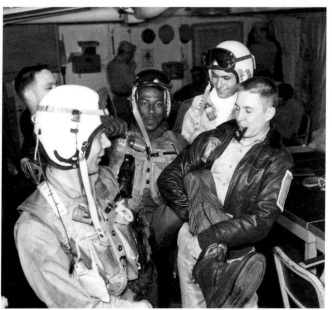

After missing his landing on the first try, Jesse had to pay the customary fine to the squadron coffee fund. Left to right: Lee Nelson, Jesse, Marty Goode, and Bill Koenig.

The *Leyte* and *Valley Forge* at anchor in Sasebo harbor. In the distance lies the British carrier *Unicorn*, on reprieve from operations off Korea's western coast.

Sailors and locals mix in Sasebo's Black Market Alley, also affectionately known as Robber's Row.

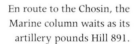

En route to the Chosin, the Marine column waits as its artillery pounds Hill 891.

These Chinese soldiers were captured near Hill 891. Here, they wear their reversible uniforms with the brown facing outward.

A *Leyte* Skyraider returns from a mission at the time of the bridge strikes.

The *Leyte*'s "special mission" Skyraiders and Corsairs on a mission in early November.

Jesse as seen through a Corsair's windscreen in late November 1950.

The bridges of the Yalu. After the *Leyte* Skyraiders' strike, smoke engulfs the Korean end of the highway bridge. Planes of the *Valley Forge* will pummel the railway bridge next.

During the November 26 photo shoot for *Life,* Dick Cevoli (left) and Jesse play backgammon.

The photo shoot took Jesse onto the flight deck . . .

The *Life* photo shoot ended with this last shot of Jesse high on the *Leyte*'s tower.

. . . and into the cockpit of a Corsair.

After the snowstorm that forced Tom and Jesse to land at Wonsan, *Leyte* deckhands work to clear the deck.

The Chosin Reservoir at the time of the battle.

Stalin propaganda posters were prized souvenirs. This Marine liberated one from an enemy bunker near the Chosin.

Marines press onward through the Chosin's relentless cold.

Marines keep the Chinese at bay during a rare daytime firefight at the Chosin.

Marines watch the effects of air strikes against enemy troops near Koto-ri.

Nicolas Trudgian's painting *Off to the Chosin* depicts Tom's takeoff on December 3.

Gareth Hector's painting *Wingmen to the End* depicts Jesse and Tom as they support the Marines' withdrawal from Yudam-ni.

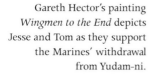

An HO3S from Charlie Ward's unit prepares to lift off from Hagaru. A wounded man's feet can be seen jutting from the open window.

Matt Hall's painting *Devotion* depicts the events of December 4.

During the withdrawal to the port of Hungnam, the living often walked while the dead rode.

Marines of this mortar squad manage to smile during the evacuation of Koto-ri.

Marines follow the precipitous mountain trails toward the port of Hungnam. "Retreat, hell! We're not retreating," General O. P. Smith famously said. "We're just attacking in another direction."

With sailors assembled to spell the ship's name, the *Leyte* returns to San Diego in February 1951.

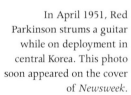

Coderre's parents visit him in a Rhode Island hospital in 1951.

In April 1951, Red Parkinson strums a guitar while on deployment in central Korea. This photo soon appeared on the cover of *Newsweek*.

Casings slapped Red's back; he shouted and squirmed in pain. He shielded his eyes and barely caught a glimpse of a plane zipping over the ridge. Another plane roared past, and then another. Red buried his face in the snow and kept it planted. His arms began shaking, then his shoulders, then his entire body. He couldn't help it; he was laughing. "They're Corsairs!" Red shouted. The planes had made it.

Against a backdrop of stormy clouds, four Corsairs were looping back around. White numbers stood out clearly on the planes' dark noses. Corsair 210 was up there, flown by Marty Goode. But it was the tails that caught Red's eye. Each sported a tall, white letter *K*.

Red and the others rose to watch the Corsairs.

"It's the Ks!" a Marine shouted.

"They're *Leyte* birds!" added another.

At Crete, the Marines had watched these same planes fly too high and slow for their liking. But this was different. This was the best air show they had ever seen. Corsair after Corsair thundered past at eye level, then Skyraider after Skyraider, each slung with ordnance, each in a hurry to free the embattled column.

Red took his rifle in his fist and raised it for the passing pilots to see. He shouted the first word that came to mind: "Hallelujah!"

Meanwhile, near the front of the column, Marines snapped off shots. The sky was blank, and the air smelled of gun smoke and diesel exhaust. No planes had come for them, only more White Jackets on the ridgeline.

Fifteen minutes had passed. The men looked up. Still, the sky was empty. *Are we just stuck on our own out here?* they asked one another.

Then came the buzzing sound. Tired and wounded men raised their faces. Everyone glanced down the line of vehicles. The buzz grew louder, then louder still.

A flight of blue planes suddenly burst into view. They peeled up from the valley with a furious roar. There were Corsairs and Skyraiders, each with a white *K* on its tail. The planes raced alongside the column. A cheer rose from the men.

With a rightward flick of their wings, the Skyraiders banked toward the ridgeline. Since they were the flying tanks, the first target always went to them. The Corsairs kept following the road, bound for another target of their own. They had spotted Chinese troops ahead of the column, in a patch of woods. The enemy were hidden beside the MSR, just waiting to spring another ambush.

Tom raced across the snowy landscape. Three planes ahead, Cevoli led the flight lower, almost even with the treetops. Tom fought back a smile. He had seen the Marines waving below and was glad to be there for them. And he knew that the Skyraiders behind him were chewing up the enemy ridgeline by now.

"We'll lead in with napalm to stir 'em out," Cevoli radioed, his voice unusually serious.

Tom's face twisted. Napalm was among the most dangerous fire bombs, a spare fuel tank filled with jellied gasoline and sealed with a white phosphorus detonator. Tom had dropped it on enemy buildings and vehicles before, but never on troops. Yes, they were fighting one another. But they were young men, just like he and his American buddies were.

The woods appeared before Cevoli's plane. They looked cold, brown, and deserted—that is, until Tom and the others could make out white shapes. Two hundred White Jackets were racing into the snowy field to form a firing line. Hundreds of flashes exploded—clearly, the enemy had come out for a clearer shot at the incoming planes.

"Whoa," Tom muttered as he reeled back in his seat. "Watch it, Dick!"

Cevoli's plane snaked through the air while bearing down on the soldiers below. Tom held his breath. Just before Cevoli reached the enemy line, he released his napalm and climbed hard.

The egglike napalm bomb tumbled end over end. In a bright flash, it cracked in front of the White Jackets and ignited. A three-thousand-degree wave of flame bubbled and rolled like an orange carpet over the middle of the Chinese line.

The enemy's padded uniforms burst into flames. Men fell writhing, fully engulfed, while others stumbled from the fire. From his Corsair, Jesse could make out the face of one man in particular. Jesse gasped at the horrific pain the man was clearly in. Meanwhile, a black cloud billowed from the boiling napalm. Cevoli's wingman burst over the enemy and through the black cloud. Jesse followed him intently, his heart racing.

Tom's stomach flipped at the damage done as he swooped

across the field. A herd of White Jackets were sprinting for the tree line to the right, so Tom steered his glowing crosshairs onto them. Some soldiers tripped and fell, some stopped to fire up at him. Tom's eyes tightened.

He clenched the trigger. With a roar, yellow shock waves burst from his gun muzzles. Orange tracers chewed a path through the scattering troops. Tom lost sight of his targets. He blasted blindly into the black wall of smoke and was momentarily swallowed. A burned, oily smell flooded the cockpit.

The Corsair punched out the other side and climbed through the air. The woods and fire sank far behind.

Over the snowy hills, the flight looped back around. Tom released a long breath and wiped his nose with his sleeve. That harsh, burned smell clung to his nostrils; he knew what he was smelling, and his face scrunched with disgust.

As the flight passed over the woods, Tom glanced down and saw the enemy dragging their wounded beneath the trees. They were down, but not out. They still posed a threat. The flight crossed over the MSR during a turn to come back around for another strike. Tom glanced beneath his wings. Below, Marines were taking cover behind vehicles and in ditches. Some lay sprawled, probably wounded, screaming, bleeding out as their buddies held them.

Tom might have known them. They might be the same boys who had been in the South of France with him, or the same ones who had tossed their love letters from the *Leyte* into the waves, to hide their mail from their mothers, to save them any shame if their sons died in battle.

And now they were dying. Tom was seeing it happen.

The Chinese had attacked a column of tired, frostbitten, wounded men intent on destroying them. Tom's lip curled. The smell in his nostrils no longer bothered him. He had a duty to protect his fellow Americans.

Ahead, Jesse snapped his wings level to begin his attack. Tom could tell by the sharp, deliberate way that his friend was flying—Jesse was feeling the urgency, too. One after another they rolled in to drop their napalm.

After the planes with the *K*s on their tails were finished attacking, exhausted Marines stood on the MSR and glanced up and around. The enemy gunfire had stopped. Craters and scorch marks pocked the ridgeline beside the column. More than five hundred dead Chinese troops lay there. The Marines would later give the battle a title: the "Great Slaughter."

Grunting and groaning, Marines pushed destroyed vehicles from the road. Trucks and jeeps crunched into roadside ditches. The men boosted the wounded back into trucks, while the remaining men and boys fell into ranks. Everyone stood a little straighter. Snow-caked tires and treads began churning.

Finally, the column rolled onward.

Overhead, the Corsairs orbited over the smoldering battlefield. Cevoli broke from orbit and the others followed. With five Corsairs following, he raced over the road, straight over the MSR.

Below, Marines cheered and waved their helmets and gloved

hands in reply. A Black Marine squinted as the third Corsair roared over him. The plane's wing dipped toward the road and the Black Marine saw the pilot, as clear as could be. The pilot was smiling and waving down at him.

The Corsair blurred past. The Black Marine watched the plane race down the road. He turned to one of his white buddies, who was shaking his head in wonder.

"You saw him, too?" the Black Marine asked.

"See who?"

"That Negro pilot!"

"Really?" the Marine replied. "I didn't know we had Negro pilots."

"I guess we do now." The Black Marine smiled.

In a jeep ahead, the FAC rode in the passenger seat and his radioman sat behind him. The FAC raised the radio handset as the Corsairs raced toward the reservoir.

"Well done," he radioed. "If we ever meet, I owe you fellas a beer!"

CHAPTER 36

INTO HELL TOGETHER

That night, December 3, 1950
Aboard the USS *Leyte*

Christmas music was piping throughout the cabin, but Tom and the others were too tired to celebrate.

The squadron mates waited around a table in the admiral's dining room. Tom puffed a pipe, and Jesse and Cevoli conversed somberly at his side. Their arms were folded, their voices hushed.

The *Leyte*'s captain had opened the cabin as a reward, a place for the pilots to enjoy a drink, and each squadron was given a turn to relax—or at least to try to. The walls were pale green, the chairs white and fancy. A framed Pacific map hung on the wall. Outside, the wind howled in the darkness, thick with flurries.

"I just can't get it out of my mind," Jesse said. "That one guy running, all covered in fire. After everything, he bothers me the most."

Tom took a puff on his pipe. "The problem is you can't see the guys you saved today, like you can see that guy on fire."

Jesse nodded reluctantly.

"That's not the only problem with napalm," Cevoli said, lowering his glass. "From here on out, you'd better not get shot down."

The men knew what Cevoli was saying—a pilot couldn't drop a weapon as vicious as napalm on the enemy and expect anything less than torture if he was captured.

Tom and the others yawned as the stress of the day hit them. In another group, Marty slowly sipped brandy. That morning, he had essentially saved the day by helping lead everyone in the direction of Chosin. But he brushed it all off as another day's work.

An officer entered the cabin with news that the lead elements of the Marine column had rolled safely into Hagaru. A collective sigh rose throughout the room. Tom and Cevoli grinned, and even Jesse relaxed a little. Still, they knew there were more men out there, and there was more fighting to be done.

An outburst of conversation and backslapping followed. Cevoli stepped front and center. "Okay, fellas, let's wrap things up," he said. "Tomorrow's gonna be a big one."

A little after midnight, under the light of a lamp, Jesse's pen swirled across the page. As he wrote a letter, his eyes fixed on each word.

In the dark, Koenig lay in the lower bunk. The ship's hum coursed through the walls. Now and then Koenig checked his watch. Both he and Jesse were slated to fly the next day and needed eight hours of sleep, or else they'd be removed from the roster.

Jesse slid aside a page after filling it with neat, upright cursive. He started writing a second. The incomplete drawing of his dream house was still propped against the desk. Koenig heard Jesse sniffle. He caught a glimpse of his roommate wiping his nose with his sleeve. Koenig closed his eyes. He felt shy about witnessing such profound emotion, so he pretended not to notice.

Jesse gripped the pen tightly and wrote a third page, then a fourth. Finally, he set the pen on his desk and slid whatever he had written into an envelope.

The desk lamp snapped off and Koenig heard Jesse's footsteps in the darkness. Jesse climbed quietly to his bunk, careful not to rouse his roommate. But Koenig was still awake. Above him, a flashlight clicked on. Koenig saw a glowing light on the ceiling and knew that Jesse was reading his nightly Bible passages. He had stopped sniffling, too.

Some time passed, maybe thirty minutes, maybe more. Koenig stared at the ceiling and waited.

Finally, the flashlight clicked off and the room became dark. Jesse was ready.

The following day, December 4, around 1:45 p.m.

An envelope sat in a wire basket on a table in the ready room. The basket was labeled OUTGOING MAIL, and the envelope was addressed to Mrs. Daisy Brown.

Outside on the flight deck, Corsair 211 rolled slowly forward.

Inside the cockpit, Jesse gently pushed the throttle with his left hand, where his Rolex encircled his wrist. Tom was assigned to be his wingman. Tom waited behind Jesse in Corsair 205.

Beside Jesse's propeller, a deckhand wrapped his arms over his shoulders, then fanned his arms wide: *Spread wings!*

Jesse lowered a lever and the wings unfolded like draw-bridges. As they lowered fully, an incredible sight greeted Jesse. Up and down the tower, sailors and aviators crowded every deck, their arms draped over railings. Boyish awe filled their faces.

Marty, Wilkie, and other pilots watched from Vulture's Row, and Jesse's fan club crowded every other deck. The stewards had come out, as had cooks, mechanics, even snipes from the engine room. At the foot of the tower, the deckhands and the crash crew gazed up at the pilot in his cockpit. Everyone knew where the flyboys were headed, and more men than ever had come out to show their support.

Now they could see that the next pilot was about to launch.

From behind Jesse, Tom saw it. On the tower, a man outstretched his arm and flashed a V-for-victory sign. Another man raised his fingers in a V. Then another, and another, until men on every deck were flashing Vs to Jesse Brown.

Jesse looked up and extended a thumbs-up to the men on the tower. He turned back to his instruments.

It was time to go.

The ten Corsairs flew two by two over the wintry valley. Slants of sun cracked through dark clouds overhead. From the perch of his Corsair, Tom leaned over to scan the terrain five thousand feet below. Everyone knew that the Chinese occupied the hills leading up to the Chosin. Yet from the air, that same valley appeared cold and empty.

The hour-long flight had passed in silence. Ahead of Tom, the Corsairs of Cevoli and his wingman bobbed in the rough air. Beside him, Jesse flew tight-lipped. He caught Tom's attention with a wave and pointed forward.

At the end of the valley, Tom saw they'd reached it—the American base at Hagaru. Before them lay a sea of green tents surrounded by wisps of rising smoke. A tiny village lay to the base's right, and defensive lines ringed it all. To the left of the tents lay a dirt runway, and behind the scene stretched an icy reservoir. Everything looked small from so high up.

"We're ten F4Us, checking in."

"Welcome back," the base dispatcher's voice crackled. The dispatcher described their objective: a stretch of road for the flight to patrol, where ten thousand Chinese troops had been spotted that morning, moving toward Hagaru. Tom glanced at his kneeboard map. The course would take them up the MSR to Yudam-ni and then deeper into the wild. They'd be in enemy territory all the way. Tom reached and flicked his gunsight to life. Someone had to do it.

Cevoli steered the flight around Hagaru. He leveled his wings toward the hills west of the base to begin the patrol. "There they are, boys!" he announced. "One o'clock!"

Tom edged forward in his seat for a glimpse. A dark line of

vehicles and men snaked down from the snowy hills and inched into the base.

The column—the last of the Lost Legion—was returning.

Once the Marine column trickled in, the base's garrison would stand a fighting chance. Already, the two-thousand-man garrison had been joined by a relief force of four hundred Marines, soldiers, and British Commandos who had fought their way up from the south. Then a thousand survivors of the army's task force had limped in from across the ice. And now came the last of nine thousand Marines from Yudam-ni. Within the hour, the Marine air wing commander at Hagaru would radio the *Leyte* and *Philippine Sea* to say: "[I] saw the Fifth and Seventh Marines return. They thank God for air. I don't think they could have made it as units without air support. . . . Tell your pilots they are doing a magnificent job."

From his cockpit, Jesse glanced over at Tom. A smile stretched across Jesse's face. Tom nodded. They could both see the column of Marines snaking down from the hills, and they both knew it.

There was hope.

Ten minutes later

Against a backdrop of gray clouds, two blue Corsairs dived toward the snowy mountains. Tom's and Jesse's planes plummeted side by side. Jesse's helmeted head scanned back and forth, his eyes searching for a place to crash. He was going down, seventeen miles northwest of Hagaru, deep inside enemy territory.

None of the pilots had heard the gunshots over their engines.

None had seen the weapons rise or fall from the snowy field. But now a vapor trail oozed from the belly of Jesse's Corsair: a bullet had punctured the oil line. With every passing second, the oil was bleeding, the friction was rising, and the plane's eighteen pistons were melting inside the engine.

High above, Cevoli and the others tried to lend eyeballs to the search. Tom, too, scanned the terrain beyond each wing. Rugged mountains stretched as far as they could see. The mountains bristled with woods and dipped into dark gorges. Patches of sun camouflaged the terrain, distorting its contours.

Jesse glanced to his left. A high, flat pasture lay atop one of the mountains.

"I'm going for it," he radioed Tom. His Corsair broke leftward and he steered for the pasture. Tom peeled after him. Following a short chase, he resumed his place beside Jesse's wing.

Tom glanced ahead. The pasture appeared to be about three hundred yards deep and as level a runway as they were going to get. But as they neared, Tom's eyes widened with alarm. The pasture was anything but smooth—small trees and boulders jutted from the snow. Jesse saw them, too, and steered toward the left side of the pasture where the land sloped uphill. The snow there looked white and flat.

Jesse steadily lowered his goggles over his eyes.

From above, Cevoli and the others watched the two fighters descend, side by side, into the pasture.

"One fifty! . . . One forty! . . . One thirty!" Tom called out their speed so that Jesse could keep his eyes on the pasture. As the Corsairs went lower, the trees and rocks appeared taller.

The propeller blades on Jesse's plane began to slow until the four flat blades windmilled. His wings rocked—the plane was sinking. Jesse aimed for the slope, struggling to glide with a melted engine.

"One twenty!" Tom called. "One ten! . . . One hundred!"

The white pasture and slope widened before them.

"Two hundred feet!" Tom shouted. "One hundred feet! Hold it steady—fifty feet—here you go!"

Tom gunned his throttle, hauled back on the stick, and climbed. He looked over his left shoulder and twisted to maintain a view.

Jesse's plane was bucking, struggling to keep its nose up. Without an engine pushing, the Corsair's wide wings lost lift. It was as if someone had cut the string that was holding the plane up. The twelve-thousand-pound fighter suddenly quit flying.

With a perilous crash, it dropped the final twenty-five feet to earth.

The plane's nose slammed the slope in a burst of snow. Shattered propeller blades were flung in every direction, the engine ripped from its bolts and cartwheeled away, and the tail smacked down hard. Groaning, the Corsair skidded to a stop.

Tom orbited over the crash site, just above the mountain peaks. A cloud obscured Jesse's plane.

Come on, Jesse, Tom thought. *Cue the radio.*

The snow slowly settled and Jesse's plane appeared. Tom inhaled sharply. Ahead of the cockpit, the Corsair's long nose was bent so far to the right that it nearly snapped off. Behind the tail stretched a path where the plane had skidded. The snow had parted and revealed sheer rock beneath. Jesse's canopy had slammed shut and remained so.

Then Tom saw it. Inch by inch, the canopy cranked back.

Relieved voices flooded the airwaves. Tom had almost forgotten about the four pilots orbiting above him. Jesse waved but didn't leave the cockpit.

"What's he waiting for?" someone asked.

"He's gotta be hurt?" Koenig suggested.

Cevoli tried to call Jesse over the radio but got no reply.

"I'm going upstairs to call for a helicopter," Cevoli announced. By calling from a higher altitude, he could beam a clearer transmission down to Hagaru. "Fellas, maintain orbit," Cevoli continued. "Tom, once Jesse gets clear, destroy the plane."

Tom agreed. He knew the rule: Never leave an intact plane and its technology in enemy territory. Otherwise, the enemy could familiarize itself with the way American planes worked— and even copy them.

Cevoli climbed from the circling planes into the dark clouds.

At separate altitudes, Tom and the others kept orbiting. Minutes passed and Jesse kept waving.

Cevoli's voice crackled over the radio. He was still above the clouds. "Okay, a chopper's coming," he said. "But it's going to be twenty minutes or more. I'll keep you posted."

Tom's face twisted. If Jesse was hurt, he might freeze to death in that time.

Wisps of smoke began floating from the twisted nose of

Jesse's Corsair. *A fire.* And the plane's 230-gallon fuel tank lay dangerously near his feet.

"Come on, Jesse, get out!" Koenig radioed urgently.

Jesse looked to be struggling. Tom's eyes tightened. He watched the nose of Jesse's plane and dreaded the thought of flames. *Lord, don't let him burn!* Tom prayed. If he could see the fire, then the Chinese soldiers could, too. And then what? They were probably already on their way.

Tom took a deep breath. There was one last option.

The Tom Hudner who'd reported to Fighting 32 in December 1949 would have kept orbiting. From above, he might have watched Jesse burn and told himself there was nothing he could do. A downed pilot was to be left alone—the skipper had said so. It was his rule and he'd court-martial any man who broke it. It was probably the navy's rule, too, written in some manual.

But this was not 1949.

Tom lowered his black-rimmed goggles.

"I'm going in," he radioed.

Above, Koenig and the others remained silent. Cevoli was still away and they either didn't understand what Tom meant or didn't want to encourage what he was thinking. So they watched.

Tom dipped his left wing and swooped down toward the pasture.

It was time to break the rules.

Jesse must have known that a Corsair was approaching him.

He must have felt the blast of wind at his back and heard the metallic crunch. In his rearview mirror, he must have seen the plane rushing toward him like a powerful blue wave. And he must have seen it stop in a violent lurch and toss a whiteout of powdered snow.

When the whiteout had settled, Jesse didn't need to see the number on the nose or the face of the pilot behind the shattered windscreen.

He must have known who had come to try to save him.

High above, Koenig muttered in admiration: "Of all the guys, it would be Tom."

Tom lifted his head from the seat back and released a deep breath. When he'd woken up that morning, he hadn't known he'd wind up intentionally crash-landing on a rural mountain. Still, his brow lifted with relief. "My God, it worked," he muttered. His plane's windscreen had shattered and the props had folded backward, but Corsair 205 had held together. More importantly, he himself had survived a carrier-style landing on a mountaintop.

Fifty yards ahead lay Jesse's plane, still smoking. Tom came to his senses and clawed at the latch on his chest. He cranked open the canopy and frigid air flooded the cockpit. *Damn, it's cold!* he thought. The pasture sat so high he could even see the Chosin Reservoir in the distance.

Tom pushed himself from his seat. A wave of pain shot up his back and he grimaced. He sank back down with a groan. He figured he had possibly fractured a vertebra. Eyes tight with pain, he stood again. This time he swung his leg over the rail and lowered himself down to the right wing.

Tom slid from the wing and his boots sank into the snow. The sun was gone, and dark clouds now rose around the peaks as if hungry to swallow the two men and their wrecked planes.

Tom took a step and winced, then managed a second step. Gritting his teeth, he stumbled around the steaming engine and kept going. Frigid wind whipped his tan flight suit, while snow stuck to his goggles. Doubled over, Tom hobbled uphill toward Jesse in a race against time.

CHAPTER 37

ALL THE FAITH IN THE WORLD

On the mountaintop

From a distance the sight must have looked odd—the pilot plodding through the snow, his life preserver flapping in the wind.

With every step, Tom panted. Snow gripped his boots. He glanced at Jesse's plane and could see his friend sitting high in the cockpit, smoke rising around him. *Hang on, Jesse!* Tom thought.

Halfway between the planes, Tom stopped. His eyes locked on a pair of footprints that dotted the snow in front of him. *Chinese soldiers!* They might belong to one man, they might belong to a hundred men. The White Jackets were known to march strategically in the same footsteps, so that it would never be clear how many of them there were. Tom drew his .38 revolver.

His eyes followed the tracks to the end of the pasture. There sat a wooden shack with a boarded-up window. A farmer probably worked the pasture during the warmer months. The wind howled, and Tom's helmet muffled his hearing. He could have sworn he heard voices. He whirled, pistol in hand, searching. Dead trees creaked and snow swirled.

Tom raised the pistol skyward and fired. The shot echoed. No one emerged from the shack or stepped from the trees. He fired again. Nothing.

Tom plowed ahead and approached Jesse's right wing from the rear. Jesse waved weakly.

"Tom, I'm pinned," he called down, his voice strained.

"Don't worry, Jesse," Tom shouted up. "A helicopter's on the way." *All he needs is one good tug to get him out,* Tom thought.

Tom inserted a gloved hand into a high handhold on Jesse's plane and leaned his left foot out from the wing. He kicked a spot in the fuselage, and a metal foothold folded down. Tom rested his boot on the foothold. With his weight distributed between the foothold and the wing, he grabbed the canopy ledge and stood face to face with Jesse.

Tom drooped at the sight. Jesse's lips were blue and his ears looked frozen and brittle. He was shivering wildly, his arms folded, his breath puffing. The cold had curled Jesse's fingers into claws. Jesse looked up with glassy eyes and said simply, "We've got to figure a way of getting out of here."

Tom nodded rapidly. "Let's see what's got you pinned." He raised his goggles and leaned into the cockpit. Wisps of smoke seeped through the shattered instrument panel. The smoke was the reason that Jesse couldn't close the canopy to escape the cold—it would asphyxiate him.

"It's this one," Jesse said, tapping his right thigh. Tom waved the smoke away and saw it: when the plane's body—its fuselage—had buckled, it had crushed Jesse's knee against the part of the instrument panel that ran between his legs.

Tom's eyes narrowed. Jesse's helmet was lying next to his left foot. *So that's why he wasn't responding,* Tom thought. The helmet contained Jesse's microphone and earphones. His gloves lay on the floor as well, out of reach. In Jesse's hurry to flee a potential fire, he had discarded his cumbersome gear and only then realized that he was trapped.

Tom grabbed the chest of Jesse's leather jacket. Jesse's hands gripped the canopy ledge.

"On three," Tom said. "One. Two. *Three!*"

Tom tugged while Jesse pushed upward. Jesse's eyes clenched with pain, his bottom raised from his seat, but the metal gripped him fast.

Jesse lowered back into his seat. He leaned his head against the headrest and gasped. Tom surmised that his friend had internal injuries, a shattered back at least. He hated to try again and put Jesse through pain, but one glance at the plane's nose reminded him that a fire could spark at any second.

"Okay, Jesse, let's try again," Tom said.

Jesse nodded.

Tom placed his full weight on the foothold. He gripped Jesse and pulled, using his whole body for leverage. Tom strained, his arm shook. Jesse groaned and pushed, but his knee wouldn't budge.

Convinced that Jesse was immovable, Tom knew he had to buy time. "I'll be right back," he told Jesse. He lowered himself to the wing and slid down to the plane's broken nose. He hurried around to the empty engine cavity. With gloved hands he shoveled snow into the cavity, toward the source of the smoke. After several heaps, the smoke settled into a trickle. Tom raised his goggles and squinted inside. He couldn't tell what was burning. He didn't know if he had squelched the fire or just barricaded it.

Tom scampered back to the wing and up to Jesse's side. Wisps of smoke still filtered through the instrument panel, but fewer than before. "Fire's contained," Tom reported. "If it hasn't erupted by now I don't think it's going to." Jesse nodded, his teeth chattering. Tom unzipped his jacket and retrieved the black knit cap he always carried. "Hold still," he said. Jesse's eyebrows rose. Tom flopped the cap over Jesse's head and pulled it down over his friend's frozen ears.

"Thank you," Jesse said.

Tom glanced down and tugged the silk scarf from around his neck. "Jesse, give me your hands," Tom said. Jesse raised his hands but averted his eyes—the sight was too painful. Tom wrapped Jesse's hands tightly in the scarf and Jesse settled his hands back to his lap.

"We're going to need an ax to cut you out," Tom said. "So I'm gonna go get a message to the chopper to make sure they bring one."

"Okay." Jesse nodded.

Tom slapped Jesse on the shoulder and climbed down. He couldn't believe it: Jesse's composure was settling *him* down.

As Tom plodded downhill, he noticed that the snow, the Corsair, the peaks, all were turning a deeper shade of blue. Time was slipping away.

* * *

Several miles to the southeast, they ran through a snowy field between two mountains, like a pack of upright wolves. White Jackets, a hundred or more. Their black sneakers crunched the snow, and weapons bounced on their shoulders. They ran for the distant mountain, the one where the smoke had risen, where planes now circled.

Three thousand feet above the mountain, Koenig boiled with worry as he followed the planes ahead of him. Something was terribly wrong; fifteen minutes had passed and Jesse was still in the cockpit.

Cevoli swooped down from the clouds and slid back into the lead. "Helicopter's halfway here," he reported, his voice high with hope. After an orbit or two he asked, "Where's Tom?"

"Lead, you might want to look down," Koenig replied.

Cevoli's right wing dipped for a better view. "Holy cow," he muttered.

Far below his circling friends, Tom lowered himself into the seat of his crashed Corsair. He used the radio to call for their attention. His chest heaved as he glanced upward.

"Go ahead, Tom," Cevoli replied.

"Jesse's alive but pinned inside," Tom said. "I think his back's broken. Tell the helicopter we need a fire extinguisher and an ax to extract him, and tell them to hurry, please."

Tom cupped his earphones tightly to hear the reply. "Helicopter's already in the air," Cevoli said. "I'll relay your message. If there's no ax aboard, there may be a delay while he goes back for one."

"Okay," Tom said, his face twisting. "Thanks for sticking around, fellas. Jesse's in rough shape—but he has all the faith in the world." Tom tugged the cord from the radio to return to Jesse's side. He had been gone long enough.

In his Corsair above, Koenig slid the radio dial to number 7, the Guard Channel. He couldn't wait for permission—Cevoli was busy on the horn with the helicopter. "Calling all transports," Koenig said. "If anyone's listening, fly over grid Charlie Victor 40-96 and drop a fire extinguisher—we've got two pilots down and they need one desperately."

Static crackled.

"Any transport, come in?" Koenig shook his head.

Cevoli's voice returned to the airwaves. He sounded somber. "The chopper's turning around to get an ax," he told the flight. "The rescue's going to be a while." Koenig's jaw clenched at the news. In silence, the flight kept circling.

But there was still fighting to be done.

Suddenly, the radio hissed to life. Koenig looked up—someone was listening.

"This is Split Seam flight," a pilot announced, "Heard you've got pilots down?"

Koenig glanced toward the Chosin—in the distance, four Corsairs were approaching. Koenig checked his knee chart.

"Split Seam" was the call sign of a Marine squadron called the "Devil Cats." Cevoli welcomed the newcomers. In no time, chatter burst across the radio.

"Enemy in the open!" another pilot reported.

"Oh, I see 'em!" shouted another.

Koenig's eyes traced the commotion. Enemy soldiers were pouring into a field between two mountains.

One at a time, the Corsairs dived toward the field with smoke puffing from their wings. They were attacking the Chinese troops with all guns blazing. Each plane disappeared behind a snowy rise, then rose again from the trees.

Again, the radio crackled. "This is Attack 35, coming on station." Two *Leyte* Skyraiders banked over from the Chosin to fall in with the Marine Corsairs. Cevoli welcomed the Skyraiders and urged everyone listening, "Keep 'em off our boys!"

On the mountaintop, Tom dangled from Jesse's canopy ledge, shivering. Without an ax to free Jesse's leg, there was nothing more he could do.

Overhead, Tom could see his shipmates clearly. Their bent wings tilted toward him as they circled.

Thumps of gunfire sounded. Tom and Jesse glanced across the pasture, but a mountain peak mostly blocked their view of the fighting. They only saw their air support, when a Corsair climbed high or a Skyraider turned wide. As the daylight faded, the temperature plummeted. The sweat on Tom's skin froze like a layer of frost and he shivered.

Tom's eyes wandered to his watch. It was already 3:40 p.m.

Darkness would arrive around five. Cevoli and the others still had an hour's flight ahead of them. If they were to reach the ship before dark, they'd need to leave. Tom gulped. *We're going to be alone soon.*

But he couldn't let Jesse quit.

Tom looked up.

"Jesse, look," Tom said, pointing upward. "They're going clockwise." By the direction of their orbit, the others were signaling that a chopper was coming.

Jesse glanced up. "Yes, they are," he said. His voice was labored and his breathing shallow.

Meanwhile, aboard the *Leyte*

Marty lowered his magazine and leaned forward from his seat in the ready room. He was on standby duty, ready to launch in the event of a threat to the ship. His eyes settled on a teletype machine nearby. White letters clicked across its flickering green screen. A message was coming through.

"Fellas, get over here!" Marty shouted to the others in the room. "*Leyte*'s got a pilot down." The others crowded around as more words formed on the teletype.

ENS Brown, VF-32. Shot down.

Marty's eyes blinked wide, and the others looked at one another in disbelief. More words appeared.

LtJG Hudner, VF-32. Intentional crash landing.

"What?" someone muttered.

"This can't be right!" Marty said. The words kept trickling.

Both pilots awaiting evacuation.

Cevoli providing air cover.

Helicopter en route.

"Thank goodness!" someone said. Marty let out a sigh of relief. If Cevoli's flight was on the job, he had faith that things
would be okay. He knew firsthand that the Corsair pilots could
keep an enemy army at bay.

Marty settled his eyes on the screen. The others remained in
place, but their chattering slowed. Everyone watched and waited.

On the mountaintop, Tom's muscles ached and his knees quivered. In the cockpit, Jesse clutched himself, shivering silently.
His head drooped forward. His puffs of breath were getting thin-
ner. Forty minutes had passed since his crash, and twilight was
settling across the pasture.

Beyond the peaks, Cevoli broke from orbit and led the others
down toward Tom and Jesse. Tom glanced forward, and Jesse
slowly lifted his head. Cevoli's wings stretched wider and wider
as he descended.

Jesse had seen such a sight before. As a young sharecropper,
he'd stood tall while a plane buzzed him in a cotton field, its
pilot eager to see him run. But this plane was different. From a
distance, the pilot began wagging his wings. He kept wagging
them as he skimmed over a peak, over the pasture, and over Tom
and Jesse.

Jesse raised his bundled hands in a feeble wave. Tom's face
sank. Wagging wings sometimes meant "Good luck" and sometimes "Goodbye."

Cevoli's wingman's Corsair roared overhead next, its wings wagging. Jesse raised his hand. Then came Koenig and finally his wingman.

Tom glanced over his shoulder and watched the planes shrink away toward the Chosin. The last pilot wagged his wings as long as he could.

"They're still waving, Jesse," Tom said.

When he turned back, Jesse's chin had slumped to his chest. His eyes were closed. Tom could see his chest barely rising and falling.

The clouds turned darker. Tom felt his revolver at his hip. What would be the best course of action if Chinese soldiers came? To avoid torture, should he shoot Jesse and then himself? Or take a chance as a prisoner of war? He knew a POW camp would be brutal. For Americans held prisoner by the Chinese and the North Koreans, that winter would be known as the "starvation months," when more POWs died than at any other time.

Tom glanced at his watch. It was nearly four o'clock. *Maybe the helicopter isn't coming after all,* he thought.

Jesse slumped heavily forward. Tom reached out and shook his shoulder. Jesse raised his head. His eyes slowly opened. They were glassy and blank. Then they closed again. *This can't be happening,* Tom thought. He wanted to slap his friend's cheeks to bring the light back into his eyes.

A weak voice uttered Tom's name.

"Yeah, Jesse?" Tom said.

With only his eyes, Jesse looked up at Tom. He drew a shallow breath. "Just tell Daisy how much I love her."

Tom nodded. Jesse closed his eyes and slumped heavily again. His breathing became so shallow that his shoulders barely rose.

Tom lowered his head. The finality was setting in.

Whomp, whomp, whomp. A bass sound traveled on the wind. Tom's eyes lifted. *Whomp, whomp, whomp.* The sound echoed across the pasture and grew sharper. An engine was whirring. Tom shook Jesse again, in the hope that he'd rally.

"Hey, buddy, hang in there!" Tom said. "The helicopter's here—I'm going to go flag him down."

Jesse's eyelids opened heavily. He barely nodded.

Tom stumbled through the snow. In a furious burst of noise, the helicopter banked in front of him. The chopper was a buglike HO3S. The helicopter pilot turned the glass bubble nose toward Tom and hovered closer. Tom shielded his face as it landed on the snow. A door swung open from the right side of the helicopter and a short, stocky pilot jumped out. The man wore a hip-length parka, paratrooper boots, and a black knit cap. Tom ran to greet him. Then he stopped short with surprise.

The pilot was Lieutenant Charlie Ward, the jovial Alabamian who had once joked to Tom and Jesse that he didn't know the meaning of *fear* because he didn't understand big words. Over the engine, Ward shouted, "Hi!"

Tom pointed to Jesse's plane and shouted, "We've got a pilot pinned inside and a fire in the nose. You have the ax?"

Ward nodded. He handed an ax to Tom and grabbed a fire extinguisher for himself. The duo sprinted for the Corsair.

Tom hopped onto the wing. He glanced back and saw Ward stopped in his tracks, his eyes fixed on the pilot in the cockpit.

"Is that Jesse Brown?" Ward shouted.

"Yeah."

"Aww, shit."

Tom climbed to the cockpit. Jesse appeared unconscious; his breath had stopped puffing. Tom focused on the outer fuselage, where the metal pinned Jesse's knee. With a sidearm swipe, Tom hauled the ax back, then swung it forward.

Clang!

The steel blade skipped from the metal. The blade had barely made a dent. In a frenzy, Tom swung the ax again and again and again. Clang after clang sounded. The ax wasn't cutting, and worse, Jesse hadn't flinched.

More leverage! Tom thought. He lowered himself to the wing and raised the ax high over his head. Pain rippled up his back. Tom clenched his teeth and slammed the ax down against the fuselage. *Clang!* But still the ax had barely dented the frozen metal. Tom's feet slid from under him and he slammed down onto the wing.

Tom handed Ward the ax. Ward leaned in to look Jesse in the face. "Hey, Mississippi—you hang in there, okay?" he said. "Hey, buddy?"

Jesse didn't stir.

In an outpouring of angst, Ward swung the ax blade against the Corsair again and again, but his frenzied blows had the same effect—barely a dent.

"We need a cutting torch," Tom said. "They must have one at Hagaru!"

Ward shook his head and pointed a thumb back toward Jesse. "Jesse ain't moving. I don't want to admit it, but I think he's gone."

Tom looked away. He shook his head in denial.

Ward scanned their surroundings. The peaks had turned inky blue; soon they'd be black with night. "We gotta go," Ward said. "I don't have instruments for night flying." He looked Tom in the eyes. "You coming or staying?"

Tom glanced up at Jesse, slumped in the cockpit. If Jesse had been mumbling or even breathing, Tom's decision would have been easy. He'd have stayed.

"Decide quickly," Ward said. "But remember—you stay here, you freeze to death."

He hustled toward his helicopter.

From the ground, Tom looked up to the cockpit. "Jesse, we don't have the right tools to free you!" he shouted to his motionless friend. "We're going to go and get some equipment. Don't worry—we'll be back for you!" But Jesse didn't stir.

Tom turned and followed Ward's footsteps to the helicopter. He rolled inside, then shut the door and slumped against a bulkhead.

Up front, Ward glanced at Jesse through the glass and mumbled a quick prayer. He turned in his seat. "Ready?" he shouted to Tom over the whining engine. Tom didn't reply. He had pressed his face against the window.

The helicopter lifted off—one wheel, then two, then three. Tom gazed down and saw Jesse still slumped in the twisted cockpit. His eyes remained locked on his friend as the helicopter flew up and away.

CHAPTER 38

FINALITY

Forty minutes later
Twelve miles south of Hagaru

In near darkness, the helicopter touched down. Inside the craft, Ward removed his earphones and shouted to Tom, "All clear!"

Tom slid the door open and winced at the bitter wind. A winter storm was swallowing any glimpse of the darkened sky.

This was Koto-ri, an American supply base below Hagaru, at the end of the valley. Rows of pyramid tents surrounded the helicopter landing pad. The tents fluttered in the wind like partially collapsed parachutes. Ward led Tom toward them. As Tom limped through the snow, he stared at the ground. *We left Jesse out there in this,* he thought.

Tom followed Ward into a long tent lit by lanterns. A wisp of warmth brushed Tom's face, but he could still see his breath. The tent was crowded. More than a hundred fighting men were standing, eating from tins. Most were Marines, many were army, and a few wore the green berets of the British Royal Marine Commandos.

Ward took a box of rations for himself and offered one to Tom, who shook his head. Ward pointed to steaming cups of coffee, but Tom declined those, too. Ward shrugged.

Tom fiddled with his gloves, his eyes intense. "If we find a torch, can we go back first thing in the morning?" he asked Ward.

Ward's face scrunched with frustration. "There's not a piece of equipment anywhere on this peninsula that could get Jesse out," he said. "You'd have to dismantle the damned plane."

Tom nodded, but his eyes stayed intense.

Between bites, the nearby Marines and soldiers eyed Tom with curiosity. His tan flight suit was dark up to the knees, wet from the snow. He still wore his helmet and he wasn't eating, as if he was itching to leave. Finally, a young Marine asked, "Sir, how'd you wind up in this mess?" The other Marines turned to Tom with anticipation.

"Crashed my plane up in the mountains," Tom said somberly. He motioned to Ward. "He came and rescued me." Ward shrugged and kept eating. For him, it was just another mission in a dangerous line of duty.

"Well, you're pretty safe here," the Marine assured Tom. The others nodded.

"A word of advice, though," the Marine added. "Avoid using the latrines after dark. The crapper's always the first thing to get hit!"

Ward laughed with the Marines.

Tom forced a smile.

That night, Tom stayed at the base. For now, there was no way he could get back to the *Leyte*. He and Ward ducked inside a tent. In sleeping bags, eight Marines slept on a dirt floor, helmets and rifles at their sides. Ward laid out his own sleeping bag. Tom flapped up his fur collar and stretched out on the ground. He rested his helmeted head on the dirt.

"You sure we can't hunt you down a blanket somewhere?" Ward whispered.

Tom shook his head.

As he lay there, he kneaded his fingers to encourage circulation. The wind flapped the canvas above. Near the entrance of the tent, a flashlight clicked on. The bobbing light approached Tom. A Marine crouched with a sleeping bag draped in his arms.

"Sir, you'll need this." He set the bag beside Tom.

"I can't take your bag," Tom said.

"Sir, you'll need it a lot more than I will," the Marine said with a grin. "I'm on duty tonight."

"I'd take it," Ward muttered.

Tom reluctantly accepted the bag and thanked the Marine.

Tom spread the bag and climbed inside.

"Charlie," he whispered.

"Yeah?"

"Thanks for coming to get me."

Charlie paused. "You did good yourself, Tom."

"No," Tom said with resignation. "I'm gonna get court-martialed when I get back."

Ward rolled over. "Nahh," he muttered.

Tom stared at the ceiling. Outside, the wind was howling.

Three days later, December 7, 1950

The Skyraider came to a halt on the USS *Leyte*'s flight deck. Crewmen swarmed the plane as a pair of boots descended to the deck. Tom Hudner emerged without a word. He paused and gazed across the empty rear deck. The early-morning sun swept the wood as the deck crew scurried to reset the cables.

Tom had been away for three days, but the carrier was back to business as usual. He lowered his face and hobbled toward the tower. A deckhand opened a door and Tom stepped inside, where an officer was waiting. "Lieutenant Hudner, the captain wants to see you on the bridge," the officer said.

Tom removed his helmet and tucked it under his arm. After days on the ground, his hair was matted, his uniform soiled. And now he was going to be punished. *Let's get on with it,* he thought.

A Marine guard opened a door and Captain Sisson, the captain of the *Leyte,* stepped inside wearing a green parka. His face was round and ruddy, his nose pointy.

Tom snapped a salute. "At ease, son," the captain said, his Southern accent thick. Tom lowered his shoulders a little.

Sisson's blue eyes were piercing. Golden wings adorned his

left breast. As a young aviator, he'd flown search missions for Amelia Earhart over the Pacific, then during WWII he'd planned the carrier strikes for the invasion of North Africa.

Sisson slapped Tom's shoulder. "We're glad to have you back, son."

Tom's eyes opened wide with surprise.

"Personally," Sisson said, "I've never heard of a more wonderful act than what you pulled out there."

Tom's face softened. He thanked the captain.

Sisson meant it. Two days earlier, in a *Leyte* press release, he'd praised Tom's rescue attempt by saying: "There has been no finer act of unselfish heroism in military history. From the time of the first reports, we all prayed that our shipmate's life would have been saved thereby."

Sisson's smile faded. He told Tom that he'd sent two recon planes over the crash site that morning. "They saw Ensign Brown's body still in the wreckage," he added softly. "He'd been stripped of his jacket and gear."

Tom looked down at his feet. The finality was hard to accept.

The enlisted sailors stood aside as Tom limped back down through the corridor. Their eyes lowered from his matted hair to his soiled flight suit. They might or might not have recognized him. That morning, Sisson had formally announced Jesse's death to the entire ship and concluded by saying: "The country needed Jesse Brown."

Tom passed through the mess hall, his helmet under his arm.

Officers dotted the tables and stewards cleaned up from breakfast. No one said a word.

Tom approached the ready room. When he entered, the squadron stood from their magazines and board games.

Tom lowered his head. It was hard to face them, having returned without Jesse at his side. The pilots set their coffee mugs aside. In a bunch, they swarmed Tom. Koenig, Marty, and Wilkie slapped his back, and Dad Fowler shook his hand. Voices overlapped. Cevoli gripped Tom by the shoulder, his eyes misty.

The crowd parted as the skipper barreled through. Tom's shoulders sank. *Here it comes,* he thought. He braced for the words *Your court-martial will convene on . . .*

With everyone watching, the skipper extended his hand. Tom shook it.

"Thanks for risking your life for Jesse," the skipper said. "We're all mighty proud of you."

Tom glanced around. The others were nodding, their eyes filled with gratitude.

"Cevoli says that what you did was the finest act he's ever seen," the skipper added, "and that's sayin' something."

The skipper placed an arm over Tom's shoulder and steered him from the circle. "Be sure to get to sick bay to tend to that limp. And stay off your feet as long as you need."

Only later would Tom realize what had changed. The skipper's edict—"It's bad enough to lose one pilot. We can't lose two"—was based on the concept of a nameless, faceless downed pilot. But when that pilot was Jesse, everything changed. The skipper never mentioned a court-martial for Tom. He'd later write the squadron's combat history and record Tom's actions as "outstanding heroics."

Tom's brow was still furrowed, his thoughts far away, focused on someone Jesse had spoken about endlessly. Tom's mind now held a single question.

Does she know yet?

CHAPTER 39

WITH DEEP REGRET

A day later, December 8
Hattiesburg, Mississippi

Arms laden with shopping bags, Daisy followed her best friend, Snook Hardy, into the apartment building of Snook's parents. It was a Friday afternoon, around 4 p.m.

Snook was tall and thin, and glasses encircled her cheerful eyes. Back when they were children, the two had lived next door to each other. Everyone called them "Pete" and "Repeat" because whenever one was seen, the other was nearby. Daisy and Snook sank into couches and laughed together as they slid paperboard boxes from the bags.

Daisy held up a colorful new dress. She had purchased it in preparation for her upcoming trip to the Bahamas with Jesse. Daisy's other bags contained Christmas presents for Pam. In a letter, Jesse had suggested presents Daisy should buy for the baby.

The phone rang and Snook bounded into the kitchen. "Yes,

ma'am, she's here," Snook said, then shouted over her shoulder, "Tootie, your mama's calling!"

Daisy entered the kitchen and held the phone to her ear.

"Come home, child, you have company," her mother said simply. Her voice sounded strange. Daisy asked who had come to see her but got no answer. Daisy's brow furrowed. She hung up the phone and turned to Snook.

"All she'd say is there's someone there to see me," Daisy said.

Daisy gripped her shopping bags as she shut the car door and hurried to her mother's apartment. *It must be someone from* Life *magazine!* she thought. The magazine's photo-essay on Jesse was due to be published that month. Daisy wondered if they had come for some photos of Jesse's hometown. She pattered up the back steps and into the kitchen.

Her mother, Addie, came to her side. Addie was robust, with a strong, oval face. Her eyes normally beamed, but not today. "Give me your bags, Daisy Pearl," she said, her voice shaky. "I'll take them upstairs."

Daisy's face twisted. She handed over the bags and her mother disappeared. Daisy heard murmuring, and she stepped into the living room. Her younger sisters and brother were there, and Jesse's close friend M. L. Beard. Everyone turned to face her. In confusion, Daisy glanced from one somber face to the next.

M.L. approached Daisy. He was twenty-five and tall, but his thin mustache made him look older and wiser. His eyes were bloodshot.

"Shouldn't you be at home in bed?" Daisy asked. M.L. usually had to sleep during the day because he worked nights, stocking a local department store while saving up for medical school.

The young man glanced at his feet and told Daisy her mother had called him. He didn't look up. "When was the last time you heard from Jesse?" M.L. asked, his voice quivering.

"I got a letter from him today," Daisy said. "Why?"

M.L. walked over to the family's radio against a side wall. The radio was square and tall, like a small jukebox. Daisy's mother always placed her mail on top.

There sat what looked like a white postcard.

"We just received this," M.L. said. He took the postcard, passed it to Daisy, then turned away. Daisy saw M.L.'s shoulders bobbing. He was crying.

Daisy noticed that the "postcard" was actually a Western Union telegram. Her knees became weak. She lowered her purse to the floor. Her legs automatically carried her to the couch and she sat down. She glanced around the room again. Her siblings were crying and M.L. was looking away. In the kitchen, Daisy's mother paced in circles with Pam in her arms.

Daisy gasped, and the telegram shook in her hands. She read a few words: *It is with deep regret* . . . She looked away and held the telegram at arm's length. Her tears began flowing as waves of horror came crashing down. Daisy peeked back at the telegram. Through blurry tears she read it.

It is with deep regret that I officially report the death of your husband Ensign Jesse Leroy Brown. . . .

The telegram fell from her fingers. Daisy buried her face in her hands. She felt someone sit beside her and pull her close, but she didn't lift her head. She sobbed and sobbed into her hands. Her chest heaved.

After some time, Daisy lifted her face, sniffled, and sucked in air. She saw M.L. at her side. Someone gave her a handkerchief. She wiped her eyes and nose. Her rib cage ached. A vision of Jesse's parents entered her mind. John and Julia lived alone in the countryside, without a phone. Their children had all grown up and moved away.

Daisy staggered to her feet. M.L. moved to steady her, but Daisy waved him away. She retrieved her purse from the floor and rummaged through it, produced her car keys, and started for the back door. Her mother blocked her way with Pam in her arms. Addie shook her head. Her eyes were sad but stern. She had been widowed at the age of thirty and never imagined that this would befall her daughter, too.

"I've got to get to the Browns'," Daisy said, her voice shaking. "I want to be there before they get the news."

"Child, you're in no state to drive," her mother asserted.

Daisy turned to M.L. "Will you drive me?"

M.L. nodded. Daisy passed him the keys and led the way out the door.

Twenty minutes later, Daisy climbed the rickety steps to the Brown family's porch. Before she entered, the wails stopped her where she stood. Daisy nearly broke down herself but took a deep breath and entered the cabin. M.L. followed.

On one side of the room, John Brown sat rocking in his chair.

His wife, Julia, sat across his lap. Her arms were locked around him and she sobbed with her face pressed against his shoulder. Julia glanced up and saw Daisy. Julia ran and embraced her and the two cried together. M.L. knelt at the side of Jesse's father. John Brown kept rocking, his eyes fixed blankly across the room.

Julia was gasping for breath and clutching her chest. Daisy guided her to a chair at the kitchen table where Jesse and his mother had once played the "word game." Now, instead of a dictionary, a telegram sat on the table. Daisy moved it out of sight and held Julia's hand.

Daisy glanced over and saw John Brown still rocking, locked in a stupor. Daisy stood. "M.L., bring Daddy Brown to the car," she said. "We're going to the doctor."

Daisy led Julia down the rickety steps toward the Wayfarer. M.L. followed with both of his arms wrapped around John Brown to keep him from collapsing.

This time, Daisy got behind the wheel and drove.

That night, Daisy clutched the railing as she climbed the back steps of her mother's apartment in the dark. Her mind felt hazy. The doctor had given Jesse's parents sedatives. They had insisted they'd be okay. *One last task,* she thought.

Daisy staggered into the kitchen. There were more voices in the living room. Snook appeared in the kitchen and approached with open arms. After a long tearful hug, Daisy picked up the telephone from its cradle. She asked for the long-distance operator.

For some time, Daisy talked in a low voice, pausing only to

wipe her eyes. Finally, she hung up and turned to Snook. "Now Jesse's brothers know," Daisy said. In search of better opportunity, Fletcher, Lura, Marvin, and William had moved to Chicago, where they lived in an apartment building owned by their uncle.

With Snook at her side, Daisy entered the living room. Her pastor, Reverend Woullard, was waiting with her family. Daisy hugged the older man, then excused herself to freshen up.

As she started up the stairs, her feet felt heavy. The lightbulb overhead began swirling. Tunnel-like darkness squeezed her vision from the sides, turning everything blacker and blacker.

Daisy fell unconscious to the stairs.

CHAPTER 40

TO THE FINISH

Three days later, December 11
Northeastern North Korea

Red watched his own shadow hobbling alongside him. The shadow was hunched. Its breath puffed in the frigid air.

Red himself looked like a survivor of a polar expedition. His red beard had filled in and bristled with ice crystals. Dark bags hung beneath his eyes.

The road before him snaked downhill through a corridor of rock.

Yudam-ni lay seventy-eight miles behind his detachment. They had fought their way here, to Korea's eastern coast, in a grueling trek that the men were calling the "Big Bug-Out." Once sixty Marines strong, the detachment had been whittled almost in half, to thirty-five men. Among their losses was the detachment's only MIA—Charlie Kline. No one had seen him since his disappearance.

Men mumbled now and then. No one talked anymore—they

lacked the energy to even finish a sentence. Alongside them, drivers steered jeeps and hauled the wounded. Red caught glimpses of other units ahead, snaking downhill, and he heard orders shouted from units behind him, around the bend. His eyelids drooped as he slogged along. He hadn't showered in fifty-three days. He sporadically slapped his cheeks to stay awake.

Red glanced to the side and his eyes widened. Far below lay a harbor. Sunlight glistened on the sea. There, rows of American transport ships could be seen, their doors flung open. The road ahead wound down to a tent city on the beach. Cranes transferred cargo onto the ships. Marine units were marching to the ships. Planes buzzed in from aircraft carriers beyond.

The column slowed and men wandered to the roadside. Red almost bumped into the man in front of him. Everyone's eyes feasted on the sights.

This was the ramshackle port of Hungnam. One of those ships would be Red's ride out of North Korea. At that moment, he knew it: *Devans was right.*

At the base of the hill, Red hiked faster, surging with a desperate rush of adrenaline. He panted and struggled to keep his footing. The gate to the tent city—the finish line—lay a field's length away.

Behind the gate, Shore Patrol sailors directed traffic, waving in each unit of Marines, urging them to move faster. The Americans and British were evacuating North Korea. Fourteen thousand fighting men were arriving from the Chosin, not to mention the units from other areas.

Red swore he would collapse in joy when he crossed that line in the dirt. Then the gunny's Kentucky twang rang out: "Hold it up!" Red's face sank. Everyone stopped.

Gunny Sawyer paced back and forth along the line. "Double column!" he shouted. "And look like Marines! Cinch them straps. Tuck in them loose ends. Stand like you've got a spine."

Red plodded into a line. Others straightened themselves up. Even wounded men hobbled from jeeps on frostbitten feet, using their rifle butts for balance. The wounded fell in with the others, and the two columns came to number roughly fifteen men in each. As the gunny passed to inspect them, Red and the others stood taller.

"Forward march!" the gunny called.

Sixty boots began thumping the snowy gravel. Red's eyes fixed ahead. His eyes perked up and he raised his chin higher. In step beside the columns, the gunny started singing: *"From the halls of Montezuma . . ."* A chorus of voices picked up the tune: *". . . to the shores of Tripoli. We will fight our country's battles, in the air, on land, and sea. . . ."*

The men sang as they marched through the gate. Young voices blended with older ones, Northern voices with Southern. From the corner of his eye, Red saw others watching—the SPs, the interpreters, refugee mothers with babies, squatting old men, bundled little boys and girls.

Inside the tent city, the song ended and the gunny called a halt. Red and the others lowered their last boot heavily. The wounded swayed, desperate to keep balance. Everyone fought to keep their backs straight. They once had been Boy Scouts and soda jerks and baseball players in sandlots. But now beneath the stubble and grime, they were veterans.

Even the enemy looked on, seemingly impressed.

Off to the side of the compound, hundreds of Chinese prisoners watched from the fence of a wire pen. Blankets were wrapped around their shoulders. They were loosely guarded, and their casual posture suggested they had accepted their fate. They were due to be evacuated, too.

Red's eyes focused ahead.

The gunny pointed to a ship that was currently taking aboard tanks and told the men they'd be boarding soon. The ship would carry them to Pusan, on the southeastern tip of South Korea. The gunny showed them where to assemble on the beach, two hundred yards away. "Y'all got ten minutes to grab a snack," the gunny said, raising a thumb to the trailers behind him. "Ten minutes, no more! Lotta Marines are coming in behind you."

Red and the others grinned.

Stretcher bearers approached and the gunny told the wounded to fall out to the side. "Everyone else stay on your feet!" the gunny added. "No plopping down—I ain't gonna drag your asses the last mile—it's un-damn-dignified!"

For the first time in a while, the men laughed.

On the beach beside their ship, Red and his buddies dropped their packs and relaxed. They'd grabbed coffee and cookies and settled down to snack in peace.

Up and down the line of ships, Marines from other units were climbing gangplanks to board. Trucks and tanks drove into the vessels' cargo holds. One hundred and eighty ships were already waiting or en route to Hungnam. Over nearly two weeks, the ships would take aboard 100,000 fighting men, 17,000 vehicles, and 91,000 South Korean civilians—most but not all of the refugees who had flocked to the harbor.

Red opened his canteen and took a sip of coffee. It was perfectly hot and bittersweet. He fished an Oreo from his pocket and crunched down gratefully on the cookie. His jaw had nearly forgotten how to chew.

The others ate cookies and drank their coffee in silence.

They made no victory toast. But there had been a victory of sorts at the Chosin Reservoir. The Marines, the army, and their U.N. allies—roughly nineteen thousand men—had bested more than a hundred thousand enemy troops, nearly destroying the Chinese Twentieth and Twenty-Seventh armies.

"We shouldn't be leaving," a Marine commented. His eyes scanned the vast piles of supplies. "We should just regroup here."

Red shrugged. "Here or down the coast," he said. "What's the difference?" The others nodded. In a month, they'd get their wish. In January 1951, the First Marine Division would be returning to battle.

"Heya, look at that," one Marine said. He pointed to a nearby ship. Red's eyes focused on the ship's anchor chain. Halfway up the chain, two North Korean peasant boys were climbing to sneak aboard.

Their small faces were clenched. Their hands clutched the

iron chains and their small bodies dangled over the frigid blue water.

They might have been brothers. They were probably orphans. Whoever they were, they were desperate to escape the Chinese. Red glanced at the boys and knew exactly why the Korean War mattered. There, on the anchor chain, he saw why he had come to this land and why Devans had given his twenty-one-year-old life.

"That about says it all," Red muttered.

At his side, the others nodded.

CHAPTER 41

THE GIFT

Sunshine streamed into the apartment's living room. Local folks, Black and white, men and women, dotted the sidewalk in front of Daisy's mother's apartment. They spoke softly and somberly. Ever since the local paper had announced Jesse's death on the front page, a constant stream of visitors had come to express their condolences. For many white visitors, it was their first visit to Hattiesburg's all-Black neighborhood. Almost every visitor had brought banana bread or a casserole or their mother's recipe for this or that.

After they had gone, Daisy sank down onto the couch. She had never expected to become a twenty-three-year-old war widow. She wasn't angry at Jesse for leaving her, nor at God for taking him. When a writer for *Ebony* magazine asked how she was coping, Daisy said, "I guess it was the will of the Lord to take him. I'm glad, proud that he died fighting as a navy flyer.

He would have wanted it that way more than anything in the world."

Still, Daisy felt hollow.

The house was silent. Her mother was out and Pam was napping. Daisy was glad Pam was asleep. Anytime Pam heard an airplane fly over, she ran for the windows shouting, "Daddy! Daddy!" and it broke Daisy's heart all over again.

Later, Daisy's mother, Addie, entered through the back door and set a small sack on the kitchen table. She emptied the contents and a pile of mail poured out. Citizens across the nation were writing to Daisy to express their sympathies. Even Tom Hudner had written from the *Leyte* to tell Daisy of her husband's bravery, but the letter went missing in the deluge of mail.

Daisy's mother leafed through the pile surreptitiously. Whenever she found a newspaper, she tore it in two and threw it in the trash. She couldn't bear to let Daisy see what the papers were saying—it was too terrible.

The story of Jesse and Tom had become front-page news across America. The papers were all quoting a report that had been wired from the *Leyte* immediately after the crash, before Tom had returned to the ship. But the report got the story wrong, and so did the papers.

In Tom's hometown, the Fall River *Herald News* wrote, "The 26-year-old Hudner landed in the same field and ran to Brown's help knowing, the Navy said, that his own chances of escape were slim. But Brown was dead when Hudner reached him. Hudner radioed for a helicopter to take Brown's body back to friendly territory."

In Hattiesburg, many Black folks read the *Afro-American* newspaper's account: "Navy rescue planes rushed to the scene of the crash, but Brown's plane became enveloped in flames before he could be removed from the cockpit. . . . the Marine helicopter arrived and Ensign Brown was removed from the plane. He was dead."

Daisy's mother thumbed through the envelopes to see who had written. She didn't realize that her efforts to protect her daughter were in vain. Daisy had already gathered clues from her visitors, who openly lamented the senseless, gruesome way that Jesse had died. She had heard how her husband had died alone, before anyone could reach him. And she surmised what no one would tell her—that Jesse had burned to death.

"It's for you," Daisy's mother said as she set an envelope on the coffee table in front of her daughter and then hurried away. Daisy sat up, curious. "I'm going for a walk," her mother announced from the kitchen. The back door opened and closed.

Daisy picked up the envelope. Her eyes went wide. She recognized the handwriting and the return address: *Fleet Post Office San Francisco, USS Leyte, VF-32—Ensign Jesse L. Brown.*

The tears began streaming. Daisy slowly opened the envelope and unfolded four handwritten pages.

At Sea, Sunday Nite
3 December 1950

Daisy held her mouth and shook her head. Jesse had written this on the night before his death:

> *My own dear sweet Angel, I'm so lonesome I could*
> *just boo-hoo. But I try to restrain myself and think of*
> *the fun we're going to have when we do get together, so*
> *only a few tears escape now and then. I love you so very*
> *much, my darling.*

Daisy could hear Jesse's voice in her mind. She held the letter closer.

> *The last few days we've been doing quite a bit of*
> *flying, trying to slow down the Chinese communists*
> *and to give support to some Marines who were*
> *surrounded. . . . Knowing that he's helping those poor*
> *guys on the ground, I think every pilot on here would fly*
> *until he dropped in his tracks.*

Daisy's eyes raced left to right.

> *Don't be discouraged, Angel, believe in God and*
> *believe in Him with all your might and I know that*
> *things will work out all right. We need Him now*
> *like never before. Have faith with me, darling, and*

*He'll see us thru and we'll be together again before
long too.*

Daisy flipped through the pages. Jesse spoke of the past they
shared and of the future he longed for with her. It was as if he
had a premonition that they might part.

*I want you to keep that pretty little chin up, Angel,
come on now, way up. I want you also to be confident
in this and that is: Your husband loves his wife with
all his heart and soul—no man ever loved a woman
more.*

Daisy turned to the final page. The end was coming.

*Darling, I'm going to close now and climb in the
rack. I honestly dread going to bed, but I usually dream
of you, so I'll manage to make it until we'll share our
bed together again—darling, pray it'll be soon.*

Daisy's eyes savored each word.

*I have to fly tomorrow. But so far as that goes my
heart hasn't been down to earth since the first time you
kissed me, and when you love me you "send" it clear
out-of-this-world.*

Daisy gripped the letter tightly.

I'll write again as soon as I can. I'll love you forever.
            Your devoted husband
            lovingly and completely yours
            forever
            Jesse

Daisy clutched the letter to her chest. She leaned back against the couch and closed her eyes. New tears slipped down her cheeks as a look of calm settled across her face. She knew that this letter was a blessing, a means to hear Jesse's voice again and again for the rest of her life.

Soon after

Each morning before their shifts, they came up to the corridor in the *Leyte*'s tower.

They were white sailors, Black sailors, men in T-shirts from the boiler room, stewards in white high-collared coats, deckhands in colorful shirts, and others. The tower was the officers' area, a place where the sailors rarely ventured.

Still, they came with an envelope in hand. At a steel door, each man knocked. The door opened and each handed over his envelope.

Officers came up too, holding envelopes. Tom knocked on the office's steel door. So did Koenig, Marty, and Wilkie. Captain Sisson came from the bridge and handed over his envelope.

This was Commander Wally Madden's office.

His staff had placed the morning's collection on his desk,

and each day the pile of envelopes cascaded like a landslide across the desktop.

Today, the envelopes contained cash. Everyone in Squadron 32 had heard Jesse say, at one time or another, that his dream was to provide his daughter with an education, so the *Leyte*'s crew had taken up a collection to create a scholarship for baby Pam. As the air group commander, Madden had been chosen as custodian of the funds.

The ship's crew didn't normally take up collections. They couldn't possibly do it for every casualty. But, as Madden explained in a *Leyte* press release, "We felt this way about the loss of Jesse. He was a hell of a swell guy. We figured that his little girl was going to have a rough row to hoe without any daddy, so we wanted to do something for her in his memory."

Some sailors gave one dollar, some a couple of quarters. Someone leaked that Captain Sisson had contributed forty dollars— equivalent to nearly four hundred dollars in present-day money.

In the end, nearly every man on the *Leyte* knocked on that steel door with an envelope in his hand.

Six weeks later, February 3, 1951

A line of pilots descended the gangway of the *Leyte* and stepped onto the pier of North Island Naval Air Station in San Diego, California. After three months at war, the *Leyte* had returned to the United States.

The sun shone brightly as crowds of civilians cheered. A navy band belted out marching music as drum majorettes high-stepped to the beat. Nearby was a telephone trailer for the pilots to use to call home.

The crowd searched the pilots' faces for friends or loved ones. They parted as the skipper, Cevoli, and Dad led the squadron through. The pilots wore green tent caps and leather jackets, and they carried seabags over their shoulders.

The men of Fighting 32 remained in line. Marty grinned at some of the women in the crowd but didn't try to flirt. Wilkie eyed the telephone trailer but didn't dart away to call his wife. Tight-lipped, Tom passed the clamoring dignitaries.

He carried two seabags—one his, the other Koenig's. Koenig followed behind, arms wrapped around a box. The *Leyte* had sailed to war with nearly three thousand men, and three had been killed in action. The box belonged to one of the fallen.

It was heavy with books—Plato's *Five Great Dialogues,* and *Love Poems, Old and New,* and Jackie Robinson's life story. There were a well-worn Bible and the drawing of a single-story red dream house that would never be built.

Eyes set forward, the squadron left the crowd and the carrier behind. They were a squadron of veterans now, far from the days of Cannes. This time, the skipper didn't need to ask.

Everyone stuck together.

CHAPTER 42

THE CALL FROM THE CAPITAL

Almost two months later, March 31, 1951
Fall River, Massachusetts

Under the ceiling light in his childhood bedroom, Tom scribbled a note at his desk. He had returned to Quonset Point with the other pilots, and from there had gone on to his parents' house. Envelopes lay piled beside him, some open, some sealed. A sack of unopened mail sat on the floor nearby.

For months, countless Black Americans had written to thank Tom for trying to save Jesse. Some letters contained photos or good-luck charms. For weeks, Tom had come home every weekend to answer the mail. He responded to each letter with a quick note and a clarification: "I'm no hero, I just did what was right to do."

The phone rang. Tom lowered his pen. *At this hour?* It rang again. Tom walked into his parents' bedroom and picked up the phone.

"Mr. Hudner, I'm trying to reach your son, Tom."

Uh-oh, Tom thought. "This is he."

The man introduced himself as the White House naval liaison officer. He was a lieutenant commander and he sounded all business. "Lieutenant," he said. "You've been approved to receive the Medal of Honor for your actions in northern Korea."

Huh? Tom's heart skipped a beat. The Medal of Honor was the military's highest award. It was so rare that Tom had yet to see anyone wearing one. Tom lowered himself to his parents' bed and kept listening. He had heard rumors that Captain T. U. Sisson, the captain of the *Leyte,* had nominated him for a medal, but he had never believed them—until now.

"In two weeks, the president will be presenting the medal to you here in Washington, on April thirteenth," the commander added. "It'll be a brief ceremony. Your travel and lodging arrangements will be forthcoming. Any questions?"

"No, sir." Tom's voice was low. *Is this really happening?* he wondered.

"Good. This will be the first Navy Medal of Honor since World War Two."

The commander hung up and Tom sat, stunned. He knew the medal came with responsibility—he'd be placed on a pedestal as a figurehead of the military.

Tom's face sank as his thoughts raced to Mississippi. He lowered his head. *What will Daisy think of this? Jesse's gone and I'm getting an award?*

Two days later, Hattiesburg

Seated behind a gray dashboard, Daisy clutched the Wayfarer's metal steering wheel as she drove. Snook sat beside her on the striped fabric seat. It was a Monday afternoon, and the two were running errands.

"So are you going to Washington?" Snook asked over the engine's purr. The White House had invited Daisy to attend the Medal of Honor presentation, all expenses paid.

"I don't know," Daisy said. "It's just going to bring it all back."

Snook nodded slowly.

It had been a long, sad winter. First came Jesse's memorial service. Then came Christmas, when Jesse's cousin Ike and his wife, Gwen, came home to Hattiesburg, distraught. Then Jesse's mother died. Thirty-one days after her son's death, Julia collapsed while making her bed. The coroner said she had died from a stroke, but the family considered her a casualty of the Korean War, killed by the pain of Jesse's death. John Brown's depression only deepened.

"Someone should represent Jesse at the ceremony," Daisy said, thinking aloud.

Ten days later, on her way to Washington, D.C., Daisy looked at her toes as she walked down the plane's aisle. She wore a long tan coat and a small hat. Behind her, the sounds of revving aircraft engines slipped through the plane's open door. It was just another busy day at Hattiesburg Airport. From seats on both sides of the aisle, white passengers glanced up at her as if she didn't belong there. It made her deeply uncomfortable.

Daisy wanted to turn and flee back to the terminal. She had never traveled alone before. *You're representing Jesse!* she reminded herself. She dropped into a seat beside a round window. Behind her, baggage thumped as it was loaded aboard.

Daisy took a deep breath and fastened her seat belt.

The following afternoon, Friday, April 13, 1951

From the backseat of a Cadillac, Daisy glanced side to side with wonder. To the left stretched the National Mall, its green lawn warm in the afternoon sun. On her right stood the stately buildings of Washington, D.C., with their wide steps and tall stone columns.

Daisy held a bouquet of roses on the lap of her coat. The bouquet was a gift from the secretary of the navy, who would be present at the ceremony.

At Daisy's side sat her escort, Seaman First Class Clara Carroll. Clara was a young Black woman. Her navy uniform flowed into a skirt, and she wore a white hat with a short brim. Her face was round and her hair curled behind her ears. The White House had arranged for Daisy to stay with Clara because most of Washington's hotels didn't permit Black guests (and would not admit them until later in the 1950s).

Daisy gripped the roses, her feelings mixed. Already, she was overwhelmed by the navy's generosity. Earlier that morning at Quonset Point, the air group had announced their scholarship for Pam. The *Leyte*'s crew had raised $2,700, equivalent to more than $24,000 in present-day money. It would pay for Pam's college education.

Daisy hadn't forgotten Jesse's instructions for her, either. His life insurance money had arrived, and she knew he wanted her to spend it on her education and become a teacher like his mama. But Daisy was hesitant to spend the money on herself. She had Pam to raise, in addition to looking after Jesse's father.

For now, she tried to focus on her surroundings, and to be strong for the ceremony.

"Have you met Lieutenant Hudner before?" Clara asked her.

Daisy's face scrunched. "I'm sure I have, I just don't remember him because Jesse and I lived off base. All I really know about him is what the papers said—he tried to save Jesse, but Jesse had already passed."

Clara nodded.

"He was very brave to try," Daisy added.

Beneath the covered entrance to the White House, the driver opened Daisy's door. She stepped from the car. A navy-blue dress peeked from beneath her tan coat, and she wore white gloves. Her hair was curled beneath a hat, and a borrowed mink stole draped her shoulders. From behind a wrought-iron fence, tourists snapped photos. The spring air was crisp.

A White House staffer led Daisy forward. She could see

a chandelier inside and a small army of staffers waiting to greet her.

She took a deep breath and stepped inside.

Tom and his family entered the White House Cabinet Room behind the presidential secretary. Tom wore his navy-blue uniform with the usual black tie and white shirt, and his hair was swept back.

Tom's family admired the long table where the president held meetings. Thick leather chairs surrounded the table, and light poured in from tall windows beside it. Tom's mother was all smiles in her thickest fur wrap. His father stood quietly content in a gray three-piece suit. Tom's sister and brothers were there, along with his three uncles and their wives.

Tom turned to the secretary. "Where can I find Daisy Brown?" he said. "I really need to talk with her."

The secretary told Tom that Daisy was waiting outside but that Tom couldn't go out yet—he needed to meet the president first.

"Okay," Tom muttered.

He had tried to find Daisy at the hotel, but she hadn't been there, either. Tom's uncle stood quietly by. He knew why Daisy wasn't at their hotel, but he held his tongue, not to spoil Tom's day.

The uncle was from Tom's mother's side, and his last name was Brown, like Jesse's. He'd decided to come to Washington at the last minute and called the stately hotel on Sixteenth Street, where the White House was housing the Hudner family. The uncle told the reservations clerk the reason for his visit and asked, "You've heard about Jesse Brown, the colored pilot who died in Korea?"

After a pause, the clerk replied, "I'm sorry, Mr. Brown, but we're all filled up."

Tom's uncle found this odd. So he called a friend in Washington and asked him to try to make a reservation for the same night. His friend called him back with a disturbing update. "You're all set to stay there," the friend said. "The problem was that when you said your last name was Brown, they thought you were a Negro, someone from the Hattiesburg Brown family."

"Everyone, please gather around," the secretary said. He then turned to Tom and said, "Just a warning, but expect to see a lot of cameras—far more than usual." The secretary sounded annoyed at the thought. Tom knew why the media were turning out.

Two days earlier, President Truman had made a controversial decision.

With the battle lines in Korea seesawing along the thirty-eighth parallel, Truman's administration was suggesting peace talks with the Communists.

For now, though, the focus was the Medal of Honor. The door to the Cabinet Room opened and Tom turned. From the hallway, the president's snappy Midwestern twang sounded.

"I want to meet this young man!" Truman said loudly. "Where is he?"

As Tom and President Truman stepped onto the porch, thunderous applause erupted. Countless flashbulbs popped, and Tom blinked. Dignitaries lined the sides of the staircase, and more than three hundred people crowded the Rose Garden lawn below.

Truman flashed a cheery grin and waved to the crowd. His face was round, his nose sharp, and he wore wire-rim glasses. A red tie provided a splash of color against his gray suit. Few presidents had ever made as many impactful decisions as he had. Truman had authorized use of the atomic bombs in World War II, strikes that leveled the Japanese cities of Hiroshima and Nagasaki but ended the war. He had also ordered the desegregation of the military in 1948, and he'd sent American forces to the war in Korea.

Tom scanned the faces along the staircase. Halfway down, on the right, he spotted Daisy. She was facing him and smiling, tight-lipped but friendly. She held a bouquet of roses in the crook of her arm and was clapping. Tom released a breath of relief. Daisy stood between Seaman First Class Clara Carroll and a middle-aged officer. A thin mustache lined the officer's oval face; he was Lieutenant Dennis Nelson, and during World War II he'd become one of the navy's first twelve Black officers.

Truman turned to Tom and asked, "Shall we?"

Tom nodded and followed him down the stairs.

★ ★ ★

President Truman stepped to the podium. Tom took his place at the president's side.

Cameramen hunkered down behind movie cameras and photographers raised handheld still cameras. Reporters flipped open notepads. Behind the press pool, a large portrait of Jesse in his uniform stood on an easel.

Truman looked across the audience and began in a steady voice: "The President of the United States takes pleasure in presenting the Medal of Honor to Lieutenant Thomas Jerome Hudner Jr., United States Navy."

Applause sounded.

When the crowd quieted, Truman recited a summary of Tom's actions while Tom stood at attention, his eyes locked forward. He saw men in fedoras and women in shin-length dresses. Admirals and generals dotted the crowd. Captain Sisson was among the brass, too. In the background, the Washington Monument stood tall against a blue sky.

Truman's voice lowered as he read the final line: "Lieutenant Hudner's exceptionally valiant action and selfless devotion to a shipmate sustain and enhance the highest traditions of the U.S. Naval Service."

The president removed a felt-covered box from the podium. He opened the box, revealing the bronze, star-shaped Medal of Honor. "You earned this," Truman said to Tom. "This is the greatest honor anyone can get." He draped the medal around Tom's neck and snapped the blue ribbon closed.

"Thank you, sir," Tom said.

Truman shook Tom's hand but didn't let go. His eyes lowered to the medal. With his free hand he lifted the medal from Tom's neck and said, "I would rather have this than be president."

Tom grinned.

A cameraman shouted from the press pool: "Mr. President! Can you stay there so we can get some close-ups?"

"Sure," Truman said. "Let's do even better." He turned to Daisy and called, "Mrs. Brown—would you be willing to join Lieutenant Hudner and me?"

Daisy nodded. She descended the stairs proudly. Truman wrapped his arm around her. Daisy glanced at Tom and smiled; not a single tear had slipped from her eyes.

She's just like her husband was, Tom thought. *An extraordinary person.*

Truman turned to face the press with Daisy on his right and Tom on his left. "Okay!" he said loudly. "Get your shots, movie men."

Cameras flashed and movie cameras panned on their tripods. Daisy had never been under a brighter spotlight. *So this was Jesse's world,* she thought. Her husband was special, she had always known it.

Daisy smiled across the sea of cameras and didn't blink.

The president's secretary indicated that Truman needed to be going. The president nodded and shook Tom's hand heartily. Truman then turned to Daisy and said, "Mrs. Brown, the nation is grateful for your husband's sacrifice."

"Thank you for remembering him, Mr. President," Daisy said. She explained that she had brought a photo of Jesse and left it with his secretary.

Truman's eyes turned moist. He shook Daisy's hand and said simply, "Thank you," before he turned to climb the steps.

Tom stood alone with Daisy as the dignitaries and photographers dispersed. Tom's family watched from the steps. A few admirals lingered for a chance to speak with Tom, but everyone gave Tom and Daisy space.

"There are some things I've been wanting to tell you," Tom said softly. "There's just no easy way to do it."

"Tom, it's okay," Daisy said. "Say whatever you need, I'll be all right."

Tom glanced at his toes. "Jesse was so calm through it all, I've never seen anything like it," he said. "When we were on the ground, he was calming me down, when I should have been the one calming him down."

Daisy cocked her head. "How could he have calmed you? The papers said he passed before you reached him."

Tom looked up with surprise. "Oh, they got that all wrong." New life flowed into his eyes. "Jesse was alive. We were together for forty minutes—I was up along the canopy and we were talking."

Tears welled along Daisy's eyelids. She shook her head in disbelief.

"When I left the plane to wave in the helicopter," Tom added, "that's when he let go."

Daisy squeezed the bouquet of roses tightly.

Tom looked Daisy in the eyes. "He was thinking of you. He even gave me a message to tell you."

Daisy gulped.

Tom's voice choked. "He said, 'Just tell Daisy how much I love her.'"

Daisy lowered her head and her tears flowed. Tom glanced away, his eyes blurry. Everyone watching became emotional, and some wiped their eyes.

Sniffling, Daisy pulled herself together. She blotted her eyes with a handkerchief. But Tom's head remained lowered. Jesse's death still weighed on him enormously.

"So, Jesse wasn't alone," Daisy said, her voice warming. "That means so much, Tom."

Tom didn't look up. "I'm just sorry the result wasn't happier," he muttered.

Daisy ducked to see Tom's face. "Tom?"

He finally looked up.

"I'm just so grateful that you tried to save him," Daisy said. "Jesse was lucky to have a friend like you."

Tom's face slowly loosened and his shoulders lowered.

After a pause he said, "Well, I guess we'd better be going."

Daisy agreed. Cars were waiting to whisk them to a dinner. That weekend they'd do a radio show together, in Baltimore; then the next month they'd travel to Chicago to be honored by the *Chicago Defender* newspaper. Over the years, Tom and Daisy would make numerous appearances together to perpetuate Jesse's legacy. This was just the first.

Tom and Daisy turned and walked up the steps. Behind them, the press pool had thinned and the portrait of Jesse had come into sight.

On the steps, Clara took her place at Daisy's side and asked, "How are you holding up, Mrs. Brown?"

"I'm doing as well as I can," Daisy said. "This is the price of marrying an exceptional man."

CHAPTER 43

THE MESSAGE

Six days later, April 19, 1951
Fall River, Massachusetts

Tom waved sheepishly from the black Cadillac convertible as it cruised his hometown's Main Street. Around him, a crowd of all ages waved and cheered. More than forty thousand townspeople of Fall River filled the sidewalks. Some had to stand on their toes for a glimpse of the officer in the navy blazer and white hat. There were local children, businessmen, housewives—even Tom's childhood bully-turned-friend, Manny Cabral, might have been there. It was a brisk, gray Thursday afternoon and the city's largest celebration since WWII had begun, an event that the town fathers had named the "Hudner Day Parade."

Tom's eyes darted about with confusion, even discomfort. He couldn't fathom why so many people had turned out to see him. Tom's parents and sister sat in a separate Cadillac behind Tom's, and a marching band followed several lengths behind. Farther back stretched a motorcade of dignitaries, and behind them came the marching soldiers of an all-Black National Guard unit.

Tom continued waving, his smile tight and awkward. This was only the beginning, and he knew it. *Life* magazine wanted to interview him. Invitations to a quiz show and a movie premiere were forthcoming.

Tom hadn't yet committed to a thing. Secretly, he wanted to put his newfound notoriety behind him. On his blazer he wore a small blue award ribbon to represent the medal, but nothing more. Around his neck, Tom wore his navy-issue black tie—he had left his Medal of Honor at home.

A roar bellowed from behind. Tom glanced over his shoulder as four Corsairs raced low over the parade route, then over his head. White *K*s stood out on their tails. Their noise caused children to cover their ears. Another four Corsairs buzzed Main Street, then came another four. The crowd cheered.

As the Corsairs sped away, Tom shook his head in wonder. His friends were at the controls, including Cevoli, Marty, and Wilkie—all flying to salute him.

I really don't deserve this, Tom thought.

At the end of the parade route, the vehicles stopped in the city's South Park. Tom stepped out of the Cadillac and headed over to a stage. A cold bay of ocean lay downhill. Behind Tom, the crowd funneled into the park.

Dignitaries lined up on the stage to greet Tom. He shook hands with the mayor, representatives from the state, and even the commander of Quonset Point, a rear admiral who'd later say in his speech: "I am very proud to wear the uniform that Tom Hudner wears."

At the end of the receiving line waited a cluster of women. Beneath their hats they wore their hair in buns. One of the town fathers introduced them to Tom as the town's Gold Star Mothers. They'd each lost a son in war, most in WWII, a few very recently in Korea. Tom stepped into the half-circle of women and warmly shook each mother's hand. With teary eyes, one mother told Tom how brave he was for trying to save Jesse. Another pulled him close and hugged him tightly.

Tom could sense their grief, the same emotional wound that had killed Jesse's mother. Yet the women all looked at Tom with admiration. Each wanted to shake *his* hand. As Tom conversed with the Gold Star Mothers, he began to realize the powerful responsibility that came with the medal.

Someone has to speak for those who paid the ultimate price.

Next, eager faces watched Tom step to the wooden dais. Against a backdrop of trees he addressed the crowd.

"This has been one day I shall never forget," Tom said. "Concerning the incident that happened in Korea last December— just as sure as I am standing here now, if I had been down, it would have been Jesse Brown who would have helped me out."

Tom kept his remarks short, then concluded by saying, "To the fellows there now and to those who will never come back from this horrible conflict, I want to thank you all. And to this committee and the people of Fall River—God bless you all."

For the day's final presentation, a judge from the city's superior court stepped forward and handed him a check in his name for $1,000—equivalent to about $9,000 in present-day money. Tom shook his head in disbelief.

When he returned to his seat, one of the town fathers tapped him on the shoulder, leaned in, and asked in an excited whisper, "So, how are you going to spend all that money?"

The next day, Tom climbed the steps to Fighting 32's briefing room at Quonset Point. Clad in his leather jacket and green pants, Tom moved with a bounce in his step. He carried an envelope containing his check from the city of Fall River.

Tom entered the squadron briefing room and set the envelope in the outgoing mail bin. The envelope was addressed to Mrs. Daisy Brown, T-116 Robertson Place, Hattiesburg, Mississippi. Inside, Tom had signed the check over to Daisy. His decision had been easy.

If the Leyte's *putting Jesse's daughter through college, then Daisy should go, too.*

Tom dropped into a seat beside his buddies and readied a pen to take notes. The skipper was coming, the briefing about to begin. Tom was back, right where he belonged.

Five months later, Labor Day weekend, 1951

In a dark blur, the Corsair raced low over the Massachusetts coastline. Midmorning sun glowed over cottages and train stops. From his seat in the Corsair's cockpit, Tom flew with a mischievous gleam in his eyes.

Marinas stocked with sailboats zipped beneath his right wing, so close his wing tip nearly clipped their masts. Tom had never flown this low before—never stateside, anyway.

It was September 1, the Saturday of Labor Day weekend. Everyone had gone home from Quonset Point for the holiday, so Tom had seized the opportunity to pursue a personal mission, one he'd been considering since his first flight with Jesse.

Tom thought of Jesse often, and Daisy, too. Daisy had written Tom a gracious letter and had used his gift to enroll at Alcorn College, about three hours from Hattiesburg. She was in classes now, on her way to becoming a home economics teacher.

One day she'd remarry, after waiting seven years. She'd find someone whom Jesse would have approved of, an army medic named Gilbert Thorne. From the start, Gilbert would admit to Daisy, "I know I can't take Jesse's place, but I'll do the best I can for you." Gilbert would love Pam as if she were his own, and together the family would move to Germany on a deployment. There, in a quaint village, Daisy would secure her dream job, teaching kindergarten to the children of military parents. And there, she'd buy a red Sunbeam convertible and race the autobahn.

But that was all to come. On the horizon, Tom's target appeared. His eyes tightened. Ahead and to the right lay swaths of green grass along the coastal cliffs. Neat clumps of trees dotted the green. This was it.

Tom nudged the throttle forward and steered the Corsair lower.

★ ★ ★

A golfer flexed his knees and the spectators turned silent. He swung his club and hit the ball. As the ball rolled to a stop, the spectators clapped politely. The golfer waved, then walked to make his next shot, and the small crowd followed. The Acoaxet Country Club's annual golf tournament was in full swing.

Tom's father was on the green, wearing khakis and his polo shirt with the club logo on the front pocket. He and several friends had founded the club in 1919, and he never missed a tournament.

Tom Senior didn't see the black W-shaped silhouette diving from the sky behind him. None of the club members did. But the silhouette stretched larger and larger, aiming straight for them.

Tom steered the Corsair's nose at the crowd on the golf course. As a boy, he'd spent his summers at the club, sailing from its beach. Back then, he loved everything about the place. But lately, he had become frustrated with certain members—namely, his father's friends. In Korea, the battle lines were still locked in a bloody stalemate around that same border, the thirty-eighth parallel. But his father's friends had stopped following the news. They were back to worrying about the stock market and their golf scores, as if young men weren't still dying in Korea, as if there weren't even a war going on.

Rather than sit idly by, Tom had written a letter to the Fall River newspaper in which he encouraged his neighbors to extend the same support they had shown him to the troops overseas.

"With all the cold, the mud, the blood and horror they are

living in," he wrote, "there is never anything so demoralizing or dangerous as the feeling we at home don't have too much interest in what they're doing and going through."

Tom didn't know if the letter had an effect or if anyone had even read it. So he devised another way to get his message across.

Gotta be low enough! Tom thought, his eyes tightening as the crowd came closer into view. *They need to see that this is a navy plane.*

With a furious roar, the Corsair ripped over the crowd at 250 miles per hour, flattening the sea grass and blowing hats from heads. Golfers dropped their clubs and spectators sank to their knees, soiling their clean khakis. The plane's shadow crossed the green and kept going.

The spectators glanced up and saw a flash of curved wings, a white star, and the word NAVY on the plane's flank. A puttering sound trailed the Corsair's tail.

The plane kept running out over the sea, now low above the waves.

From their hands and knees, the golfers and spectators scowled.

"Who the hell is that?" someone shouted.

"He should be grounded!" yelled another.

Someone chuckled nervously. One by one, the faces turned to Tom's father. He was cowering on the green like the rest of them, a grin lining his face. The others glared at him and shook their heads. Tom's father just shrugged.

The perturbed golfers and spectators stood. They pranced around, trying to clean their knees off. In his cockpit, Tom could see them through his rearview mirror. He broke out in laughter. They looked just like storks.

Tom remained low and fast over the leaping waves. He almost shook his head with wonder.

Jesse was right.

He should have done this long ago.

≡ AFTERWORD ≡

After the Battle of the Chosin Reservoir, the **Korean War** raged for an additional two years and seven months along the thirty-eighth parallel, the prewar border. Neither side gave or gained much ground.

Four months before the war ended, **Joseph Stalin** died, having seen his dreams of Communist expansion crushed by the free world. After his death, with the Soviet Union gripped in a leadership struggle, the Chinese and North Korean Communists abandoned their demands for mandatory prisoner repatriation and returned to the peace table.

In July 1953, the Korean War concluded after claiming five million lives—nearly thirty-seven thousand of them American. Of the Communist prisoners captured by U.N. forces, thirty percent of the North Koreans elected to remain in the south, and seventy percent of Chinese prisoners chose not to return to Communist China.

Today, the Korean War is often called the "Forgotten War." But the men who fought there know it by a different name: the Forgotten Victory. Thanks to the United States and United Nations forces, some fifty million South Koreans live in freedom.

In January 1955, **Dick Cevoli** was on duty in Florida when his wife, Grace, gave birth at Quonset Point. Their fourth child—Richard Jr.—was born mentally disabled.

After hearing the news, Cevoli took off in rough weather in a Cougar jet to hurry home. When a priest entered Grace Cevoli's hospital room, she thought something had happened to her baby. Instead, the priest delivered the news that Dick had crashed and died.

Today, a post office in East Greenwich, Rhode Island, is named in honor of Dick Cevoli.

After his tour in fighters, **Marty Goode** became a navy helicopter pilot. Whenever he came in to land, sailors and aviators would line Vulture's Row to see a helicopter land like a fighter.

Marty later became a navy test pilot at Sikorsky and retired as a commander, far from his humble beginnings as an enlisted seaman. Along the way, he met a beautiful Hungarian artist named Paula at a theater performance. Then and there, Marty's days as a ladies' man ended; he was certain that Paula was the girl he'd been looking for. He married her and adopted her two daughters from a previous marriage.

For the rest of their days together, Marty and Paula went out weekly to dance the Argentinian tango.

Bill Koenig remained in the navy and became a master naval parachutist and commander who oversaw the development of ejection seats and escape systems.

In civilian life, Koenig remained close with the Brown family. In 2005, he took Jesse's granddaughter, Jessica, on a special trip to Oceana Naval Air Station so she could see why her grandfather had loved carrier aviation. Together, they visited Navy Fighter Squadron 32. The squadron's pilots suited up Jessica in flight gear and showed her how to preflight an F-14 jet.

Today, Jessica calls Koenig "Uncle Bill."

Richard "Dad" Fowler commanded the carrier *Ticonderoga* during the Vietnam War and retired as a rear admiral, the equivalent of a two-star general. No one who knew him was a bit surprised.

Bill "Wilkie" Wilkinson transitioned to the Naval Reserves in 1952. While continuing to fly fighters on weekends, he took a weekday job with American Airlines and became a commercial airline captain when he was only twenty-four years old. Thirty-five years later, he made his final flight for American as a 747 pilot.

In their later years, Wilkie and his wife, Mary, enjoyed sailing a twenty-foot sailboat from their home in Maine. During quiet times at sea, Wilkie reflected on his life, and his thoughts sometimes roamed back to the Yalu bridge strike and the North Korean children he flew over.

He hoped their lives turned out okay.

★ ★ ★

During a layover at Norfolk Naval Base in 1954, Wilkie reported for dinner in the officers' club and was seated two tables away from **the skipper—Dug Neill**. To Wilkie's surprise, the skipper invited him to his table, and afterward the two went out for beers, like old friends. The following year, Marty Goode bumped into the skipper at Naval Air Station Key West and enjoyed the same hospitality.

Wilkie and Marty would later come to the same conclusion: the pressures of leading a squadron had made the skipper's personality more stern and strict for a reason—out of concern for his young pilots.

The skipper would later become a university professor.

John "Red" Parkinson had trouble readjusting to civilian life. He drifted by day, and at night he couldn't sleep under blankets for fear he'd be caught unprepared.

Then in 1952, everything changed. While driving to his uncle Anton's farm, Red was crossing a four-way intersection when another driver's brakes failed. The other driver broadsided Red's car and rolled it. Red emerged with scrapes but was otherwise okay. He noticed that the other driver was a pretty twenty-one-year-old girl with hazel eyes and curly blond hair. Her name was Virginia.

In the hospital, the two struck up a friendship. Red borrowed a friend's car to drive Virginia home. Two years later they married and settled down on a dairy farm.

Every November 27, on the anniversary of the Chosin Reservoir battle, Red would climb a hill near his farm at night. In the cold, he'd sit and remember.

Red hadn't seen **Charlie Kline** since Yudam-ni but never forgot how Charlie had steered him to his faith. In tribute, Red began volunteering with the Gideons International, the organization that had given him his pocket Bible during his Marine days.

In 1985, Red attended a Gideons convention in Philadelphia as a delegate. As Red was introduced to the audience, a man stood abruptly at the rear of the hall, nearly flipping his chair. "We finally got ya!" the man shouted. Red looked closely and saw the thick chin and wide grin of fifty-six-year-old Charlie Kline.

Charlie hadn't died at Yudam-ni after all. He had been searching for his bazooka when the Chinese came, so he took shelter in a culvert. After three days in hiding, he escaped, but with both lungs damaged by the cold. The Marines transported Charlie in the column to Hagaru, then airlifted him to Japan and hospitals from there.

In the middle of the Philadelphia convention hall, Red and Charlie embraced to thunderous applause. Until Charlie's death in 1999, the two were inseparable.

On a brisk October day in 1955, **Sergeant Bob Devans**'s remains were returned from North Korea to his hometown of Wilkes-Barre, Pennsylvania, during one of the few postwar exchanges of remains. As his coffin was lowered into the earth, his brother, sister, father, and mother were present.

And so was his high school crush, Audrey Johns.

Fletcher Brown became a mechanic in the air force during the Korean War, and **Lura Brown** served in the Eighty-Second Airborne, a unit held stateside in anticipation of a Soviet attack on Europe. Both men later followed their mother's wishes and sought higher education. Fletcher earned an MBA from Pepperdine and Lura studied horticulture at UCLA.

In 2000, the brothers and Daisy represented Jesse at a Korean War commemoration in Sacramento. A tall Black Marine in his seventies approached them. Five decades earlier, he had been the square-faced Marine who had watched Jesse fly at the Chosin.

"I can still see him overhead," the Marine said, as his eyes filled with tears. "If it hadn't been for him and the others, none of us would have gotten out alive."

In 1966, **Tom Hudner** attended a Christmas party in Miramar, California. He was a captain then and navigator of the carrier *Kitty Hawk*.

Across a crowded room he saw a striking brunette, a tall Jackie Kennedy look-alike. Tom's friend told him that the brunette's name was Georgea Smith. She was a widow whose husband, a pilot, had been killed three years earlier.

Tom's friend tried to steer him toward any other woman.

Georgea had three children—and she was taller than Tom, too. But Tom had already made up his mind. As Georgea was putting on her jacket to leave, he stopped her at the door.

Two years later, they married and had a son together, Thomas Jerome Hudner III.

After thirty years of service, in February 1973, Tom delivered a speech just days before his retirement from the navy. At the Boston Navy Yard, with Daisy Brown in the audience, he dedicated a new frigate—the USS *Jesse L. Brown*.

In civilian life, Tom served as a state commissioner for veterans' affairs, as president of the regional USO, and as treasurer of the Medal of Honor Society. During his many speeches to military officers, veterans, and schoolchildren, he always remembered his last words to Jesse: "We'll be back for you!"

For more than sixty years, Tom's promise went unfulfilled. Ever since the war, relations hadn't thawed between America and the North Korean regime, and the U.S. military had been unable to search for the remains of its nearly eight thousand MIAs, Jesse Brown included.

Then, in summer 2013, at the age of eighty-eight, Tom decided to take matters into his own hands.

His family tried to dissuade him. His fellow veterans urged him to reconsider. The U.S. State Department advised Tom that they'd be powerless to protect him. But Tom had learned a lesson in wartime: sometimes you have to break the rules.

In July 2013, in a drizzling rain, Tom stepped off a plane in North Korea. Officers of the North Korean army were waiting for him and his traveling party. Two days later, in the capital,

Pyongyang, Tom clipped his Medal of Honor around his neck. Soldiers led him into a conference room, to a seat across from a North Korean colonel and his staff. For sixty-three years, Tom had waited for this moment.

With cameras of the world media rolling, Tom asked the North Koreans to begin a search for Jesse Brown's remains.

At first, the North Korean colonel remained silent. He glanced at his notes where his reply had been prewritten. News of Tom's arrival had already coursed through the ranks of the North Korean military and the government, and into the ear of the nation's new, thirty-year-old Supreme Leader—Kim Jong-un.

The colonel began to read a message from the Supreme Leader to Tom.

Kim Jong-un was impressed that Tom had come so far, after so long, to keep a promise to a friend. In tribute to Tom, the North Korean leader granted approval to his army to resume the search for the remains of MIA American servicemen—beginning with Jesse Brown.

Back in Hattiesburg, eighty-six-year-old **Daisy Brown** was following Tom's journey to North Korea and the tremendous outpouring of national support. A news network sent cameras to Daisy's home to gauge her reaction. "I never dreamed that this would happen," Daisy said in an interview, "and yet if it's successful, I'm sure that it'll bring some closure to us and they can bring him back and give him a final resting place."

With renewed hope, Daisy waited. Sixty-three years had

passed since Jesse's death and she knew it could take longer, even decades, for anyone to locate two burned Corsairs in a range of desolate mountains. Most of all, Daisy was thankful to Tom for trying.

In July 2014, after a long illness, Daisy died in her home. But before she passed, she told her daughter, **Pamela Brown**, that she had decided where Jesse should be buried if his remains ever returned to his native soil. At first Daisy had thought Jesse should rest in Mississippi. But then the schoolteacher in her had a better idea.

Daisy decided that Jesse should one day rest in Arlington National Cemetery so people of all ages and races could visit his grave and be inspired by his story. Because, to Daisy, her husband isn't done serving his fellow man.

In her last days, when she looked around her, Daisy came to one final conclusion:

The world needs people like Jesse Brown and Tom Hudner, now more than ever.

At Sea
Sunday Nite
3 December 1950

My own dear sweet Angel,

I'm so lonesome I could just boo-hoo. But I try to restrain myself and think of the fun we're going to have when we do get together, so only a few tears escape now and then. I love you so very much my darling.

I've been trying to get a chance to write you for the last three days but without much success. I'd like to write you every night. I love to tell you that I love and adore you, and, although I never quite succeed in getting it across, I like to try and tell you how much I care and how much you really mean to me. So you see, my darling, not only do I like to hear you tell me that you love me but I like telling you also that you're the sweetest woman in the world. I love you angel and I want you to know that my heart belongs to you.

It was a little past midnite when I started this, but who cares. We're in love and thats what matters, not the time. Right darling?

The last few days we've been doing quite a bit of flying to help slow down the Chinese communists and to give support to some marines who were surrounded when the Chinese launched their big drive. Knowing that he's helping those poor guys on the ground, I think every pilot on here would fly until he dropped in his tracks. This morning we were flying in weather so bad we could hardly see each other at times — snowing. Yet the air was full of planes. Navy planes for close support of the troops, Air force transport dropping supplies by parachute, etc. We know a few of the marine officers down on the ground because they were with us in the Med. But my biggest hope still is that somehow, thru the mercy of God, this war can come to a close without us getting into an all out war with China.

Know what darling? I love you with all my heart and soul. I'm so deeply and completely in love with you until nothing else in life matters to me at all except you angel. Occasionally Lee Nelson will show me a certain portion of one of his letters from Lee. The reason I mention that is because her letters to him always remind me of yours to me and mine to you. I guess people who are really and truly in love do think quite a bit alike — different couples I mean As for us, our thoughts and mind seem to run exactly alike and I know that it isn't just a coincidence. When we were married darling, our bodies, minds, hearts, and souls were also wed. I guess that is why making love to you is such an exquisite joy, because we belong to each other and we give ourselves to each other without reservations at all. In Lee's letter to Lee she was telling him how she needed him and how she was praying and trusting in God to bring him home soon.

Darling, heaven alone can know how much I need you and how badly I want to see you. I need you and want you angel far more than I have the ability to express. If only my heart could talk — if only my hungry, lonely, arms could enfold you darling, I love you with a passion that is beyond description. I love you with a true love, an everlasting love, a love that says that I am yours alone, only yours darling, and that I always shall belong to you. Sweetness, my very soul is dedicated to you.

I'm so lonesome for you and I need you so much darling. I guess you've always thought I was a big cry baby, but honest darling you're my weakness and I can't help it. I love you so much darling, and even though usually it seems that instead of tears flowing from my eyes they flow down into my heart and stay there and hurt, sometimes this loneliness just wrings the tears of my aching heart. Often when I climb into my rack at nite all the loneliness of the day seems to descend upon me and I'm haunted by seemingly a thousand sweet memories of you. Then all the tears that I've been holding back all day long refuse to be held any longer, and I just lay there in loneliness and misery and cry my heart out. I pray so earnestly to God to see my tears and grant that thru his pity and mercy we may be together again soon. Then I feel His comfort and yours and I go to sleep

Oh darling, please, please try and realize what you mean to me and try and understand how much I care. I need you so much darling. Please help me Dassy, please my darling.

Don't be discouraged angel, believe in God and believe in Him with all your might and I know that things will work out all right. We need Him now like never before. Have faith with me darling and He'll see us thru and we'll be together again before long too. I want you to keep that pretty little chin up angel, come on now, way up. I want you also to be confident in this and that is, your husband loves his wife with all his heart and soul — no man ever loved a woman more.

You know how I feel now? I feel like I feel when we've just laid in each others arms a long time just talking. We usually kiss and whisper sweet words of love to each other and say softly over and over "I love you angel." Then after vowing all over again to always love each other we're ready for the loving

4

of our lives. That is one of the times when our loving
is sweet and gentle. Thats the way I'd like to love you right
now angel, sweet and gentle. I'd like to whisper sweet things
in your dainty ears, kiss your sweet lips, play in your
hair and caress your smooth skin, frame your beautiful
face in my hands — hold you close and enjoy the thrill of you
taking my breath away — raise up at times just so I can
look at you and admire you.

Darling, I'm going to close now and climb in the
rack. I honestly dread going to bed, but I usually dream
of you so I'll manage to make it until we'll share our
bed together again — darling pray that it'll be soon. I have
to fly tomorrow. But so far as that goes my heart hasn't
been down to earth since the first time you kissed me, and
when you love me you "send" it clear out-of-this-world.

I'll write again as soon as I can. I'll love you
forever.

Your devoted husband
lovingly and completely yours
forever
Jesse

≡ Acknowledgments ≡

I'd like to extend my deepest thanks to the following people for their help with *Devotion*:

To Tom Hudner, the gentleman I met in the hotel lobby eight years ago. Thank you for entrusting me with your story and allowing me to accompany you on your mission to North Korea. You're a real-life "Captain America" who has given us all a timeless gift—an example worth emulating.

To Daisy Brown Thorne. A half century after you lost Jesse, I asked you to relive the memories of your times together, for this book. On July 6, 2014, soon after we completed our work, you left this earth. I'll never forget your words after one particularly long interview: *I just love talking about Jesse.*

To the supporting stars of *Devotion,* in order of appearance: Lura Brown, Fletcher Brown, Marty Goode, Bill Koenig, Halley Bishop, John "Red" Parkinson, Ed Coderre, and Bill "Wilkie" Wilkinson—your stories are each worthy of a book of its own. Thank you for giving *Devotion* humor, poignancy, and depth.

To Tom Hudner's wife, Georgea Hudner, thank you for your faith in this book from the start. When your husband decided to travel to North Korea, you could have dissuaded him—as many wives would have—but you encouraged him to fulfill his promise to Jesse. You're proof that beside every great man stands a great woman.

To Pamela Brown Knight—Jesse's daughter—whose blessing made this book possible. As Daisy's protector, you could have said "enough" and our history-gathering would have ended. Instead, you welcomed me to Hattiesburg and opened the doors to your family's history. You're everything one would expect from the daughter of Jesse and Daisy Brown.

To Marine Sergeant Dick Bonelli, one of the legendary warriors of Fox Company at the Chosin Reservoir. In 2013, when Tom Hudner returned to North Korea, he included Dick in his traveling party to represent the Marines. Although *Devotion* lacked the pages to cover their adventure, I assure you—*Bonelli was there.*

To the veterans' families and friends, thank you for the stories, photos, and documents you shared that enriched this book. Special thanks to: Sue Burton, Steve Cevoli, Ed Coderre, Jr., Wanda Perkowska Coderre, Dr. Frank Cronin, the Danaher family, Don Devans, Kelli Fernandez, Richard C. Fowler, Ellen Franks, James Hudner, Mary Hudner, Phillip Hudner, Rick Hudner, Thomas Hudner III, Audrey Johns, Jamal Knight, Jessica Knight, Jim and Diane McMichael, Jenny Parkinson, Edward Sisson, Charlotte Ward, and Karen Ward.

To my dedicated agent, David Vigliano, who guided *Devotion* into the hands of the team at Ballantine Books. To my editors, Ryan Doherty, who recognized the power of this story and coached me through its early days, and Mark Tavani, whose deft hand polished the manuscript to its final form. To the president and publisher of Random House, Gina Centrello, and the publishing team at Ballantine Bantam Dell: Libby McGuire, Jennifer Tung, Richard Callison, Susan Corcoran, Greg Kubie, Quinne Rogers, Betsy Wilson, Evan Camfield, and everyone on the sales and marketing team, thank you all for bringing *Devotion* to the world.

To this book's aviation advisor, Rob Collings, a modern-day Corsair pilot with the Collings Foundation, and to Valada Flewellyn, who works tirelessly to preserve Jesse Brown's history through her traveling exhibit *A Pilot Lights the Way*. Thank you, Valada, for guiding my first visit to Hattiesburg and introducing me to your friends Daisy and Pamela Brown.

To the historians and researchers of the Marine Corps Archives, the USMC History Division, the Naval History and Heritage Command, and the National Archives: Francis Alexander, Rita Cann, Jenny Crabb, Lisa Crunk, David Fort, Joe Gordon, John Hodges, Kenneth Johnson, Kara Newcomer, Nathaniel Patch, Kevin Pratt, Jonathan Roscoe, and Nancy Whitfield.

To the early readers who lent a discerning eye to this manuscript: Dianne Castelli, Franz Englram, Joe Gohrs, Patty Gohrs, Jaime Hanna, Tricia Leupp Hoover, Carolin Huber, Tony Hughes, Elizabeth Makos, Betsy Rider, Peter Semanoff, Agata Twarowska, Kyle Warren, and Bob Windholz.

To the experts, friends, and supporters who contributed in a myriad of ways: the Honorable Ray Mabus, Bill Bartsch, Jennifer Baxter, Lt. Andrea Cassidy, Mark "Goober" Connolly,

Richard Downes (Coalition of Families of Korean & Cold War POW/MIAs), Herbert Fahr Jr. (USS *Missouri* Association), Mary Faria (the *Herald News*), David Friant, Craig Fuller, Joe Galloway, Chip Gibson, Matt Hall, Paula Hancocks, Gareth Hector, Steve Herman, Jeff "Growler" Hogan, Chester Makos (Seventh Infantry), Jean Lee, Kevin "Joker" Mastin, Ken McLaurin (USS *Leyte* Association), Joseph Pickard, John Powers, Dan Sheahan (Fall River Main Library), Lindy Smith, Dave Stecker (Quonset Air Museum), Anthony "K-Bob" Sweeney, Justin Taylan (Pacific Wrecks), Pauline Testerman, Joanna Williams, Vickie Wilson (Johnson Publishing Co.), Richard D. Winters, Bill Woodier, and Le Grande Van Wagenen (USS *Leyte* Association).

To Marcus Brotherton, the veteran author and coauthor of twenty-five books who mentored my writing. From the first chapter to the last, you were always trimming, sharpening, and sharing the tricks of your trade to help me become a better writer. I'm lucky to count you as a friend.

To my grandfather Mike Makos, who passed away during the process of this book. You always told me about those postwar years when Soviet fighters intercepted your B-17 off the coast of Japan. Only now do I realize the dangers you faced.

To my sisters, Erica Makos and Elizabeth Makos, and my mother, Karen Makos, thanks for being my proofreaders and toughest critics. Your feedback helped shape this book. To my dear friend Helga Stigler, thanks for looking out for me from afar.

To my grandparents Francis and Jeanne Panfili, who brought countless lunches and dinners to my brother and me during those endless days and nights at our desks. Your love and encouragement always lifted our spirits.

To my dad, Robert Makos, and my brother, Bryan Makos, who led our research team and even traveled to North Korea for this book. Your task was lofty: to conduct interviews and gather historical facts across three continents, seven countries, and both sides of the Korean War. Few could have done the job that you did.

Lastly, thanks to you, the reader, for purchasing *Devotion*. I hope this story will inspire you and remain in your mind. If you find yourself hungry to learn more, you'll find film of Tom's trip to North Korea, an eerie ghost story from Daisy, and other bonus content on my website: AdamMakos.com.

On behalf of Tom, Daisy, and the heroes of *Devotion,* I now pass the torch to you. Keep the flame alive. The legacy of great men and women lies in your hands.

▰ Photo Credits ▰

p. iii: Bill Wilkinson
pp. 332–333: U.S. Navy
pp. 334–337: Daisy Brown Thorne, via *Ebony*

Jacket Art

Front jacket photographs: courtesy of U.S. Navy (two airmen); courtesy of Bill
  Wilkinson (flying planes)
Front jacket flap photographs: courtesy of Thomas J. Hudner, Jr. (Tom Hudner);
  courtesy of the U.S. Navy (Jesse Brown)
Back jacket photograph: courtesy of the U.S. Navy

First Insert

Teenage Tom Hudner with his siblings: Thomas J. Hudner Jr.
Nineteen-year-old Tom during a visit home: Thomas J. Hudner Jr.
Daisy holds Pam: Courtesy of the Jesse Leroy Brown family
Jesse as an ensign: U.S. Navy
Jesse and Daisy with Pam: Courtesy of the Jesse Leroy Brown family
Marty Goode aboard the *Leyte:* Martin Goode
Jesse in the Quonset Point chapel: U.S. Navy
A *Leyte* LSO signals: U.S. Navy
Marty catches the last cable: Martin Goode
Fighting 32 during the Mediterranean cruise: U.S. Navy
Leyte deckhands prepare a Corsair: U.S. Navy
The beach at Cannes: W. Carl Jeckel
Elizabeth Taylor, Nicky Hilton, and friends: U.S. Navy
Elizabeth Taylor dines with the officers: U.S. Navy
Sixth Fleet Marines practice: U.S. Navy

Red Parkinson and his platoon: John E. Parkinson
A Marine aims an M20 Super Bazooka: U.S. Marine Corps
Ed Coderre during a visit home: Ed Coderre
Enjoying watermelons on Crete: John E. Parkinson
Marines assemble aboard the *Leyte:* U.S. Navy
Red Parkinson naps: John. E. Parkinson
Jesse during a stop in Tennessee: Courtesy of the Jesse Leroy Brown family
Jesse plays with Pam: Courtesy of the Jesse Leroy Brown family
Bill Wilkinson during flight training: Bill Wilkinson
Wilkie's photo of a practice flight: Bill Wilkinson
Jesse and Koenig in their cabin: U.S. Navy
On the *Leyte*'s first day at war: U.S. Navy
Squadron 32 at the front of the pack: Bill Wilkinson
Tom in the cockpit: Thomas J. Hudner Jr.
Sailors muscle a Corsair onto an elevator: U.S. Navy
"Dad" Fowler as a Hellcat pilot: U.S. Navy, via Richard E. Fowler Jr. family
Dad Fowler launches down the center line: Bill Wilkinson

Second Insert

Marty and others review maps: U.S. Navy
Sisson and the skipper with captured flags: U.S. Navy
Jesse's buddies carry him: U.S. Navy
At anchor in Sasebo harbor: U.S. Navy
Black Market Alley: U.S. Navy
Artillery pounds Hill 891: U.S. Marine Corps
Chinese soldiers captured near 891: U.S. Marine Corps
A Skyraider returns from a mission: U.S. Navy
Jesse as seen through a windscreen: U.S. Navy
The *Leyte*'s special mission planes: U.S. Navy
The bridges of the Yalu: U.S. Navy
Cevoli and Jesse play backgammon: U.S. Navy
Jesse checks the rockets: U.S. Navy
Jesse up high on the *Leyte*'s tower: U.S. Navy
Jesse in the cockpit of a Corsair: U.S. Navy
Leyte deckhands clear the deck: U.S. Navy
The Chosin Reservoir: National Archives
Stalin propaganda poster: U.S. Marine Corps
Marines press onward: © David Douglas Duncan, Harry Ransom Center,
    University of Texas

Daytime firefight at the Chosin: U.S. Marine Corps
Marines watch an airstrike: U.S. Marine Corps
Nicolas Trudgian's *Off to the Chosin:* ValorStudios.com
Gareth Hector's *Wingmen to the End:* ValorStudios.com
An HO3S at Hagaru: U.S. Marine Corps
Matt Hall's painting *Devotion:* Matt Hall and ValorStudios.com
During the withdrawal: © David Douglas Duncan, Harry Ransom Center, University of Texas
Marines manage to smile: U.S. Marine Corps
Marines follow the precipitous trails: U.S. Marine Corps
Ed Coderre's parents visit him: Ed Coderre
The *Leyte* returns to San Diego: U.S. Navy
Red Parkinson strums a guitar: John E. Parkinson

≡ About the Author ≡

Hailed as "a masterful storyteller" by the Associated Press, **ADAM MAKOS** is the author of the *New York Times* bestsellers *A Higher Call* and *Spearhead*. Inspired by his grandfathers' service, Makos chronicles the stories of American veterans in his trademark fusion of intense human drama and fast-paced military action, securing his place "in the top ranks of military writers," according to the *Los Angeles Times*. In the course of his research, Makos has flown a World War II bomber, accompanied a Special Forces raid in Iraq, and journeyed into North Korea in search of an MIA American airman.

AdamMakos.com